Peter Rees has had a long career as a journalist covering federal politics and as an author specialising in Australian military history. His books include *Anzac Girls*; *Desert Boys*; *Lancaster Men*; *Bearing Witness: The Remarkable Life of Charles Bean*; and *The Missing Man: From the Outback to Tarakan, the Powerful Story of Len Waters, Australia's First Aboriginal Fighter Pilot*.

Sue Langford has been a practising psychologist for more than thirty years, the past twenty of which have been in private practice, working in both clinical and organisational roles. She has provided consultancy services to the Department of Defence and other government agencies over the years. Her particular interest is in trauma management.

A WEEK

A STORY OF ENDURING LOVE

IN

FROM THE BURMA RAILWAY

SEPTEMBER

PETER REES & SUE LANGFORD

HarperCollins*Publishers*

HarperCollins*Publishers*

Australia • Brazil • Canada • France • Germany • Holland • Hungary
India • Italy • Japan • Mexico • New Zealand • Poland • Spain • Sweden
Switzerland • United Kingdom • United States of America

First published in Australia in 2021
by HarperCollins*Publishers* Australia Pty Limited
Level 13, 201 Elizabeth Street, Sydney NSW 2000
ABN 36 009 913 517
harpercollins.com.au

A catalogue record for this book is available from the National Library of Australia

ISBN 978 1 4607 5942 4 (paperback)
ISBN 978 1 4607 1304 4 (ebook)
ISBN 978 1 4607 8917 9 (audiobook)

Cover design by Andy Warren, HarperCollins Design Studio
Cover images: Sky by shutterstock.com; jungle landscape by freesvgclipart.com
All photographs courtesy of Doug Heywood unless otherwise noted
Author photographs by Peter Rees and Sue Langford
Maps by Map Illustrations, www.mapillustrations.com.au
Typeset in Sabon LT Ltd by Kirby Jones
Printed and bound in Australia by McPherson's Printing Group
The papers used by HarperCollins in the manufacture of this book are a natural, recyclable
product made from wood grown in sustainable plantation forests. The fibre source and
manufacturing processes meet recognised international environmental standards, and carry
certification.

To the memory of Scott and Marge Heywood.
Their love endured the worst of times in anticipation
of the best of times.

He who has a why to live can bear almost any how.
Friedrich Nietzsche

Contents

Preface   1

Prologue   3

1   A Spray of Orchids   7
2   Keeping Close   19
3   Daydreaming   28
4   Thunder Be Buggered   41
5   Where Are the Planes?   56
6   Battle Stations   66
7   Rats in a Trap   75
8   Naked Existence   81
9   The Photo   92
10 Unforgiving   104
11 A Safe Space   114
12 Inner Life   122
13 Doctor's Orders   129
14 The Last of the Human Freedoms   142
15 Eyes Right   149
16 The Ring   157
17 Hope   166
18 What Will Be Will Be   173
19 The Tree   180
20 Dying Is Part of Your Job   187
21 Tall Tales   196
22 Fighting Despondency   202

23　The Gang   211
24　White Japs   218
25　No Cause to Celebrate   227
26　A Promised Land   233
27　Three Good Years Lost   240
28　The Pact   250
29　Cooee   256
30　Slow Boat to China   266
31　Wretches   272
32　A Welcome Diversion   277
33　Rollercoaster   283
34　Black Friday   292
35　The Shoebox   298
36　The Camphor Chest   307

Authors' Note   319
Endnotes   321
Bibliography   341
Acknowledgements   346
Index   348

Preface

Scott Heywood jealously guarded the paper he scrounged to write letters – paper that had to be hidden from guards.

The practice carried with it an inherent risk: if the guards discovered the cache, not only would the letters be destroyed, the punishment would be swift and unforgiving. As the months turned into years, the risk grew with the letters' increasing bulk. Even knowing they could not be posted, Scott kept writing.

He was a young Australian soldier who had volunteered to go to war, becoming one among the 13,000 Australians who were forced to work as prisoners of war of the Japanese on the infamous Burma Railway (also referred to as the Thai–Burma Railway) during World War II after the surrender of Singapore. Nearly 2650 Australians died on the railway, 479 of them on the Burma section.

So comprehensive are the 389 letters Scott wrote as a POW (among 570 letters in total) that they form a diary of the war as it played out in Malaya and Singapore, and then of Scott's captivity in Burma. Unintended but powerfully buried in the words is an uplifting and optimistic treatise on how to survive in extreme circumstances. At the same time, they are tender messages of love: hundreds of unsent letters, all addressed to Marge, Scott's young wife, at home nurturing their two young sons in rural Victoria.

Scott's experience of captivity in Burma bears an uncanny resemblance to another story, happening 7000 kilometres away in Europe around the same time. Viktor Frankl, a psychiatrist, was rounded up with his wife and family and sent to the Auschwitz concentration camp in September 1942.

Both Scott Heywood and Viktor Frankl were incarcerated and wrote of their means of surviving, albeit in very different situations. Both had in common the struggle to withstand deprivation and cruelty while living with the ever-present prospect of death. How they did so was uncannily similar.

Scott's story would have been like that of many other POWs, men with similar attributes and strategies that helped inoculate them against the effects of bashings, disease and starvation. And luck, of course, played its hand many times. But what makes Scott's experience unique is that he wrote it down, daily, preserving the immediacy of the moment.

Viktor Frankl told his story in his best-selling book, *Man's Search for Meaning*. Scott Heywood's story has not been told. Until now.

Prologue

The news Margery Heywood had longed for leapt out at her from the morning paper. It was 15 September 1945. After years of captivity as prisoners of war, the men of the 8th Division of the Second Australian Imperial Force (AIF) were coming home. A photo of diggers at the Yokohama railway station holding a handmade Australian flag said it all. Under the slouch hats were haggard faces, but now they were wearing broad smiles.

A month before, Japan had surrendered. These men had borne the brutality meted out by their Japanese guards – and survived. The ex-POWs were arriving in successive waves every few days and the newspapers picked up on the excitement and were capturing moments of reunion on their front pages.

Milling on the platform at Spencer Street Station in Melbourne, the diggers and their loved ones searched the crowd for a familiar face. Then the instant of recognition and embrace – joy mingled with relief. After the dark years of war, this was the moment they had pictured in their minds, over and over. And these were the moments the photographers waited for.

What excited Marge was news that more 8th Division ex-POWs would be following. No definite dates were available, but as her husband, Scott Heywood, was part of the 8th Division, he had to be in one of these arriving groups. She would fling her arms around him, just like those people in the paper.

Marge had not seen Scott since mid-1941; it had been a void filled with anxiety and silence – and telegrams. Those ominous, simple slips of paper that signalled the news of a man's life – or death. She had been beside herself for so long, fearful of Scott's fate. No news only increased the anxiety, feeding the different scenarios that played out in her mind. She had received the first telegram in October 1943. It broke twenty-one months of silence – twenty-one months of not knowing whether Scott was living or dead. The telegram informed her that Scott was alive and a POW in Burma. Her relief was overwhelming – and then came more silence. For a year.

A second telegram, in October 1944, finally broke this awful silence, starkly and dispassionately informing her that Scott was missing, feared dead. A Japanese transport ship taking him and hundreds more Australians to Japan had been torpedoed. Six weeks after that blow, Marge had received a further telegram, confirming the news. It began with 'I regret to inform you ...' She knew what was coming. 'It is feared that your husband ... lost his life.' Scott's records would now be endorsed with a sentence that made Marge shudder: 'Now reported Missing believed *Deceased* on or after 12/9/44'.

These words, so clinical in their announcement, seemed so final. Scott was missing, but the government's belief was that he was dead. Scott dead! Grief struck. Marge had two small boys who barely knew their father and would now have to face life without him.

It was an agonising three months before Marge's world was turned upside down again, when yet another telegram arrived in January 1945. This one began: 'It is with pleasure that I have to advise you ...' And she knew what that meant: Scott was alive! Still a POW, but he was alive!

In this topsy-turvy world of war there was relief and joy for Marge and the whole family. There was hope again. She could now contemplate a future. A follow-up telegram bolstered her even more. A Japanese propaganda radio announcer read a short statement from Scott urging her to 'keep smiling'. Marge knew it was from Scott – it was just what he would say. This was something to hold on to, in a time of so little news due to the fractured communications of war.

Reading the news that Saturday inspired her, and she resolved to go to Melbourne and wait. She would go to Spencer Street Station each day until he arrived. She was barely able to contain her excitement, eager for the night to end. Her suitcase was packed and her parents would look after the children. The next day she'd make the 300-kilometre trip from Hamilton, in country Victoria, to Melbourne. She would be there, in her best coat, smiling and waving, when Scott stepped onto the platform, and she would hold him tight and let the memory of the past few years melt away. She could see it.

The next morning, Sunday, 16 September 1945, Marge was brimming with anticipation as she opened the front door on her way to catch the bus. 'Beau View' was a simple Edwardian weatherboard bungalow, and on the verandah stood the boys' rocking horse. Nearby was the Hamilton police station, where her father was the officer in charge. Spring flowers lined the brick path that led from the front door to the gate, a gate that held so much symbolism for both Marge and Scott. Through letters, they had an agreement that the gate was always to be left open, like the proverbial light in the window. For Scott, that image had never dimmed:

> Before I go to sleep each night, I look at all our photos
> and my favourite snap, you holding the gate open for me.
> You are looking at me as I write, still with the gate open. I
> like that snap best 'cause it is so natural, and one of these
> days you are going to close the gate behind me.

The moment was near. Marge had a well-rehearsed picture in her mind: she would return from Melbourne with Scott and close the gate, putting the war behind them.

As she reached the gate on that crisp, September morning, she turned to wave to her parents, who were standing at the doorway, holding the hands of her young sons. Out of the corner of her eye she saw someone approaching.

1

A Spray of Orchids

Scott Heywood couldn't have been happier on Sunday, 4 February 1940, the day he would marry Margery Hawkins. They would put family pressures to one side and push the war into the background. This day was theirs. Marge was the daughter of a police sergeant, and Scott the son of the well-respected owner of the Heywood's Cordial factory. She was eight years younger, but this concerned neither of them. They were deeply in love. Scott thought her beautiful and would often seek confirmation of this fact, proudly showing her photo to his mates, who would respond appropriately. Looking at her velvety brown eyes and soft brown curls, they thought him a lucky man. And so did he.

The Heywoods were prominent in the Stawell 'establishment' in Victoria's Wimmera region. They were closely involved in the local business community and conspicuous in the town's activities. The Heywoods were early settlers in Victoria, tracing their roots in the infant colony back to 1839. Indeed, they had a direct lineage to the second Duke of Cambridge, which afforded the family quite some social standing. Scott's mother could trace her lineage back to mad King George III, although she wasn't given to advertising this fact.

Born in the town of Daylesford on 4 March 1911, Scott grew up in the shadow of the Great War. His was a family with a strong military tradition: his father, Fred, served with the 3rd Victorian Bushmen in the Boer War in South Africa, while his uncle, Jack Heywood, was in the group that landed the first gun at Gallipoli. Wounded there, he went on to the Western Front in France, where he was again wounded.

In Australia, schools played their part by fundraising and morale-building; news of the war was read out at school assemblies. Fêtes were organised and children were encouraged to raise money by doing jobs for their neighbours, all in the name of the war effort. Scott began his schooling midway through the war, and this period would have been a potent influence on him, likely sowing the seeds of patriotism and duty.

As was common at the time, Scott left school at fifteen, having achieved the Merit Certificate. A natural move was to join the family business. He began by delivering cases of soft drinks, before moving to the manufacturing side of the business that proudly advertised 'Quality First!' Scott's young adulthood seemed to be running to a predestined course, with his future in the cordial business assured.

As a teenager in the 1920s, he enjoyed the social life of Stawell and took part in local sports: he was a tennis player, a cricketer and an enthusiastic member of the local football team, with a premiership to boot. Scott was a joiner. His medium height and lean physique gave him an advantage as a runner. As a good Stawell citizen, he ran in the Stawell Gift Carnival in 1932, notching up a series of respectable fourth-place finishes. According to family lore, one year he missed a carnival: he'd had too good a time the night before. This did not go down well with those Stawell townsfolk who had money on him. At the age of twenty-one, responsibility could be a fluid thing. There was always next year.

Without the diversions of city life, skylarking with mates on weekends was a not-uncommon diversion in country towns. The local paper reported that Scott, in what could have been a serious accident, had a 'remarkable escape' from injury when he slipped off the bonnet of a moving car and suffered severe lacerations to his thighs from a model aeroplane mascot on the radiator cap.

But at the same time, Scott was growing restless. Perhaps motivated by his father's and uncle's war service, and by Stawell's reverence for the sixty-two men from the district who had died in the Great War, Scott joined the militia in September 1934. Neither the poor pay nor the dowdy, ill-fitting uniforms of the nation's volunteer citizen army deterred him.

The annual militia training requirement was hardly excessive: six days' home training and a six-day camp. Twelve days' training a year. Morale was low. It was hard to retain volunteers for the full three years, let alone attract them from among the unemployed, yet Scott remained in the militia for five years.

He was signalling a commitment to military service at a time of increasing international instability, even when love came along in the form of Margery Hawkins. Her family had moved to Stawell in 1930 when Marge's father, Sergeant Jack Hawkins, took charge of the police station. The Hawkins were newcomers to a town with an established tight social network. So years later, when Scott took an interest in the much younger Margery, his parents were concerned. Social standing mattered. In a quiet country town, the young couple courted against a background of discernible disapproval from family.

This was also a time when the standing of the Victoria Police – not least in Stawell – was at a low ebb. In mid-1936 the new chief secretary in the Victorian government recognised the need to rehabilitate the reputation of the force – something that the *Horsham Times* welcomed. The paper editorialised that the prestige of the force had been 'affected in a variety of ways in recent months', leaving confidence badly shaken. One constable under Jack Hawkins' command had just been convicted in the Stawell Court of assaulting a local youth, and in a small country town such a conviction undermined trust in the police force.

If Scott was concerned by such considerations, he did not allow it to affect his relationship with Marge. What was concerning was an accident involving her in their early days together: the eighteen-year-old Marge was struck by a motorbike while walking. The head injury she suffered left her with permanent poor balance.

Elsewhere, the world was rapidly spinning out of balance as the drumbeat of war grew louder. In Vienna, an earnest young doctor, Viktor Frankl, was also courting the woman he would marry. They had met at the hospital where she was a nurse and he a psychiatrist. He was attracted by her beauty, but it was her 'understanding heart' that convinced him. For her twenty-third birthday, Viktor bought Tilly a tiny pendant, shaped as a globe, with the inscription 'Love makes the world go round'.

Viktor and Tilly were the last Jews to be married in Vienna. Barred from travelling by taxi, they walked home after the ceremony, Tilly still in her white veil. Nothing could hide the yellow star each was forced to wear. Happy as the moment was, their future was looking increasingly perilous.

Closer to home, the Second Sino-Japanese War had erupted. Japanese troops invaded Nanking, the then capital of China, and launched a campaign of atrocities against civilians. In mid-1938, Scott, already committed to his army training, felt compelled to transfer from the militia to the Permanent Forces.

At this time, Marge's father was transferred away from Stawell to be officer-in-charge of the Dandenong police station. If Scott's parents were pleased with this transfer, in the hope that his love for Marge would fade, they were to be disappointed. As Marge settled reluctantly in Dandenong, Scott missed her badly. He brooded as he waited for her letters. Even the Stawell Hospital debutantes' ball did not cheer him up. And he certainly didn't want his photo taken with the debs, as he wrote to Marge:

> First of all, with regard to the ball, it was a lousy turnout. I didn't enjoy myself at all – it may have been because you were not there to dance with ... Everyone told me I looked miserable and so I was.

The permanent army meant serious training – and training meant longer separation from Marge. Letters now became their main means of communication. Whatever the symbolism of nine o'clock, the couple agreed it would be the time each would focus on the other.

> Have you remembered nine o'clock? I haven't missed yet. We were sitting here when I came last night and I went

into a trance for two minutes, and they all wondered what was wrong.

As he prepared to travel to Sydney for training, Scott found it hard to comprehend that he was finally leaving the town of his childhood. But his future with Marge was assured, and that was enough.

As with everything he undertook, Scott threw himself into the small arms course with the Australian Infantry Corps. He knew the training was crucial, as he expected he was likely to be tested in war. The memory of the Great War, only twenty years earlier, had not faded. Scott understood the importance of leaders who were well trained, and that the modern conditions of war put more and more onus on junior leaders – and he was training to be one of them.

With the 'real thing' closing in, he recognised that leaders had to instil discipline in troops to the point that they would instinctively respond 'to cope with any situation that may arise'. In what is now an old and faded notebook, with 'C of A' on the cover, Scott made neat handwritten notes, headed 'Principles of Training and the Instructor'.

As senior non-commissioned officers (NCOs) – sergeants and warrant officers – were closer to the men who formed the other ranks (ORs), their influence was considerable. As such, 'they may exert discipline of the required British nature'. This was held up as the model for the Australian Army, and regarded as preferable to that of, say, the Germans, who were seen as being controlled by fear. 'Prussian discipline was faulty in that men were treated as machines and no consideration to their human status was given,' Scott noted with prescience.

On 1 July 1938 Scott Heywood left the militia and joined the permanent army with the temporary rank of sergeant. A career in the military beckoned as war loomed.

About eighteen months before her marriage to Scott, Margery Hawkins had to leave Stawell when her police sergeant father was transferred to Dandenong, where this photo of her was taken in 1939, outside the police station residence.

Sergeant Heywood emerged from his time at the school as an instructor with knowledge of small arms as well as the fundamentals of military organisation, discipline and training. This led to his promotion to Warrant Officer Class 2.

Now settled in Dandenong, Marge entered the public service as a typist. She joined a choir and wrote long letters to Scott. Letter-writing became a preoccupation for them both. In one letter, a popular colloquialism of the day helped Scott explain just how much his mates were ribbing him about her: 'The lads have been giving me Larry Dooley about writing to you every day, but I love you and so I just don't take any notice.'

Being so far away from Marge, Scott sought to reassure her of his feelings. After a weekend's leave in Dandenong, he wrote that their time together had been wonderful. 'It was one of the happiest I have ever spent, and I think it has made us love one another even more. Didn't want to leave you this morning ... but I have to work to get the bankroll up to a decent size.' Friends, he said, told him that he was 'an extra faithful boyfriend'.

In psychological terms, they were immersed in a state of limerence in the first few months of letter-writing. But as their time apart lengthened, Marge began to worry. In August 1939, she expressed doubts about Scott's commitment to her, and suggested they should end the relationship. A devastated Scott urgently attempted to allay her fears, writing to her that he could 'hardly think straight': her concerns had hit him hard. He sought to reassure her just how much he loved her and sought her forgiveness.

If you say it's the end, I will never see you again, God forbid it ... I'm very near tears so I'd better finish now ...

at present I can't think of much else but the fact that in perhaps one, two or three days we shall be at war.

He was right. War in Europe was declared on 2 September, and on 3 September Prime Minister Robert Menzies went on the radio to say that it was his 'melancholy duty' to announce that Australia was at war with Nazi Germany. By now the logistics for war had become urgent, as neither the part-time militia nor the full-time permanent military forces could legally serve outside Australia.

For Scott, training was ratcheted up following the federal cabinet's decision to immediately call for volunteers for a special military force of 20,000 men. This would comprise one infantry division and auxiliary units. Enlistment in the new Second AIF meant continuous service for the duration of the war, and twelve months thereafter. The government intended to call up the whole of the militia force of 80,000, providing a force of 100,000 trained men.

Scott was immediately summoned for intensive training at the Small Arms School, Randwick, for a further seven weeks. This time it was more challenging, involving men being placed in squads of ten, with an instructor for each squad. The training was exacting, physically pushing him out of his comfort zone.

In an environment where the pressure intensified and the pace of his life quickened, Scott thrived. His drill instructor was particularly demanding. 'When we work, we do so with a vengeance, and when we play, we do so likewise,' he wrote to Marge. Scott thought himself lucky to be at the school, knowing it would be a struggle to stay near the top of the course, given some stiff opposition, but 'if I just think of you, I'll do it'.

He clearly enjoyed being pushed and was keen to excel on his courses. Self-discipline and a naturally competitive nature drove him to high achievement. He sought leadership roles. He wanted to be someone the men respected. Just as he wanted Marge's respect.

Whatever had been problematic in their relationship was quickly resolved. Scott proposed, and Marge accepted. By mid-December 1939, plans were settled: they would marry in February, just a few weeks away. Marge was still living with her parents in Dandenong, while Scott was stationed at a military camp at Daylesford, 150 kilometres away. The distance and slow travel times meant life was difficult, with pressure on them both. Scott lamented that 'nothing seems to go right for us at all'.

However, they managed to spend Christmas and New Year together in Dandenong – a precious few days before Scott was to go to the newly established military training camp at Puckapunyal. This would become his base for the foreseeable future. As their wedding day approached, Scott began looking for accommodation for them in nearby Seymour, where at last they could live together under the one roof. In the meantime, Marge was feeling miserable. Scott wrote encouragingly to her:

If things get any worse for you, darling, come to me – I don't care what people say, and I'll look after you … If only this hadn't happened, still it has and we just have to grin and bear it … Blast everyone and everything in this world but you.

The wedding was held on Sunday, 4 February 1940 at St James' Church of England, Dandenong. It was a quiet affair, with Marge given away by her father. Both *The Age* and the *Dandenong Journal* carried brief reports of the nuptials. Readers would have noted certain coded messages in the description of events: Margery was unattended and did not wear white. Instead, she wore an ensemble of grey wool sheer, to which was pinned a spray of orchids. The reports said that a reception was held at the home of the bride's parents.

No photos of the bride and groom were taken. Marge was eight months pregnant.

2

Keeping Close

There was no honeymoon. Scott was back at Southern Command Training School at Puckapunyal the day after the wedding, and, as usual, took up his pen to write to his wife of twenty-four hours. Addressing her as such gave him a sense of pride: 'I am just beginning to realise that we are really and truly married. After all the worry and anxiety, at last you belong to me.'

He lamented being away at training courses during much of the pregnancy, unable to protect Marge from the inevitable disapproval of some of their conceiving a child out of wedlock, and the worry of others. However, there were surprises. 'Can't quite understand your mother being pleased to see me,' he wrote. 'I thought she hated me.' With their relationship now validated in the eyes of society, they could focus on the next big event – becoming parents. They were writing to each other most days, but Scott's requests for leave were not looked on favourably by an army that was gearing up for war.

At Southern Command, Scott was feeling the pressure. This was harder and more competitive than any course he had been through, to the point that he saw Vickers machine guns in his sleep. 'Half the fellows in my squad know more about the Vickers than I do, and they just sit around like crows waiting for me to make a mistake.' Scott did not enjoy the ragging. 'I'll be glad to see the end of this course – am sick and tired of machine-guns,' he told her. Finishing it was 'a hell of a job'.

With Marge in the third trimester of her pregnancy, Scott was determined to be as responsive to her needs as possible. When he heard she had a cold, he couldn't wait to go on leave to help out. 'Four days with you will work wonders with me cuddling you up every night.'

No sooner had he returned from leave than he fell ill and was hospitalised for a few days. Released from hospital, he went for a horse ride on his twenty-ninth birthday, 4 March 1940. Unexpectedly, the horse bolted and threw him. Adding insult to injury, the horse kicked him in the leg, fracturing it. Again he was hospitalised.

Just nine days later, John was born. Scott was still in hospital, feeling helpless. He had hoped to get leave, but the accident had 'knocked all my plans on the head again. When will things go right for us, I wonder?' Confined to hospital, he felt frustrated. When a note came from Marge's mother on 14 March letting him know that John had been safely delivered the day before, Scott felt relief that his wife had weathered the ordeal.

He immediately wrote to her. 'Thank God you got through all right, my precious. If anything had happened, I don't know what I'd have done.' He was ecstatic that he was now a father. Confined to bed 30 kilometres away, he contemplated what fatherhood might mean: 'Seems funny somehow. Probably won't be so when I'm walking the floor at nights.' He pondered how wonderful it would be watching 'his nibs' grow up.

By September 1940, with the war in Europe going badly and the threat from Japan becoming more ominous, Scott volunteered for service with the AIF. This meant overseas service. In December 1940, he transferred to the 8th Division's Petrol Company, Australian Army Service Corps (AASC). With an eye to his abilities, the unit took him on with a promotion to Temporary Warrant Officer Class 1.

Simply put, the AASC were the army's grocers and truckies: procuring, storing and distributing food and petrol, as well as transporting troops, stores and ordnance wherever it was required – essential in a combat zone. Fighting as infantry, commandos, cavalry and gunners was also within the scope of the corps' operations. Men like Scott were chosen for their leadership qualities. He had shown he had the right temperament to handle men, as well as the necessary organisational and technical skills.

However anguished Marge may have felt about Scott's decision to join the AIF, she would have understood his motivation. Australia was now at war, and this was what Scott had been training for in all their time together. As they prepared to celebrate Christmas 1940, there was a strange sense of urgency in Australia. As during the Great War, women knitted socks and volunteers packed parcels bound for overseas troops. The 6th Division of the Second AIF was fighting in North Africa against the Germans and Italians, and the Empire Air Training Scheme had been set up to train RAAF recruits for Bomber Command, Fighter Command and Coastal Command. British forces had defeated an Italian invasion of Greece, but a new attack loomed. The threat posed by Japan was intensifying.

Scott and Marge spent several precious months living as a family at Seymour. They only had a rented room but, as Scott would soon reflect, these were happy days. And Marge was now pregnant with their second child. Scott had formed a circle of good mates at Puckapunyal, among them Warrant Officer Henry Heath 'Lofty' Waters – so called because of his towering height. The two had forged a firm friendship early in their training. There was an occasion when Scott came home after a night out with Lofty and the boys and fell into a deep sleep. Marge saw an opportunity. When Scott awoke the next morning, he looked in the mirror to find that half his moustache had been shaved off. Marge liked him much better cleanshaven.

Scott liked a drink or two, not least with Marge's father, Sergeant Jack Hawkins, and the two of them would have a few at a local Dandenong hotel. According to family lore, the two once took exception to some rowdy drinkers. With Scott's help, Jack rounded up the drunks and, amid the ensuing mayhem, made use of the 'Indian death lock'. This was a manoeuvre he had learned from the popular touring American wrestler Chief Little Wolf, whom he had befriended. The drunks slept the night off in the cells.

On Christmas Eve 1940, the *Horsham Times*, in florid and wildly optimistic language, declared that 'daily amid the widespread chaos we view our assuredly indicative victory dawning into a flood [lit] peace'. As overseas service loomed, it was increasingly clear that this would be the last Christmas Scott and Marge would enjoy together for some time.

With Christmas and New Year celebrations over, Scott headed off to the Bonegilla camp, near Albury. This was home to about 8000 troops, and was another step towards embarkation – and separation. Marge wrote to Scott in late January 1941, excited about his upcoming leave. She had enclosed photos, which he immediately cherished. 'In two weeks from Thursday I'll have you again for a few days,' she wrote. 'Thank goodness.' Every day counted.

For Scott, the transition from home comforts to camp life again came as a shock. With Bonegilla on a war footing, there was strict discipline, intense activity and noise day and night. The training included open-range mock battles with live ammunition. There was no word yet on when he would leave on active service, but Scott hoped departure would be far enough away for him 'to see our little daughter'.

He was to be among a contingent of 4000 troops from Bonegilla who would march through Melbourne's streets in February. Filled with pride and patriotism, Scott badly wanted Marge to be there 'so that you can see your old man go past. You could have lunch somewhere and a sit down, and I could meet you at Flinders Street [train station] under the clocks at two o'clock. I hope you can make it.'

As she was heavily pregnant, Marge was unable to be there for the march. However, *The Age* thought 4000 bronzed and fit men from Bonegilla made an impressive show for the 100,000 cheering Melburnians: 'In summer battle dress, with rifles with bayonets fixed over their shoulders, the troops made a brave showing. To a man, they looked ready and eager to emulate the achievements of their comrades in the Middle East.'

Two months later, on 14 April 1941, Marge gave birth – not to a daughter but to their second son, Ian Douglas Heywood (henceforth known as Doug), at a private hospital in Dandenong. Doug was several weeks premature. Ever prone to larrikin humour, Scott celebrated by citing an old story. Fortuitously, he said, there just happened to be a galah in a tree outside his hut; tongue-in-cheek, he assured Marge that it had provided 'a welcome change of diet'. As the old adage

On his final leave in mid-July 1941, Scott holds his three-month-old son, Ian Douglas. The photo seems to capture his ambivalence about leaving his family and the anticipation of overseas service.

went, the galah had to be cooked in a pot of water with herbs, a dash of wine and a stone. Only when the stone was soft enough to be pricked by a fork would the bird be cooked.

A fortnight later, Scott moved to the Bathurst Military Camp in central western New South Wales, where he transferred to the newly formed 27th Brigade. In Bathurst, the men thought the training harder than in any previous camp, with more mock battles and exercises that went on for several days and nights. They slept rough, and practised on Great War–era Lewis machine guns, which, although outdated, would prove useful. Few liked the Bathurst camp: the food was mediocre and the nights cold, with icy winds off the mountains. Moreover, enjoying a beer in town meant a fifteen-kilometre walk.

Making life a little easier in the fevered preparation at Bathurst was the presence of Scott's mate Lofty, who was 'as happy as a sand-boy' now that they were together. Sharing a drink helped to lighten Scott's mood. The reality of not seeing Marge and the boys for an unspecified period of time was hitting home. Scott wrote to her warning that from now on their letters – hers as well as his – would be censored, so his might seem a little matter-of-fact. But she should just think of the time 'when we will be living in a free country and the mantle of peace has descended on us'.

Late in May 1941, knowing that his training was coming to an end and that the next phase – overseas service – was not far away, Scott was prompted to include a precious keepsake in a letter to Marge. 'Am enclosing a couple of my curls,' he wrote. 'Have no hair left now – it came off yesterday.' He instructed her to keep the curls for him to collect in the near future. 'They will keep you safe till I walk in the door again.'

Scott had his final leave in mid-July and took the train to Dandenong, a seventeen-hour overnight trip by train. The precious time he and Marge shared was not easy, though. With his parents upset, sixteen-month-old John was understandably out of sorts; as Scott saw it, the thought of what was to come 'hung over our heads like the sword of Damocles'. Parting was a challenge for them both. Dandenong station was awash with soldiers leaving for war. Scott gave Marge and four-month-old Doug a final hug, then he picked up John and, giving him a hug, said goodbye. Marge, with her father beside her, watched him go. Scott waved from the train carriage as many others were dragged away from sweethearts, pleading for just a couple of minutes more. It was a scene played out across the nation.

Scott watched Marge until she was out of sight. He felt for John, so young. 'Poor kid, he didn't know what it was all about,' he wrote. The train was packed with soldiers, whose feelings ranged from exhilaration to trepidation and worry for their families. The only thing some could do to quell their emotions was find solace in grog and forget for a while. 'Were we full by the time Benalla was reached!'

As soon as he could, Scott telegrammed Marge, urging her to keep her chin up. The troops did not know where they were going but had a fair idea it would be Singapore and Malaya. As he crossed the desolate Nullarbor Plain, he settled on a way to keep her close: 'I'm a long way from you now, but you are always in my thoughts. I have decided that each night at nine, I'm going to think of you for two minutes and see if I can't contact you.'

Nine o'clock now assumed an almost otherworldly dimension for them. Conjuring up each other's image and entering a trance was something magical they shared. As he sailed towards war, the thought of this gave Scott a sense of purpose. He could survive anything.

In training, Scott is pictured here operating a gas-operated, air-cooled Lewis machine-gun.

Scott Heywood, on the right, with mates before departure for Singapore.

3

Daydreaming

As three Australian troopships slid into Singapore Harbour after eight days at sea, Scott Heywood jostled with other 27th Brigade troops cramming the deck rails. The ships' bands played 'Waltzing Matilda' and 'A Cottage by the Sea', and small craft fussed about the harbour as the troopships berthed a week after leaving Fremantle. It was 15 August 1941, and this was the largest single convoy to arrive in Malaya since the war against Nazi Germany had broken out. The principal army units in the convoy comprised the 27th Brigade (Headquarters), the 2/26th Battalion, the 2/29th Battalion, the 2/30th Battalion, the 2/15th Field Regiment, the 2/12th Field Company, the 2/6th Field Park Company and the 2/10th Field Ambulance.

George Fletcher, a tall and solidly built 33-year-old stock and station agent from Mungindi, in northern New South Wales, was a gunner in the 2/15th artillery. He was struck by the 'wonderful and inspiring sight' of the 'huge guns of the fortress bristling in the background', and felt pride to be among those 'chosen to help defend this great stronghold', But considering the challenge ahead, it was a relatively small

Australian force, made up of inadequately trained men who were to join British, Canadian, Indian and Malayan troops in the defence of Malaya and Singapore.

The General Officer Commanding (GOC) Australian Forces in Malaya, Major General Gordon Bennett, was there to welcome the Australian force in driving rain. 'The tension here now is grave,' he said to the newly arrived soldiers, 'and the present reinforcements of well-equipped units give us added confidence that we will be able to deal effectively with any enemy. Our enemies may count their men in millions, we measure ours in spirit and determination.' It was an expression of confidence that exceeded the capacity to deliver.

The new arrivals were now part of a British and Commonwealth force of just under 90,000 men. Of these, 18,000 were AIF personnel, alongside 1100 from the Royal Australian Air Force (RAAF) and 1500 from the Royal Australian Navy (RAN).

News of the safe arrival of the convoy was eagerly awaited in Australia. During a rebroadcast through the ABC of the troops' arrival, soldiers sent messages of love and cheer to their families. Scott was one of those the ABC reporter spoke to. In his first letter home, an excited Scott was eager for Marge to hear it. 'Were you listening in to the broadcast of our arrival? If you were, you heard my melodious voice – I had a few words to say and sent you a message.' Marge had heard the broadcast. A telegram from Singapore followed: 'All well and safe, my thoughts are with you all, my love.'

On arrival, the Australian troops were immediately hit by Singapore's oppressive heat and humidity. Coming from the Australian winter, it was a shock to the body. They moved into a newly built camp about 25 kilometres from central Singapore and began to acclimatise.

Scott and his good mate Lofty Waters spent their first day in Singapore as tourists. Like Scott, Lofty had been in the militia and the permanent military forces, and had also been based at Seymour's Southern Command Training School. They enjoyed drinking at swank hotels and wending their way through thronging Change Alley, where you could 'buy anything from a pin to an anchor', as Scott told Marge. Scott thought the city a den of iniquity, but that didn't stop him enjoying being there. It was a lazy life. 'We get around in shorts and no shirt – if you do any work, the sweat soaks everything. Plenty of showers and plenty of baby powder is the only way to prevent disease.' His hair had to go: 'You said you'd love me if I was bald ... I have my doubts now, dearest.'

Another mate was Ken Dumbrell, a sergeant in the 4th Anti-Tank Regiment, who also hailed from the Wimmera region. As he saw it, nothing much had changed – except the labels on the bottles. Instead of Carlton and Foster's, it was Tiger and Anchor. The bathtub was always full of bottles, and their insatiable thirsts were amply compensated. 'There was always more than enough to keep our spirits riding high,' Ken wrote.

In the weeks that followed, Scott noticed how scratches festered and sores lingered. While the novelty of his new surroundings had not worn off, the sight of Europeans with kids playing on a lawn left him wistful. This prompted him, in his next letter home, to ask Marge for more photos. This became a constant refrain as he resumed his custom of writing most days, often with a rider: 'Another day gone, one more nearer home.'

The nights were the worst. It was then Scott had time to think; the family seemed so very far away. But at least he had his photos. 'I have the two you sent away in my wallet with all the rest,' he wrote. 'I go through them all each night.' And he focused on fulfilling the pledge he'd made to Marge before leaving Australia: 'Had a read to nine and then kissed all the family goodnight and went to sleep after my two minutes.'

At the end of August 1941, the 8th Division was allocated responsibility for the defence of Johor, the southernmost state on the Malayan Peninsula, and the west-coast state of Malacca. Scott's unit moved from Singapore to Malacca. His responsibilities included picket duty, which often meant quelling fights among drunken troops outside brothels. He wrote to Marge saying he had spent time on duty 'trying to teach one of the ladies of easy virtue' to speak English. He assured her there was no need for her to worry: 'I love you too much to even look twice at anything here.'

Scott's rank made him an authority figure, but as a married man of thirty with two children, he seemed of a different generation from the many much younger and single troops. Scott had an unwavering commitment to Marge. He may have been 6000 kilometres from Melbourne, but nothing could shake it. He was sending four letters a week, and he treasured Marge's frequent responses, especially when they came with photos. Routines came easily to him. Indeed, just as at Puckapunyal, he was often teased for his adherence to his rituals around Marge. 'Thirty-eight letters in ten weeks keeps my average up pretty well,' he noted. 'They barrack me here about my letter writing when I grab a pad and sneak off to write to you.'

Lofty was in a camp just 30 kilometres away, so they were able to catch up frequently. One lazy Sunday afternoon, Lofty and another warrant officer, Jim Walker, arrived in the mess hall. The afternoon quickly developed, and they bowled over bottles of whisky with beer chasers. 'So you can imagine that when reveille went this morning, your old pot and pan was not the brightest and best,' Scott admitted to Marge. 'We made a decent mess of Lofty. They had to unload him from the truck when he got home.'

An amused Marge wrote to Lofty, enclosing photos of the two boys. In turn, Lofty wrote to Scott, declaring: 'I have it in writing from her that we have her permission to get as drunk as we like when we get back.' Scott and Marge regarded Lofty as the boys' second father.

By and large, the 8th Division's rank and file consisted of men who, like Scott, came from the country. Although they were steeped in the racist attitudes towards Asians that the White Australia policy had generated since Federation, their new, closer relations with the Malays, Chinese and Indians inevitably began to challenge their prejudices. Such attitudes, though, could never be quickly erased.

George Fletcher realised this after he and a mate, Bill Hunter, became friendly with two schoolteachers at a prominent school. After thanking them for their hospitality, George said that if they were ever in Australia, he would try to return the favour. One of the women replied, 'I often wonder just how we would be treated in Australia – we are Eurasians, you know.' George wondered too, and was doubtful it would end well.

Located in exotic surroundings for the first time, Scott was at first dismissive of Malaya and its people: it was just so utterly foreign. Yet as time went on, and the novelty wore off, the local culture piqued his interest more and more. He became intrigued by a Chinese storyteller he visited from time to time. 'If only you could see him yourself, darling,' he told Marge. 'He is marvellous. His hands and facial expressions tell the story.'

Scott began to go further afield, photographing people and events. He was fascinated by the architecture, daily life and local ceremonies. A wedding grabbed his attention one Sunday night as he came home from church with a mate, Corporal John (Dave) Levick. A large number of Chinese sat at a table as an orchestra of six musicians played.

> The orchestra started on 'I'm Forever Blowing Bubbles'.
> You should have heard it! Never in all my life have I heard
> anything like it. There was a clarinet going up and down
> the scale, trying unsuccessfully to finish the key, the big
> bearded Sikh playing trumpet and he had the three stops
> down and all we could hear from him was 'parp parp'
> occasionally. A fellow on a wooden whistle was doing
> best. He was getting bits of the tune but was drowned by
> the bass drum. The euphonium you couldn't hear, nor the
> kettle drum. They played it four times through, each time
> different. Dave and I clapped like hell. The Sikh got up
> and bowed.

Before they'd left Australia, the imminence of war had been drummed into the troops. Yet in Malaya a sense persisted that they were marking time. Spirits were high and the troops were having a grand old time. Back in Australia, they were mocked as 'five-shilling-a-day tourists'.

A perception of calm and ordered life among the 8th Division troops, fuelled by a series of stories in the *Australian Women's Weekly* a few months earlier, had led to rumblings in Australia that the men were enjoying a holiday, surrounded by women and basking in luxury in a tropical paradise. The troops were angered, feeling that their training for battle was being

Cricket was one of the activities that kept the troops occupied as they waited in expectation of a Japanese invasion. Scott wrote to Marge in October 1941: 'The one of me in my cricket gear is worth enlarging, I think.'

downplayed. While they were there for good reason, the question was when would they face an attack. Just as there had been an eight-month 'phoney war' in Europe, so too was there a hiatus in Asia as Japan prepared to make its assault.

A report in the Sydney *Sun* quoted American naval experts declaring that 'Singapore is well-nigh invincible and could only be starved out by a blockade'. Japan could not capture Singapore without heavy losses, 'even if there was not a single British battleship in the vicinity'. The idea of an overland invasion down the Malay Peninsula was dismissed out of hand. George Fletcher wondered who they were kidding.

Although such complacency surrounded the defence of Singapore, with a dearth of combat aircraft and heavy weaponry, such as tanks, the grind of training continued. But even this was not enough: the troops needed more to keep them occupied. Sport was an obvious distraction, and Scott, a natural sportsman and a keen joiner, was happy to take part. Cricket and football competitions were formed and well attended. 'You wouldn't think there is a war on, would you?' he wrote. 'The hand shakes when I put it out for my pay.'

With British troops aplenty close by, rugby became a natural diversion. 'I played my first game of rugby today and was I short of a gallop,' Scott reported. 'I scored a try too, not a bad one for me – there's still a bit of a kick in your old man yet.' Even the band had to be occupied. 'Great war this, when the band is called out to a Chinese funeral.'

With the war far from front of mind, Scott thought that once Christmas was over he could start saving, stashing his pay away. 'Then for our new house and to settle down with our family and raise chickens and vegetables,' he wrote. In utter contrast to his daily reality, it was the simple life he craved. This daydreaming would become a preoccupation. It kept the vision of post-war family bliss alive, and bolstered Scott's optimism whenever it flagged. He would find himself feeling down at times, being so far away, with nothing but the photos and letters from Marge. He constantly pored over them. 'They laugh at me in the hut, but I don't care.'

One activity that was to become profoundly important for Scott was singing in a church choir. While it enabled him to keep his voice in trim, his singing so impressed the vicar that he asked Scott to teach the men to sing tenor and bass. Scott was amused at hearing Chinese and Indian Hindu men sing a verse of 'Abide with Me', and he took on the task with gusto. Soon singing was more than a distraction – it was something he could throw himself into, in an environment that afforded him a sense of peace. Importantly, too, as he wrote to Marge, 'I can go to church each Sunday night and feel that you, my darling, are in church with me.' Sitting in a church seemed to bring her close. 'I am going every Sunday from now on,' he said. The choir seemed to nurture a growing spirituality in Scott, something in which he could find refuge.

Meanwhile, Britain remained preoccupied with the war against Nazi Germany. To say it was going badly was a frightening understatement. Fascist Italy, under dictator Benito Mussolini, had entered the war on the Axis side. France surrendered. British cities were being bombed, and its forces were driven into the sea at Dunkirk. The Nazi *Blitzkrieg* rolled over Europe and headed for Russia.

In 1937 Britain had reaffirmed its promise to Australia that in the event of conflict in the Asia-Pacific, it would send a powerful fleet to Singapore. The city had long been a major trading port in British Malaya and, with its huge naval base

Snakes were common in the camp at Malacca. Scott wrote to Marge: 'We killed a big snake yesterday, got my photo taken with it. Quite a few Joe Blakes are getting around now.'

With the camp in flood, Scott and his mates had some fun. 'You can see them about to dump me in. How do you like me in the nude, pet?' he wrote to Marge on 31 December 1941.

With a towel around his waist, Scott (far left) joins with his mates trying to free a bogged truck. 'The one on the mudguard is Alan Campbell and next to him is Baldy McFadyen,' he wrote to Marge on the same day.

that covered some 60 square kilometres, was the cornerstone of British power in the region.

Economically, Malaya was the source of large quantities of natural resources, particularly tin and rubber; strategically, it provided a seemingly large defensive barrier to any landward advance on Singapore and its naval base. The weakness in the 'Singapore Strategy' was Britain's interwar neglect of the landward defences. As well, there were no British warships based there: they were all in the Northern Hemisphere.

Singapore had become a backwater in British thinking, and life for the colonial rulers had become pleasant and easygoing, with good salaries, comfortable houses and servants. As George Fletcher observed, most of the routine work was done by competent Eurasians and local clerks, who knew matters far better than their chiefs. 'The relaxations of their clubs, a beautiful climate and a lovely landscape, a status unchallenged by native aspirations, work that is interesting and rarely strenuous, these things make life in Malaya and Singapore very pleasant indeed for the official classes,' he wrote.

The Singapore Strategy was the key to Australia's defence policy. However, there were many among Australia's military leaders who doubted the capacity of a British fleet to make it to Singapore in time to prevent a Japanese landing in Australia. And, four years after making its peacetime promise, Britain was unable to keep it. To paraphrase British Prime Minister Winston Churchill, Britain had built a battleship 'without a bottom'.

The Japanese Army was well aware of the significance of Malaya, and began planning for an invasion in October 1940. As the Japanese threat loomed in late 1941, Britain could spare few vessels for Singapore. Only two warships had arrived by early December: the relatively new battleship HMS *Prince of*

Wales and the ageing battlecruiser HMS *Repulse*. An aircraft carrier that was intended to accompany them had run aground in the West Indies. With the lack of air cover, the two ships were vulnerable. The flaws in the Singapore Strategy were about to be exposed.

Scott was stationed with the Service Corps at Malacca, which in October 1941 underwent a reorganisation. Two new units, 1 and 2 AASC Companies, were established to meet the corps' role of supplying petrol and ammunition in the build-up to conflict. Scott's unit, No. 2 Company AASC, had a strength of fourteen officers and 362 other ranks.

By now Nazi Germany was attacking Russia, but Scott was sure the Russians would hold off Hitler's troops. Turning to the threat from Japan, he was confident 'we'll keep the yellow fellow out. Not that I think this place is worth fighting for, they should give it away. The only trouble is the Japs would hand it back again.' He was buoyed by the Red Army's success a few weeks later. 'We may be home sooner than we think,' he noted.

Scott wasn't the only one to underestimate the might of the Japanese army. Talks between Japan and the United States had broken down, and Japan was massing up to 200,000 troops in Indochina for a possible attack on Thailand or the Burma Road, which linked Burma with south-west China. A force of nearly 70,000 was focused on Malaya, ready to strike. The holiday was over.

4

Thunder Be Buggered

The rumours came thick and fast on the day the war came to Malaya. Scott began to understand something of what was in store. Early on the morning of 8 December 1941, Japanese troops landed at Kota Bharu, on the Thai border in northeast Malaya. A British squadron was mobilised to bomb the Japanese invasion convoy as they, in turn, shelled shore defences. In response, No. 1 Squadron RAAF scrambled six Hudson bombers in a desperate attempt to hold the enemy. The squadron bombed the invasion convoy, causing heavy casualties. Flying through intense anti-aircraft fire to attack with bombs and guns, the Hudson crews were the first Allied airmen to strike a blow against Japan, and sank the first Japanese merchant ship of the Pacific War. But this success was short-lived.

In the follow-up attack on Kota Bharu, the Japanese destroyed most of the RAAF's Hudson bombers, forcing No. 1 Squadron's withdrawal south. Japanese Zero fighters attacked No. 21 Squadron RAAF, destroying seven Buffalo fighters on the ground. Their tactic of bombing British airbases

BURMA

South-East Asia, 1941

N
W E
S

Rangoon

Moulmein

Thanbyuzayat

THAILAND

Ye

Burma Railway

Tavoy

Ban Pong

See p. 130

Bangkok

FRENCH

Andaman

INDOCHINA

Sea

Phnom Penh

Saigon

Victoria Point

Gulf

of

Thailand

Scale

0 100 200 300 400 500 km

MALAYA

Kuala Lumpur

Gemas

Malacca

Muar River

Muar

Johor Bahru

Sumatra

Singapore

quickly nullified the Royal Air Force's ability to either retaliate or protect troops on the ground.

The Japanese attack was part of a massive land, sea and air onslaught on six widely separated points in the Pacific. Besides Malaya, Japanese forces attacked Pearl Harbor, Guam, Wake Island, Hong Kong and the Philippines. The raid on Pearl Harbor on 7 December 1941 brought the United States into the Pacific War.

Churchill believed Singapore was an invincible fortress. The naval base, with its guns pointing out to sea, was protected from attack by water, while to the north the dense cover of jungle on the Malay Peninsula, along with the poor roads, was seen as an effective barrier. Furthermore, stationed on the island were almost 100,000 British, Canadian, Australian, Indian and Malayan troops. An attack had been expected, but victory for these forces was considered a certainty. This smugness had brought the 'Gibraltar of the East' to the cusp of crisis. Not only was Singapore at grave risk – so too, it seemed, was Australia.

Behind the attacks was Japan's need for resources. Trade embargos had left the nation increasingly desperate for rubber and oil. Plentiful supplies were in South-east Asia – on its doorstep – in countries that Western powers had colonised. The coordinated attacks brought them under Japanese control as its forces quickly overran South-east Asia. This was the war Scott had been drawn into.

At Sembawang, in Singapore, pilots of 453 Squadron RAAF watched as Japanese aircraft overflew the base on their way to bombing Singapore, their Buffalo fighters still on the tarmac. And when the squadron was finally allowed to take off, it was in a support role in what would be one of the greatest disasters of the war, the sinking of HMS *Repulse* and HMS *Prince of Wales*, in less than two and a half hours on 10 December. Scrambled too late to help, 453 Squadron's pilots arrived on the scene in time to see the last Japanese aircraft disappearing over the horizon and the *Prince of Wales* beneath the surface, taking with it 327 sailors to join the 513 who had already died on the *Repulse*.

The Japanese attacks were a stunning success, exposing the folly of the British policy. The reality was Singapore was no more than a cardboard fortress, and the advance of Japanese military forces across South-east Asia towards Australia appeared unstoppable.

In the days immediately after the attacks, Scott wrote of the rumours flying around. Although sceptical of their authenticity, he told Marge that 'it seems as if it is definitely on at last'. With the sun shining brightly, and the birds twittering in the rubber trees, Scott thought it was 'a particularly nice day for a war'. What's more, he noted, they were finally earning their pay after months of idleness.

Scott's exhilaration, in anticipation of what was to come, was palpable: this was what he had been training for. Camped in the dense vegetation of a rubber estate, he described how he was sitting in a 'gunyah, complete with all mod cons'. It consisted of two ground sheets laced together and erected over a piece of rope tied between two rubber trees.

> The walls consist of pieces of packing case I scrounged – they are designed to keep the rain from splashing in. The floor consists of strips of board with cardboard on top, and we lie on our waterproofs ... All we are waiting for is a few eggs [bombs] to be laid from the air ... Here's a plane so I am off.

He assured Marge that an aerial photo of their location showed they could not be seen from the air. 'If we get bombed, we'll be mighty unlucky,' he said.

In Melbourne, the news Marge read was grim. *The Argus* reported heavy fighting in Malaya, with Japanese planes having raided British airbases, destroying many aircraft and a British mechanised division. But the Australians had not yet been in action against the enemy. This was what she had dreaded for so long. Scott was now in a war zone, and in serious danger, however he brushed it off in his letters. This would make for an uneasy Christmas.

Scott was quickly aware that with no air cover to protect them, the two British warships had been lost, handing Britain one of its worst days of the war. In a letter to Marge, he raged: 'The bungling is criminal ... My tirades against pot-bellied politicians have not been unfounded.'

George Fletcher agreed, aghast that the war was going so quickly in Japan's favour and Penang had been evacuated. 'No protection against aircraft and worse still, no aircraft of our own,' he wrote.

It was clear to Scott that alarm was quickly developing in the AIF command. Major General Bennett had assessed that his forces were likely to be inadequate in the face of the advancing Japanese. He wanted an Australian division transferred from the Middle East to undertake offensive operations. This led to a conference in Singapore on 18 December, which agreed with the recommendation of Lieutenant General Arthur Percival, the General Officer Commanding British Commonwealth forces in Malaya, to hold the Japanese as far north for as long as possible. But the next day, Churchill countermanded this, ordering Percival to confine himself to the defence of Johor

Camped in a rubber tree plantation on New Year's Eve 1941, Scott described the occasion to Marge: 'When we sang 'Lang Syne' I had my arms crossed and [your hand] was in my right hand and my mother's in my left.'

Scott's Christmas card to Marge and his sons, 1941.

and Singapore. Nothing, Churchill said, must compete with the maximum defence of the island.

The situation quickly worsened, and it became clear the AIF would soon be called upon to defend Johor. A three-pronged thrust into Malaya by Japan's 25th Army was succeeding on all fronts, and it pressed quickly down the Malayan Peninsula towards Singapore with a speed and savagery that took the British forces completely by surprise. Their troops were ruthless, brutal and fearless, easily exposing the fallacious belief that the Malayan jungle was impenetrable. No type of ground could be considered an obstacle to the Japanese, whose attacks were mounted with great determination.

Within days, the hollowness of the Singapore Strategy had been laid bare by an enemy that was better prepared, better trained and better equipped. By 19 December, Penang Island was occupied. It seemed the fate of Kuala Lumpur and Singapore was sealed. Major General Bennett ordered his troops to prepare defensive positions at Segamat and Muar. As she read the papers at home, Marge was scared – but of what exactly she didn't know.

Scott, in a letter to her, argued that it would make more sense for Australians to send guns and men instead of Christmas hampers. As if to blank out the impending fight, he pictured being at home with Marge, in bed, 'with John on one side of the bed and Doug on the other'.

He was lavishing a mother's care and attention on 'Tommy', his submachine gun, as he knew he needed it in good working order. It was, he said, the only automatic weapon in headquarters, and he was the only one who knew anything about it. 'We are as free from any means of dealing with tanks as a frog is from feathers,' he said.

If 'Tommy' offered armed protection, there was something else that filled Scott with a sense of exhilaration: Marge's Christmas gift. He wrote to her that he hadn't been able to wait until 25 December – he'd just had to open it. Inside was a signet ring.

> Darling mine, it's beautiful. It is the best present I have
> ever received. Have put it on as a mascot. It fits my
> little finger perfectly and I've shown it off all around
> and everyone has admired it. I'm like a kid with a new
> toy at present – I don't think I've ever been as thrilled
> with anything in my life before. It shall never leave me,
> sweetheart. Nothing can happen to me now I have this on.
> It will bring me home to annoy you, my darling.

The ring came with a ribbon that Scott put into his wallet to keep 'with my other mascots'. As well, there were new photos of Marge wearing a fox fur. He thought she looked just as beautiful as ever, and told her he looked at the photo 'about every ten minutes'. When he came home, he would never leave her, even for a day.

Certain that his mascots would protect him, Scott was filled with nervous anticipation and a touch of swagger. He could feel his adrenaline rising. He told Marge he'd 'like to get a bit of blood on my bayonet'. He had an uncomplicated attitude towards the enemy, and was sure he would use the army-issue Pattern 1907 bayonet to good effect if the chance came.

And that was becoming more likely. On 23 December, Lieutenant General Percival ordered Major General Bennett to make preliminary arrangements to counter a Japanese advance down the main road from Kuala Lumpur towards Singapore.

Scott waited hungrily for photos from Marge. After receiving this one, he wrote back, 'You look swell in your fox fur and new dress and hat.' The photo entranced him.

This included taking defensive positions at the inland town of Gemas and also at Muar, on the coast south of Malacca.

Amid the deepening drama, Scott managed to send a telegram with Christmas and New Year wishes. 'All well and safe. All my love,' he wrote. For Scott, his letters were like a daily talk with Marge, bringing her closer, especially as he wrote with her photo just 15 centimetres from his nose. He reminded her of his vow: 'I have always prided myself that whenever I have been away from you, I have written every day, with very few exceptions, and the only thing that will stop me is if I get paralysis.'

As Christmas Day neared, Marge, like so many others, was despondent. It was her first Christmas without Scott, and she was alone and feeling overwhelmed. He sensed this from the tone of her letters and didn't want her succumbing to the same maudlin state of mind that he often experienced. He reassured her he would be 'there' with her when she put the boys' Christmas toys in their stockings.

Scott marked Christmas Day with a letter to Marge, lamenting that it was a lonely and miserable one, but he and his mates had stood up 'and drank to Mrs Heywood ... Perhaps next time Xmas comes around we will be together again and can watch our bairns look at their toys together.' And then he got drunk.

Scott didn't feel 'particularly brilliant' when he woke on Boxing Day, his hangover needing 'a long recovery process' and 'about three gallons of water'. More sobering was the experience of one of their supply sections, which five Japanese aircraft had bombed and machine-gunned for fifteen minutes. The crew dived for cover in trenches, and there had been no casualties. Scott wondered how he would react 'when the first one falls near me – whether I need a clean pair of underpants or not'.

On duty the next night, he sat down to write to Marge, hoping she was dreaming of him. He had the new photo of her nearby, and she looked 'swell' in her fox fur and new dress and hat. Trying to be upbeat, and to put her mind at ease, he said they had been living like fighting cocks, with cake for morning and afternoon tea, fruit salad and Christmas pudding. 'Who said there was a war on?'

The long build-up to war in the Pacific reached an extraordinary moment when, on 27 December 1941, Prime Minister John Curtin, aware of the dangerous situation developing in Malaya, warned that Australia was in grave danger from the advancing Japanese if Singapore fell. By now, Japanese forces had occupied all of Malaya north and west of the Perak River, and were continuing their advance down the west coast. In a turning point, a disillusioned Curtin broke from the British and appealed to the United States for help, inviting them to take command in the Pacific. 'Without any inhibitions of any kind, I make it quite clear that Australia looks to America, free of any pangs as to our traditional links or kinship with the United Kingdom,' the prime minister said in a radio broadcast. Any false sense of security among Australian troops was immediately dashed.

With the new year just days away, the troops were living on edge. Camped at a palm oil plantation at Kluang, Scott was soon digging trenches. He heard several planes approaching. As he watched, there was a series of crashes followed by machine-gun fire. Somebody said they thought it was thunder. Scott responded: 'Thunder be buggered, they are bombs.' Nine bombers were on the attack.

We saw the eggs fall and heard the 'crump' of the bombs and the rattle of machine-gun fire. Twelve bombs in all. We could feel the ground shake with the concussion. Was standing with another chap counting the bombs and on the edge of our trench ready to jump if we heard them any nearer. They messed up the area round the 'drome considerably and got a couple of hits on buildings in a town not far from here, but no serious damage. It was a good bit of fun and the reactions of some were funny to watch. A few needed a change of underpants.

Adding to the men's amusement, one soldier had dived into a trench that had been dug as a latrine. Scott was especially gratified that the Service Corps was the first of the 8th Division to come under attack from bombing and machine-gunning. This was a battle honour that he could boast about to his 2/29th Battalion mate Lofty.

Convinced that the Japanese were poor shots, Scott assured Marge that she need not fear him being shot. Good-naturedly, he joshed her for being worried about him in her letters. 'Come on, darling, snap out of your trance and forget this absent-minded caper and the mooning around, it won't get you anywhere,' he wrote. 'Keep your chin up, poke your chest out and get a smile on your face. Anyone would think I was at death's door.'

But Scott was not immune to the complex mix of emotions that combat, or the anticipation of it, can evoke. He could swing from exhilaration at the prospect of the fighting to the softer feelings that were immediately conjured up at the thought of Marge. At these times, contrary to the rush he had felt with the attack, he began to question whether he should have enlisted at all. Yet he reasoned that she may not have thought much of him had he 'hidden behind your apron strings as so many did'.

> Precious, do you know I love you very dearly? How I
> wish I was with you now to see the old year go. Still,
> maybe next one. I'm lonely, darling, oh so terribly lonely.
> I sometimes wish I had been one of them who stayed at
> home. Still, I guess you would not have loved me so much
> had I not done my bit.

While melancholic at times, Scott assured Marge he was in the best of health. Among his many tasks, which included laying out and supervising trench digging, he had been given a list of medically unfit men who were to go home. While a little envious, he was adamant he didn't want to be sent home that way – it was 'the cowards' way home', as he saw it. He needed to convince her that 'when I come home, I will be sound in mind and limb and the job completed. Then we can settle down to build our home together.'

The fighting was now three weeks old and the delivery of mail from Malaya to Australia inevitably slowed. Marge feared Scott may have been already taken prisoner and wrote to the Victorian Branch of the Australian Prisoners of War Relatives Association seeking any information. Already monitoring daily broadcasts from Tokyo and Batavia, they had none, but added Scott to their database. The letter was dated 1 January 1942. It was an ominous start to the New Year. A day later, Scott sent a telegram saying he was well and safe. Marge could breathe easy for the moment.

Still Scott hungered for photos from Marge. Such was his longing that he fantasised about how wonderful it would be if she could walk out of the photo and sit on his knee as he wrote. He often found himself talking to her photo. Amused, he speculated that if anyone heard him, they would think him crazy. Just looking at photos of her, he admitted, made him 'go all funny inside'. He had no doubts about how he wanted his life to play out: 'All I require is you and the bairns to make life perfect.'

They had been apart now for six months, and the separation intensified Scott's longing. He needed to be told often that she loved him as it made life easier to bear – although some of Marge's descriptions of her life at home affected him more than others. In mock tones, he chided her: 'I do think it was mean of you to mention the fact that you were lying down clad in only a pair of pale green scanties. It gave me ideas!'

Any 'ideas' were short-lived; Scott now knew that escaping the grim reality of what war meant was no longer possible. The shortage of available guns became a worry: Scott speculated that the militia back in Australia had all the Bren guns – as if 'we wouldn't need them over here!' His contempt for 'those responsible for the whole sorry mess' was deeply felt; he believed the shortage meant a waste of good lives.

An early-morning attack on the Kluang aerodrome on 5 January 1942 by thirty Japanese bombers convinced Scott that the enemy were 'fair dinkum' this time. He raced from his bunk to take cover in the trenches 100 metres away as bombers pounded the area. Even in the midst of the attack, Scott was alert to the details of the scene:

There was a most unholy din going on, the crash of
bombs bursting, the detonation of A.A. [anti-aircraft]
shells and the rattle of machine-gun fire ... It was a perfect

morning, blue sky, the sun just up, shining on the wings of the Japs as they glided in, the puffs of A.A. shells bursting followed by the noise.

The Japanese bombed the aerodrome for thirty minutes, and Scott could feel the concussion running right up his legs and through his body. The anti-aircraft gunners did a great job, he told Marge, throwing all they had into the air with lethal fire. Disgusted, he added: 'Our planes, you ask? There weren't any – the Japs just did as they pleased.' The news both scared and angered Marge. In her reply to Scott, she wrote that they had been sold out.

No. 2 Company formed armed road patrols, a curfew was imposed and anyone found on the roads was interrogated. Scott was given orders to prepare a ten-man team, with himself as leader, to work with paratroopers. He started with bayonet training, his voice so rusty that it gave out every half-hour or so. When the paratroopers landed, he took his team to meet them. Acting out the scenario in jungle became 'quite a good little show'. There were creeks to jump and logs to climb over as they worked through the training. 'I shot two and bayoneted two Japs, got the biggest bag,' Scott reported.

Simulations were one thing; the real thing was yet to come.

5

Where Are the Planes?

'MARGERY' – there it was, Scott's wife's name painted on the side of a supply lorry from his unit. It was the last piece in place essential for his safety. With his other mascots from Marge, he now felt confident. 'I can't possibly have anything but good luck now,' he told her. Something else added to Scott's upbeat mood: Marge had sent him a clipping from a Bendigo newspaper, reporting a Christmas card he had sent to two aunts who lived in the city. He was thrilled to see a paragraph in the paper about him, with a photo to boot.

Scott was confident the Australians would do as well fighting the Japanese as recent reports in the papers indicated the Allied forces had done against the Germans and Italians in Libya. But the war was closing in, with the sound of bombing close enough to be worrying. Lieutenant General Percival pulled the Allied troops back more than 200 kilometres in the face of the Japanese push down the peninsula. The troops had orders to implement a scorched-earth policy, destroying bridges and infrastructure as they went. Port Swettenham, Kuala Lumpur and Malacca were to be left for the Japanese in ruins.

On 12 January 1942, the Japanese 25th Division entered Kuala Lumpur after its defenders were ordered to withdraw. Maintaining their momentum, the Japanese divisions pressed southwards to Johor, separated from Singapore island only by the narrow Straits of Johor, where the British command were now concentrating their efforts.

Scott was ordered to organise supplies as part of the build-up for the 8th Division. 'They wanted our truck to take 700 gallons of kero up the road, so I went along. Or rather "Margery" and I went along, because you went with me, my beloved.' They were 160 kilometres from the fighting and were anticipating some action. 'But alas nothing. Yesterday they machine-gunned our trucks up there and I was ready for some excitement today but got none.'

On the way home, he thought about how good it would be if Marge was sitting on his knee listening to the rain. 'Then we could go to bed and I snuggle you up while it beat on the roof. Life without you is very empty.' His mates knew how he felt. 'The lads have just been looking at your snap and they reckon you are too good-looking for me.'

As the 2/15th Field Regiment were forced to retreat southwards, George Fletcher rendezvoused with Scott's Service Corps trucks to pick up food supplies. He thought they were doing 'a great job, up and down the roads, and bombed day after day'. What Scott saw during the same operation disturbed him. He could not help but think of Marge as he looked at the fearful, haunted faces of the local Malacca villagers from Johor's Segamat District as they evacuated, 'hurrying along with their bundles, hopeless and resigned'. It seemed like a 'city of the dead', with tragic scenes in abandoned shops and thousands of pounds of goods just left. The chaos in the households was indescribable. 'Everything upset, drawers turned out, all the pictures of ancestors left on the walls, little trinkets left, it was pitiful,' he reported. The collateral damage of war for civilians left him shocked, as it did George Fletcher, who thought it cruel and too sad for words.

Already the enemy was close, with Scott's unit reporting the capture of three Japanese within its patrol area. More trucks delivering rations to a forward battery were machine-gunned, without casualties. There were dozens of dead Japanese soldiers everywhere. Scott noted that the artillery was 'blasting hell out of them', but still there was no air cover. 'After six weeks still no fighter support,' he wrote. 'It's murderous.'

The news from up country was confused and worrying. The Japanese had won the battle of Slim River, using tanks and motorised infantry to force British troops to retreat. On 14 January, the day the Battle of Gemas began, Scott's unit moved to 'near the doings' in what was the first major Australian engagement of the Malayan campaign. A company of the 2/30th Battalion launched an ambush against the Japanese, in the hope of preventing them from advancing further south. The Japanese suffered hundreds of casualties after unsuspecting soldiers rode bicycles through a cutting and over a bridge on the Sungei Gemencheh river. Scott noted that the ambush was conducted 'without the assistance of a solitary plane ... One listens in vain for the drone of a Hurricane or the whine of a Buffalo.'

Militarily, the ambush was a great success, encouraging Major General Bennett to tell the *Singapore Times* that his troops were confident they would not only stop the Japanese advance, but put them on the defensive. Bennett's claim was wishful thinking: on the afternoon of 15 January, the Japanese called in aircraft and tanks and forced the Australians to withdraw, with seventeen dead and fifty-five wounded. It was, said George Fletcher, 'just bloody murder without air support'. The pity of it was, he added, 'they hate our bayonets. It is just a race to get planes now.'

By 17 January, the Allied forces had been subjected to constant daytime bombardment, forcing them into night-time withdrawals and delaying tactics, but this had little impact on the advancing Japanese. That day, the Australian 2/19th and 2/29th Battalions and elements of the 4th Anti-Tank Regiment were sent to support the inexperienced Indian 45th Brigade on the coast near the Muar River as the Japanese made their way down the coast. They were under pressure, with the road behind them blocked, preventing Scott's unit from getting through with supplies.

The Australian/Indian force fought a desperate withdrawal but suffered heavy casualties, as Fletcher recounted:

Many of our brave comrades stained the banks of the Muar River with their precious blood, many fell in the jungle swamps never to rise again, while others with shattered limbs, badly scarred bodies, wounds torn and bleeding made their way through trackless jungle to their own lines, but only after they had destroyed their guns, or run out of ammunition, or had seen that further resistance was useless.

Back home, Marge read morale-boosting reports of the fighting in the papers, but she couldn't help worrying. Scott's assessment in his letters to her continued to be upbeat: 'The thought of people being killed holds no terrors,' he told her. If his aim was to reassure Marge about how safe he was, these were hardly words that would do it. But with his role in supplying frontline troops, he was in a heightened state, his own survival on the line. He and others were bringing wounded troops back from the fighting in trucks, and narrowly escaping being cut off.

During down times, Scott allowed his mind to drift to the image of Marge holding the gate open for him. 'Wonder how long it will be before you really do,' he wrote to her. He thought back a year to when he was on leave with her. 'Now I'm sitting in the jungle watching the fireflies, listening to all the weird noises of the night and wondering if we'll be lucky enough to hear a Jap kick our tripwires and give us a chance to open up.'

In the face of relentless Japanese attack, Scott was manning a Lewis gun when three enemy aircraft suddenly appeared overhead. He dived for cover, said a prayer and looked at the signet ring that Marge had given him. Visceral fear took over and survival became paramount as the reality of war hit home.

It was a most ghastly feeling. I was wondering whether they could see our white skin. Over the bomber went, and I got closer to the ground. Right overhead, and then down he came and let three go on the road, and over came the next one. I thought of you and the two bairns, and wondered if we were going to collect one. We had no protection in front of us and it would have been fatal to open up with a gun. Then they started machine-gunning the area … I was anxious to have a go with the Lewis, but with no protection, it would have been suicide as we were out in the open.

Scott had begun to experience the truth of war: raw and vibrant, terrifying and full blast.

By 20 January fewer than 1000 Australians and two companies of Indians were facing more than 10,000 troops of the Japanese Imperial Guard. Withdrawing towards Yong Peng, the location of the British line, the Muar force then headed west, towards the main Allied defensive line south of the village of Parit Sulong. At dawn the next day, the exhausted force found the bridge on the withdrawal route controlled by the Japanese. Successive counterattacks failed, and the Allies were trapped.

Cut off without hope, the convoy of wounded made their way to the bridge under the Red Cross emblem, in the desperate hope that the Japanese would allow them safe passage to Yong Peng. The Japanese refused, unless what was left of the covering force – which was now under the command of the 2/19th Battalion's Lieutenant Colonel Charles Anderson – surrendered. Anderson would not agree, and the next day gave the order for all able-bodied men to break contact and escape as best they could through the jungle, first destroying all guns and vehicles.

There was no option but to leave the wounded behind. They were made as comfortable as possible and left in the care of volunteers, in the expectation that the Japanese would provide first aid. Just 271 members of the 2/19th and 130 of the 2/29th – less than a quarter of the Australians at the start of the battle – managed to escape. For his valour and leadership, Anderson was awarded the Victoria Cross.

The 110 wounded Australians and forty soldiers from other Allied units were taken prisoner and awaited their fate. First beaten with rifle butts, they were then ordered to remove all equipment, clothing and personal items. Stripped naked, they were ordered to throw away whatever small personal items they had kept – photos of loved ones and lucky charms. No shred of dignity was left to them. At sunset, the prisoners were lined up and shot. Cans of fuel were poured over the dead before they were set alight. Just one man, badly hurt, survived to tell the story at war's end.

With no news of Lofty, Scott had become deeply alarmed. Those Scott talked to did not want to discuss the fighting – the tragic look in their eyes said it all. Hundreds of good men had been sent to slaughter. Even though he knew his letter would be read by the censor before it was sent on to Marge, Scott could not help criticising the British leadership.

Where are the planes they have been going to send, and still haven't, which would have saved so many? I wouldn't be allowed to tell you the stories of some of the chaps. They speak volumes for the initiative and courage of the Aussie privates and NCOs.

All Scott knew was that Lofty and his men had been in trouble. When last seen, Lofty had his batman at one end of a ditch, 'while he was hurling grenades from the other end at a mob of Japs, cursing and swearing like a trooper. I am a bit worried about him,' Scott wrote. That same day, the unit suffered their first casualty with the death of driver Len Byng.

'Things are not too good around the place,' Scott said. He was uneasy: he and Lofty were like brothers, and he feared his mate was among the casualties. He was afraid that young Doug, who was Lofty's godson, had 'no second father now'. Scott reminisced about 'the long fellow', recalling their halcyon days at Dandenong and Seymour, of getting on the grog together and coming home to Marge. Lofty was too good to go like that – he was 'worth all the brainless incompetents who are responsible for this mess rolled into one'. He asked Marge to pray for Lofty's safety, and urged her to keep her chin up.

When the letter reached her a few weeks later, Marge was shocked. For her, the news moved from worrying to alarming. She feared for Lofty, but what did it all mean for Scott's safety? With the situation grave, Scott received orders that his unit was to prepare to evacuate to Singapore at short notice.

Opening *The Age* on the morning of 29 January deepened Marge's fear. Enemy air action was continuing day and night, the paper reported, and in the west there had been heavy fighting. The Japanese were now moving towards Singapore, with the Allied forces 'still fighting doggedly against superior numbers, delaying the enemy progress every inch of the way across Johore'. But it was not enough.

The Japanese had bombed Johor Bahru, causing mass casualties. Scott had heard Churchill say, 'We must, and will fight for every inch of Johor.' These were empty words, though, and the soldiers wondered when the planes would arrive that would enable that to happen. By now the Japanese were only 50 kilometres from the solid bluestone causeway linking Johor Bahru with the island of Singapore. Outnumbered, and flying outdated fighters, the Allied airmen were easy pickings for the vastly superior Japanese air force.

It was already too late at Johor Bahru, with bodies everywhere after 200 bombs had been dropped. Scott was deeply touched when he witnessed the body of a boy of about nine being carried away. His thoughts immediately went to John and Doug, and he understood that even the most hardened soldier could be moved by such a sight. 'Please God may you never see it,' he wrote to Marge.

Adding to Scott's distress was the utter heartlessness of the Japanese attack. With no military objectives within the vicinity, it was only civilians and their homes that were hit. He saw the surrounding roads crowded with townsfolk fleeing to the jungle, carrying all their earthly goods on poles, bikes and carts, terror-struck and bewildered.

He broke off the letter, jolted by the sudden sound of Japanese aircraft, before later resuming. 'Phew! I was right and they weren't far away,' he reported. 'I've been trying to mould my body to fit the ground for ten minutes.' He would never forget lying in the open while planes machine-gunned from the treetops. 'And you prayed they couldn't see you as you got closer to Mother Earth.'

The previous day, 29 January, Japanese troops had bombed and tear-gassed Australian troops. 'I would say this writes "finis" to the Malaya campaign,' Scott said. 'Now we begin the siege of Singapore and will we cop it.'

A day later, George Fletcher agreed: 'Have just had orders to be packed up and ready to move by 2 pm. We just live from day to day.'

Over many hours, all available Service Corps trucks cleared petrol and supply depots on the mainland. Scott helped move more than 600 tons of supplies into storage on Singapore island. After two hours' sleep, he hauled himself out of bed in preparation for evacuating troops back to the island, the same vehicles returning to the mainland under cover of darkness. He was, he wrote to Marge, about to take part in the evacuation of Malaya – 'back to the island where we make our last stand – another Tobruk, eh!'

The retreat had been fraught. The trucks went across country on bad roads all through the night and with no lights, moving troops through the deserted town of Johor Bahru and onto the Causeway to Singapore. 'Everything was very still and across we came,' Scott said. 'I thought of Lofty as we reached the other side, and of the many young chaps who were still sleeping their last long sleep, somewhere in a jungle.' Once all were across, sappers blew up the Causeway. 'So here we stay till the war goes one way or the other.'

With great relief, Scott got word, though unconfirmed, that Lofty had survived, having been slightly wounded before heading into the jungle. Scott thought of Marge and the boys and heaved a sigh of relief that he was safely across. He told Marge that the signet ring she had sent him had stood by him again. He noted wryly, 'I looked at it a lot during Friday and Friday night.'

6

Battle Stations

The situation was grim: Japanese troops were poised to invade Singapore. The withdrawal of troops to the confined limits of the island meant that the workload of Army Service Corps units was reduced, as they had no legitimate technical employment.

Brigade commanders concluded that they must make the best use possible of their manpower. On 2 February the Service Corps' Major Jack Parry was asked to estimate the number of personnel available to form rifle platoons. The next day senior commanders met with Major General Bennett, concerned at being undermanned. 'As they left,' Bennett noted, 'I realised the unfairness of asking them and their men to fight with such meagre resources.' He immediately ordered the 2/20th Battalion to form a Special Reserve Battalion from surplus Service Corps, Ordnance Corps and 2/4th Machine Gun Battalion reinforcements.

From this order, No. 1 and No. 2 Service Corps companies formed two rifle companies for use as infantry. Scott was one of the first volunteers, and was appointed company sergeant major (CSM) for No. 2 – a management role involving training and discipline. 'Am going back to the infantry,' he wrote to Marge. 'Our company is being formed into a little company as a standby in case of fire.' Scott was pleased that the officer commanding the unit would be Jack Parry, who had won his respect during training at Seymour. Drawing on his experience as an instructor, Scott was to make the rifle company an efficient unit.

He would start training as soon as their equipment arrived, and hoped it would relieve the monotony of watching Japanese bombers flying overhead. 'I'll be imagining I'm back at Seymour,' he told Marge. 'Don't be alarmed, as we will resume our role once we start to push them back.'

Major Parry was immediately impressed by Scott's efforts: 'His specialised knowledge as an Instructor, both before and then, was invaluable in making the Rifle Coy the efficient unit it proved to be, earning for itself the commendation of Lieut-Gen [sic] Gordon Bennett.'

There was an added bonus: Scott saw it as a chance to square accounts for Lofty, whose unit appeared to be the main troops affected at Muar River. There had been no further word on him yet; Scott hoped he had been able to reach the coast and be rescued by a sampan. Hundreds of men had made it back to Singapore this way in the previous few days.

Never before had so many troops from so many countries fought shoulder to shoulder on a distant rampart of the British Empire. Australian, Punjabi, Gurkha, Chinese, Malay and Indian volunteers stood alongside British troops, preparing to face the Japanese divisions that would soon mass along the Straits of Johor.

Percival gave Bennett's two brigades from the 8th Division responsibility for the western side of Singapore. This included the prime invasion points in the north-west of the island, which were mostly mangrove swamp and jungle, broken by rivers and creeks. In the heart of the 'Western Area' was RAF Tengah, Singapore's largest airfield at the time. The AIF 22nd Brigade was assigned a 16-kilometre-wide stretch of tangled mangroves, swamps, tidal islands and thick tropical coastal vegetation in the west, with few obvious landing places, while the 27th Brigade had responsibility for the zone just west of the Causeway. The infantry positions were reinforced by the recently arrived Australian 2/4th Machine Gun Battalion. Other British and Indian troops defended the rest of the island as the Japanese prepared to attack. Percival told all troops their task was to hold the fortress 'until help can come, as assuredly it will come'. Yet, as Percival knew, there was no assurance that such help would be decisive.

Watching the Japanese bombers flying overhead daily, Scott resigned himself to the reality that they were about to get their share of the 'scrap iron we sent them'. Scott's irony referred to the Australian government's 1938 decision to send 'pig iron' to Japan, sparking an angry reaction which earned the then prime minister, Robert Menzies, the nickname 'Pig Iron Bob', a sobriquet he never lived down. In Singapore, the Australians remembered.

Scott wanted to send Marge a cable for their second anniversary on 4 February, but didn't think it would get through. Instead, he wrote that he would be thinking of her, as he would later in the month for her birthday. If he could get any beer, he said, 'I'll drink your health'. He wished her a happy birthday and urged her to 'keep up the old chin'. He was thinking of Marge a lot these days, reflecting on family life and what he was missing because of war.

You seem to be very close to me all the time – that's
why I'm so sure I'll be home to you. I miss you so much,
and get very lonely at times. I want to be with you and
our bairns in our own home. I will be leaving you now
and seeing you again about this time tomorrow. Look
after your precious self, beloved, and keep on smiling.
All my love, sweetheart, and lots of xxxxxxxxxx's
from a loving husband, Scott. xxxx For John and Doug
from Daddy. xx For my precious one. God bless you and
keep you safe and our bairns safe always. I love you, my
darling one.

Scott's normal sign-off was loving, but this was unbounded
in its affection. He well knew the gravity of the crisis was
worsening quickly, with fighting on the island imminent.
Marge could not have been anything but alarmed when the
letter finally arrived. This was the letter of a man about to go
into battle, whose words to his wife carried a reaffirmation of
all that was dear to him as he faced danger. Fortuitously, Scott
did manage to get a telegram away on 6 February for Marge's
coming birthday.

Amid the hammering of shells and bombs, there was no time
now for writing letters as Japanese forces readied to invade. At
dawn on 8 February, they opened up with an intense, day-
long artillery bombardment. Dug in on the western sector the
2/15th had been ordered to defend, George Fletcher shuddered
under 'easily the worst shelling we have ever experienced in
our area. How anyone can keep alive under these conditions
is almost a miracle, as the ground all around us is being torn
to pieces. As the shells whistle and the bombs howl, down our
holes we go.'

By nightfall, it was like drum-fire, reminding diggers who had fought in the Great War of the heavier bombardments on the Western Front. The commander of 2/18th Battalion, Colonel Arthur Varley (soon to be promoted to Brigadier), was one of them. During his four years' service in the Great War, he wrote in his diary, he never experienced such concentrated shellfire over a similar period. Pozières was the heaviest shelling he had endured in that war, but in Singapore there were eighty shells in one minute in one area, sixty-seven in ten minutes in another, and forty-five in seven minutes in yet another.

Using collapsible boats under cover of darkness, two Japanese divisions crossed the Straits of Johor late on the night of 8 February along the 22nd Brigade's front. They had been expected to land on the north-east coast and had tricked Malaya Command into believing they were doing just that. But the Japanese came straight through the middle of the Australian positions and pushed in a direct line towards the city of Singapore, 20 kilometres away. They had a fight for the Tengah aerodrome, which was defended by the newly raised Special Reserve Battalion and a reserve company of the 2/4th Machine Gun Battalion.

By dawn on 9 February the two divisions were established with artillery on the island, forcing the Australians to retreat in small groups to inland positions. Many did not make it. As the 2/15th Field Regiment withdrew, George Fletcher and a mate volunteered to take a truck back to the just-evacuated camp in central Singapore to recover food supplies – only to find the Japanese had already occupied it. 'I did not lose any time in swinging my truck around and heading back for Holland Road, with many shots pinging after us,' Fletcher wrote. 'I think the Japs got the biggest surprise, never dreaming one single truck would come back, loaded with two soldiers to attack them.'

By the end of the day there were more than 30,000 Japanese troops on Singapore, and they had established a stronghold in the north-west of the island. That evening, the Japanese Imperial Guard started to land. Repairs to the Causeway took the Japanese just four days.

As delivering supplies became difficult, with cars and trucks clogging the roads amid increasing panic, Scott and the No. 2 Service Corps Company were assigned to carry ammunition to the 22nd and 27th AIF Brigades, the 12th British Brigade and the 44th Indian Brigade. At the same time, No. 1 Service Corps Company concentrated on delivering petrol and other supplies to these same units.

Scott took the infantry rifle company to the Bukit Timah rifle range, hoping to get some firing practice. But with enemy shells landing within 150 metres of their location, the company soon took up battle station in the face of day-long enemy machine-gun attacks. A hurried withdrawal to a new location followed during the night.

Early on the morning of 11 February the reserve composite force was sent to fill a gap between a reservoir and the Bukit Timah Road. Scott and the infantry company took up position on a hill about 100 metres behind George Fletcher and the 2/15th artillery. Orders came to pack up and move immediately to Government House, but no sooner had they arrived than Japanese aircraft strafed the area, forcing the Australians to take cover in dugouts.

A day later, Bukit Timah village – the highest point on the island – was captured. In the withdrawal of Allied troops that followed, a company of Special Reserve Battalion troops counterattacked with a bayonet charge to hold a line and prevent the enemy from outflanking a position. Throughout the day and night, bombs and shells rained down on the streets of Singapore. By the evening of 12 February, Allied troops had withdrawn to a final defensive arc around Singapore city, with the Australians establishing a perimeter around the Tanglin Barracks area.

At the grounds of Government House, George Fletcher helped prepare food for the gunners, but before he could reach them they were 'blown to pieces'. Shells started to fall almost on top of him and his mates. 'From then on it was hell let loose, and we all must have aged ten years during the next hour,' he recalled. When their truck was hit, the hand grenades and .303 ammunition inside caught fire. A shell hit Government House, and then another destroyed the Red Cross clearing station, just a few metres from George's dugout, killing all the Indians inside. He and his mates dived into a long slit trench, landing on top of Indians already taking shelter there. As shells fell and the hand grenades in the shattered lorry exploded, the trench shook and 'every bone in our bodies seemed as if they must surely collapse'.

When the shelling stopped, Fletcher picked up the first available truck and headed to the Union Jack Club, where he met up with the Service Corps and loaded up with rations. As he drove through the city streets, he saw hundreds of civilians lying dead. He sensed the end was near for the defence of Singapore. 'We feel the fight for the island is almost over, our chaps cannot stand much more of this. Our nerves are going to pieces,' he wrote. But there was some unexpected news. Earlier, during a raid, he had dived under a truck as someone dived under from the opposite side. It was a captain who had been looking for him. He gave George a cable which announced that his wife, Evelyn, had given birth to a baby daughter on 29 January. 'I felt like crying from joy and sadness,' he said. He did shed some tears, fearing he would never see Evelyn again, let alone his daughter.

On 14 February, as the Japanese advance neared its finale, every Service Corps vehicle was destroyed after delivering food to Tanglin Barracks and as much ammunition as possible to various units from the base ordnance depot before it was engulfed in flames. Armed patrols were established at Tanglin Barracks, and two Service Corps rifle companies moved to key positions in the defensive line, under the command of officers from the 2/30th Battalion. All positions came under heavy shelling, bombing and machine-gunning during the afternoon.

With Japanese troops soon controlling more than half the island after just a week of fighting, chaos erupted. Thousands of civilians were dying daily. Supplies of ammunition and water were running low, and Lieutenant General Percival was told they would run out by the sixteenth of the month. Defeat loomed.

On the last day that he would be a digger involved in battlefield action, 15 February 1942, Scott and his unit once more came under heavy shelling, continuous bombing and low-level machine-gun attacks over five frantic hours. Percival agreed to surrender. He didn't know it, but the Japanese were by then running low on artillery shells.

George Fletcher heard the air-raid siren sound. A driver showed him a message saying that an armistice had been signed. He and five mates – Bill Hunter, Frank Shepherd, Wally Brown (who had been awarded the Victoria Cross during the Great War), Merv Gibson and Ross Steele – decided they would not be taken prisoner but would try to escape. All they needed was a small boat. As they made their way towards the beach, the glow from burning buildings cast weird shadows on a scene of carnage and destruction. They passed hundreds of bodies, men, women and children lying in the streets. 'We saw something move among the heap of dead, on the side of the road, before we reached the beach,' Fletcher wrote. They stopped their vehicle and got out. There they saw a little Malayan boy, aged about four, who had been dreadfully injured.

> He had one leg blown off, and part of his intestines on the ground. We were all shocked, but one thing we were all decided on was that we could not leave him under these conditions to die, although he only had possibly minutes to live. It was agreed we should put him out of his misery, although I doubted if he wasn't beyond pain. Wally stuck six matches in the ground, one shorter than the others. Whoever drew the short one put the babe out of his pain. One of we six did the deed. But no-one will ever know. That was our pact.

As it was for Scott Heywood when he witnessed the body of a Malayan boy being carried away, George Fletcher and his mates were distressed by the sight of a shockingly injured child victim of war. They could not leave him to suffer. George had a daughter just a few days old whom he had not seen, and others in the group had children of their own. Each in his own way identified with this young boy. No harder act of compassion would ever be required of them.

7

Rats in a Trap

At 8.30 pm on 15 February, and without warning, an eerie silence fell over Singapore city. Orders came from divisional headquarters to cease fire. Incredulous and angry men heard the news that the Allied army had surrendered to the Japanese. As the reality of their situation dawned upon them, their sense of humiliation rose. Unthinkably, 130,000 personnel were now prisoners of the Japanese, among them 15,000 Australians. The myth of Fortress Singapore was shattered, along with British invincibility.

The AIF collected ammunition, although arms were retained. At nine o'clock the next morning, the last AIF posts and patrols were withdrawn. In shocked disbelief, some men cried with rage; others looked for a means to escape. Many were so exhausted that they simply slept.

As a soldier, Scott had been bristling with anticipation to continue the fight and, if necessary, go hand to hand to the last man. The strength of the enemy had not made him retreat; rather, he and his fellow diggers had only withdrawn under orders – orders that they found incomprehensible. The challenge he now faced was to suddenly and reluctantly change his mindset from fighting an enemy to becoming that enemy's prisoner. Just like Alice 'down the rabbit hole', he was caught in the sensation of moving from freedom and bravado to helplessness and fear of the unknown. If his fighting days were over, perhaps he would be repatriated. Or not.

In this mindless fog, there was one more thing Scott had to do before the long march from their gathering point at Tanglin Barracks to their new home, Changi Gaol. He had to bury Dave Levick. Not yet twenty-two, Dave was a mate with whom Scott had shared many fond moments, such as sitting at that table in Malaya and listening to the discordant band. Dave now lay dead, killed while helping carry wounded men to safety during the long hours of battle on that final day of freedom. Another mate from Scott's company, Private Jimmy Dickinson, was dead too, aged twenty-seven. He had been sent to the front on that last day of fighting, 15 February, and had been killed. 'Should have never been there, poor kid,' Scott wrote.

Before lowering Dave's body into the slit trench that was to be his grave, Scott helped remove the groundsheet that covered him. This was no time for florid words, just a simple description of what had happened to a mate in war. 'There he lay, huddled up just as he died, too knocked about to straighten out,' he wrote. 'As the sun was going down, we buried him.' Scott and his mates stumbled on some supplies of McEwan's beer at Tanglin Barracks and then, out of buckets, they drank the mess dry. It was a fitting last stand in memory of Dave.

Dave and Jimmy were among 191 Service Corps men lost in action in the failed campaign, while another 1907 Service Corps soldiers, together with the remainder of the garrison in

Singapore, were now in captivity. In the half-dark of Tanglin Barracks, Scott tucked into his last meal as a free man: a dish of bacon and tomatoes. It had become his favourite meal. He would remember this day – the day they lost their freedom. There were other memories he would not quickly forget: 'Our morning and evening hymn of hate from our friends the enemy.' One of the shells had lobbed in Divisional HQ, much to the consternation of the GOC and his staff.

The next day, after guns and equipment had been rendered inoperable, the Allies faced a humiliating 30-kilometre march to Changi, through crowds of victorious Japanese soldiers and stunned civilians. Scott brooded over the shame of the capitulation. 'Sold out' was the phrase Marge had used in a letter some weeks before. He hadn't wanted to believe her then, but her prescience from far away was clearer than his on the ground.

Later, as Scott looked back, there were important questions about the failure of the defence of the island that plagued his mind. Why was it that after days and days of mining, so little of the Causeway had been blown up? A gap just 20 metres wide had been created. And then there was the bridge on the Mersing Road, linking the east and west coasts – it had not been destroyed at all. Scott, like so many others, needed to make sense of it.

Subsequently, in his analysis of the capitulation, journalist Keith Murdoch summed up the woeful defence of the city:

Singapore was lost in the first day's fighting, by the fifth day its agony was intense, shelling and bombing causing casualties that could not be cleared up, hospitals without water and broken soldiers and civilians wandering the streets and hiding in the cellars. On the sixth day sectional commanders advised that further resistance was useless, and on the eighth day General Percival decided that all must surrender.

The fall of Singapore would soon be dubbed the worst defeat in British military history, and Scott was not about to defend the British government's incompetent handling of the campaign. But he knew he was a small pawn in a much bigger game in which Britain, convinced it would easily see off any attack by Japan on Singapore, had failed in the most basic planning required to defend the island. Scott and his comrades had fought doggedly during the month leading up to the surrender. Now 1800 Australians had died during the Malayan campaign and the battle for Singapore. He realised bitterly that Britain had neglected the campaign in the Far East in favour of concentrating on the war in Europe. Malaya had been a 'death trap with a vengeance'.

Scott's attitude towards political leaders was now scathing, and he felt betrayed. The troops on the ground had been told that help was on the way, that planes were coming. But the reinforcements were only newly enlisted troops, and 60 per cent of them had never fired a rifle. 'Half of them couldn't load or unload one,' he grumbled. 'And these are all they could produce from home after months and months in which to train them.' He wondered what the excuses would be.

The politicians had committed the men to a lost cause, leaving them to their fate 'like rats in a trap,' Scott wrote bitterly. 'We cursed them many a time as we lay on our bellies with Nip bombing and machine-gunning from a height of 200 feet. I said my prayers many a time, and had the wind up lots of times when they were throwing railway engines at us done up in small parcels.'

In the midst of those mad final days of fighting, escape had been on the minds of many – not least Major General Bennett, who, without Lieutenant General Percival's approval, made a daring but controversial escape by boat from Singapore. So too did George Fletcher and his five mates, after an officer confirmed the Allied surrender. 'So we told him we were going to make a break for Australia, and he said that the chance was 100 to 1 and wished us good luck,' Fletcher wrote.

Under cover of darkness, the six Australians, accompanied by three British soldiers, left Singapore in a rowing boat. Five days later they reached Sumatra, where the party was separated, leaving Fletcher and Bill Hunter to make their way together. Dutch authorities arranged for them to travel overland to Padang, where they boarded a small steamer that sailed to the remote town of Chillichap, in southern Java. From there, a Dutch ship took them to Fremantle, arriving on 7 March 1942.

On 10 February, as Singapore had burned, and three days before he was given the news of the birth of his daughter, Fletcher had taken a moment to reflect amid the frenzy and desperation. In his diary, he wrote a note to his wife, Evelyn, fearing that given the odds, he may well not survive. He wanted her to think of him in their happiest days, and know that he had loved her as he 'didn't think it possible to love any human being'. If he didn't survive the war, he wrote, he wanted her to carry on with their new baby. 'I would have loved to see him or her.' Fletcher knew the surrender would mean that he would be a prisoner of war for an indeterminate period, and he couldn't countenance that. He had an overwhelming drive to get home to Ev and the baby. It was what gave his life meaning and purpose.

In Sydney, he boarded a train for Moree, before travelling to the village of Delungra, and Ev. As the steam train chugged over the hills and plains to north-western New South Wales, all the fears he had harboured in Singapore became a thing of the past. 'Ev met me at the train and I was introduced to my daughter, who was asleep,' he wrote. 'I am sure I will soon get to know her when she wakes up.'

For George Fletcher, the nightmare was over, but for Scott Heywood and Viktor Frankl it was just beginning. They could only hope fate would be so kind.

8

Naked Existence

Half a world away in Vienna, Jews were being deported in their tens of thousands to German-occupied areas of the Soviet Union and Eastern Europe. The mass killings had begun. Vienna was under Nazi-imposed rule, and life for its remaining Jewish population was fraught. Many, including the Frankls, had been well integrated into the city's social and cultural institutions. Viktor's position as a doctor, and Tilly's as a nurse, would not protect them.

Tilly was pregnant. This caused great heartache for the Frankls, as a Nazi decree proclaimed that pregnant Jewish women would immediately be deported to a concentration camp; abortions were therefore encouraged. The choice was excruciating, but the fetus was sacrificed. Word was spreading about what happened to Jews once they were deported. It was now a waiting game, but they waited together, with increasing unease.

Scott and Marge also knew the anguish of waiting – but they had to wait separately. So much was going through Scott's mind as he tried to come to terms with being a prisoner of war. He wondered what Marge's thoughts were when she heard about the fall of Singapore. He knew it would have led to many anxious days and nights. He desperately hoped she had received his cable for her birthday. He wished he could tell her he had remembered John's and Doug's too, and had spent the day with them in his thoughts. He had come away from Australia with a precious memento: the candle from John's first birthday cake. He had carried the candle through the campaign in his respirator haversack, until the surrender. Then he had lost it at Tanglin Barracks, along with the brass tin in which he carried it.

He wished Marge could know that he and his mates had stuck together from the gut-wrenching day of the capitulation, sharing a tent at Selarang Barracks. It was here in the vast 25-square-kilometre Changi Gaol complex that most of the Australian POWs were moved on 17 February. Being with mates helped to deal with the uncertainty that filled those first days in captivity. Their initial concerns were survival in the face of the indiscriminate mass slaughter that the Japanese troops carried out against the Chinese in Singapore. Then they began to wonder how they would survive captivity, and how long it would last. Nothing in Scott's training had prepared him for this.

After the Great War, a victorious Anzac spirit had been drummed into the next generation of diggers. The Anzac legend was the template for the national character. Now these men who had proudly marched off to war as holders of the nation's faith faced the unimaginable as they wrestled with the notion of indefinite captivity. Their initial shock was giving way to a growing adjustment and a level of resignation. Amid a widespread sense of disorientation and anxiety, anger took longer to subside.

As the days wore on, the uneasy convergence of cultures – Anglo-Australian prisoner versus Japanese victor – demanded swift learning from the new POWs. Initially, prisoners were free to roam throughout the Changi complex, but in early March 1942 fences were constructed around the individual camps and movement between them restricted. A new culture began to emerge, one of captivity, with new rules, restrictions and deprivations. In the background was a growing resentment towards their commanding officers and politicians alike. As life as a POW began, morale was low.

To add to Scott's woes, he came down with dysentery – not an uncommon ailment in the tropics, and especially in the cramped, unsanitary conditions of captivity. Compounding this, the mosquito-infested camp led to a bout of dengue fever. Scott spent his birthday in bed. Before the surrender, he had derived so much comfort from writing his daily letters to Marge, and he wanted to get back to it. But he couldn't. Not only was he ill, he was depressed – there was a lot to process. Becoming a prisoner had been unimaginable, and the adjustment wasn't easy. Most of all, he did not want Marge to worry. Over that, of course, he had no control. Shame and illness interfered with his nightly 9 pm 'talk' with Marge.

What Scott couldn't know was that Marge and the children had moved back to Stawell with his parents. Desperately worried, she wrote to the Commonwealth Department of Information, hoping it might be able to shed some light on where Scott was. A formal response informed her that her letter had been passed on to the Department of the Army. Another formal response informed her that there was no information about Scott. Although regretful in tone, the letter could not escape its formulaic bureaucratic verbosity:

You are assured that your natural anxiety for
his welfare is fully appreciated, and the Military
Authorities are taking all possible action to ascertain the
whereabouts of members of AIF who were in Singapore.
It will no doubt be appreciated that as a result of
recent operations an extremely difficult problem has
been created in the manner of communication and
the obtaining of reliable information. Some time may,
therefore, elapse before the desired particulars come to
hand. Immediately any news of your husband is received
it will be made available to you.

Six weeks after the surrender, anxious and desperate for
information, Marge heard of a digger who had escaped and
recently returned from Singapore. She wrote plaintively to
the unnamed solider, saying she had heard nothing from her
husband since 2 February, and hoped that he may have come
across Scott. 'Perhaps you can help me as it's very worrying
and I would indeed be very grateful for any news at all,' Marge
wrote. 'If you cannot help me, perhaps some of your comrades
could.' If he replied, she did not keep the letter. Possibly the
digger in question may have been George Fletcher or Bill
Hunter, who had returned to Australia earlier that month.
However, they would have had no information about Scott or
any of the diggers after the night of the fall of Singapore when
they escaped. Marge's fear deepened as an information void
opened up.

Three weeks later, as Anzac Day neared, a letter came from
the Australian Military Forces District Records Office. Again,
there was no definite information about Scott. The letter
conveyed the minister's sympathies and assured her that they

were trying every possible source, including the International Red Cross, to get information about POWs.

The Victorian Division of the Red Cross followed up ten days later, but to no avail. The branch assured Marge it was making every endeavour to find out where and how Scott was. As well, it was investigating how food and clothing might be sent to the men in captivity. They asked Marge to notify the Red Cross if she received any word of her husband, as the International Red Cross in Geneva was gathering information about all POWs in Japanese hands. Marge had nothing to give. She was alone, and did not know where to turn.

Scott had become an unwilling bit player in the Japanese military's conquests. China, French Indochina, Thailand, Malaya, Singapore, Hong Kong and the islands of the Netherlands East Indies had all been conquered. And now ill-defended Burma had fallen, a country that was vital to the Allied war effort as it contained the only viable route through which the Americans could supply the Chinese in their fight against the Japanese.

When the Japanese attacked Burma on 15 January 1942, there were just two British battalions in the country, and both were below capacity. The RAF had just one squadron, with sixteen obsolete aircraft. The four principal airfields were at Victoria Point (today's Kawthoung), Tavoy (today's Dawei), Moulmein (today's Mawlamyine) and Mergui, which were vital refuelling points for aircraft flying on to Singapore. By 30 January 1942, the Japanese had captured all four towns, and it was clear the British were not going to stop what had become an unstoppable force. The only option was a retreat to India, hurriedly implemented between March and May 1942.

But at the height of their dominance, there were signs that the war in the Pacific might have begun to swing against the

Japanese. The battles of the Coral Sea and Midway in May and June 1942 had dashed Japan's hopes of neutralising the United States as a naval power, effectively turning the tide of the Pacific War. So decisive was the US Navy's victory that it greatly reduced the Japanese Navy's ability to defend the main supply routes it needed to provision and reinforce its forces in Burma, in preparation for its planned invasion of India. But there was an alternative: build a 420-kilometre railway from Thailand to southern Burma. All but 50 kilometres of the route was across rugged terrain, covered in dense, malarial jungle. It would require building more than 600 bridges, as well as hundreds of viaducts, embankments and cuttings between the administrative centre of Thanbyuzayat, Burma, and the town of Ban Pong, Thailand.

The British had surveyed the route in the 1900s, but it was considered too formidable to construct due to the mountainous terrain. The Japanese cast those considerations aside. They needed a railroad to enable the attack on India to proceed, focusing on the road and airfields the Allies were using to supply China over the Himalayan mountains. The plan was to make full use of the enormous workforce of 60,000 POWs and 200,000 local men, women and children to build the railway. They would work from more than 100 camps along the route, and build sections of the line simultaneously.

In the meantime, bomb damage to Burmese airfields and roads needed repair. POWs were the obvious answer, and Changi had POWs aplenty. Under the Hague and Geneva conventions, the detention of POWs was not to be a form of punishment, but should only aim to prevent their further participation in any conflict. The labour they undertook should be safe and healthy.

Unlike Germany, Japan had signed but, importantly, had never ratified the 1929 Geneva Convention that dealt with captured soldiers. 'A prisoner of war shall be humanely treated and in no case shall any insult or maltreatment be inflicted upon him.' When Japanese militarists insisted that their soldiers would never be taken prisoner, the Japanese cabinet agreed that expanding protections for POWs would only benefit their enemies. Within the hierarchical structure of the Japanese military, POWs were at the bottom of the ladder. Officers could ask for suitable work but were not compelled to, while non-commissioned officers could only be required to do supervisory work.

This was the background to the voyage in mid-May 1942 when Scott sailed with more than 3000 Australians in the newly formed 'A' Force from Singapore to Burma, under the command of Brigadier Arthur Varley. The three battalions were split into three separate units, with Major Charles Green, Commanding Officer of the 2/4th Machine Gun Battalion, leading Green Force, of which Scott was part.

The journey began inauspiciously, with the men herded into two rust-bucket tramp steamers – vessels they were soon to term 'hellships'. Below decks on the *Celebes Maru* and the *Toyohashi Maru* were pens built for transporting livestock pre-war between Australia and Japan. On the *Toyohashi Maru*, Scott soon found that those taller than 170 centimetres could not stand up straight; Scott, at 173 centimetres, had to stoop and crawl about. There were 1500 men in the hold and only two narrow stairways out, with another 500 men fighting for space on deck.

The air below decks was still and fetid, with the men allowed personal space of just 30 centimetres wide by less than two metres long. They slept head to feet, which meant everybody had someone's feet resting on their shoulders. The twelve toilets on board were soon overflowing, and dysentery spread. With no fresh water available for bathing, a saltwater hose was finally rigged up, which at least provided some sanitation. Food consisted of a watery soybean and seaweed mix, plus rice, in buckets handed down the steep ladder into the hold. Seasickness added another dimension to the degradation.

Scott wrote of his experience: 'The black hole of Calcutta had nothing on it. We fed, slept and stayed there most of the day. Was it hot and stinking! Particularly at night, with the rats using you for a springboard.'

On board was Captain Rowley Richards, the medical officer with the 2/15th Field Regiment. 'Our men crawled on all fours in the darkness, trying to find a place to crouch,' he later wrote. 'Jammed in like battery-caged hens, they had no room to move, no light and very little air to breathe.'

After leaving Singapore, the circuitous route took in Medan, in Sumatra, where Lieutenant Colonel Albert Coates and his medical team joined the ship. A surgeon, Bertie Coates had been posted to Malaya and the 2/10th Australian General Hospital in Malacca before the surrender. Ordered to evacuate to Java from Singapore two days before it fell, Coates' convoy was bombed at sea. He survived and made it to Padang shortly before the Japanese occupied the city, and there became a POW. He would now join the men in Burma and play a critical role in their survival.

Somehow, the POWs all survived the voyage on the two old ships, which were incapable of doing more than eight or nine knots. Scott was among 1017 men who disembarked at Victoria Point, a town on the southernmost tip of Burma, on 20 May.

At first, it seemed like the hardships of the voyage were worth it. One of Scott's comrades, the tall and spare Corporal 'Long John' Garran, from No. 1 Company AASC and the son of a prominent Australian, Sir Robert Garran, found food aplenty, including mangoes, coconuts and onions, at prices cheaper than in the market in Changi. And, he noted, the locals were sympathetic to the newly arrived Australians.

Repair work began immediately on runways at aerodromes bombed by the British before they had retreated across the Indian border earlier that month. Two work groups were formed – one of about 600 men who were housed in huts at the airfield. Lack of equipment made the task of rebuilding the tarmac close to impossible. Unexploded mines were a constant danger, as the British had booby-trapped and shot up the runway before withdrawing. The second group of more than 400 men, which included Scott, was based at the Victoria Point waterfront, and tasked with unloading ships.

*

As Scott was beginning to understand first-hand the callousness of the Japanese military, Viktor Frankl was experiencing Nazi brutality. In Vienna, the waiting game was over: nine months after they were married, Viktor and Tilly Frankl were rounded up with his parents and 1100 others. Carrying a suitcase each, they were herded into cattle trucks heading for Theresienstadt Ghetto, a transit camp in German-occupied Czechoslovakia, where they awaited transportation to a concentration camp.

Some months later, Viktor and Tilly were again bundled into cramped cattle trucks with 1500 others, going, they thought, to a munitions factory. Their hearts sank when, at dawn after several days travelling, the train pulled into the station at the Auschwitz-Birkenau concentration camp in Poland.

From the train window, Viktor took in the scene: long stretches of barbed wire, watch towers with armed guards and searchlights. On arrival, Tilly was outwardly serene; in the last few minutes before the couple was separated, she whispered to Viktor that she had smashed a clock from her suitcase so that the SS wouldn't take it. Her husband understood how she relished this small triumph.

As they climbed out of the cattle trucks, Viktor could see a tall, fit-looking man in a spotless Nazi uniform who was clearly in control. Dr Josef Mengele 'assumed an attitude of careless ease', focusing on each prisoner as he lifted his right elbow with his left hand, his right forefinger pointing in leisurely fashion to one side or the other. Such was the menace of Mengele – the Nazi dubbed 'the angel of death', and a man integral to the events at Auschwitz.

Today at Auschwitz-Birkenau, an embossed photo has been erected at the spot where Mengele once stood, showing him in front of a truckload of prisoners. The pointing finger indicated life or death, although the prisoners could not have guessed the meaning of that sinister movement. The deciding factor was whether they looked fit for work or not. A flick of the finger to either the right or the left was the difference between work and life or the gas chambers. The less fortunate would be dead within hours, having been stripped of their clothes for what they thought would be a welcome hot shower after long days packed into the airless cattle train. Instead, they stood under a lethal shower of gas.

When it was Viktor Frankl's turn, the finger pointed left for the gas chambers, but as he recognised no-one in that line, behind Mengele's back he surreptitiously darted over to the line on the right where he recognised a few colleagues. None of the Nazi guards saw him. It was a spur-of-the-moment decision that was to save his life. Along with the others to survive Mengele's selection, Viktor was stripped of all his possessions. This included his coat, into the lining of which he had sewn the manuscript of his life's work. His hair was shaved, and he had to strip for a shower – of water. He had no idea what fate had befallen Tilly. Viktor looked at the men who had travelled with him, who were now hardly recognisable. '[A]ll we possessed, literally, was our naked existence,' he later wrote.

In Burma, Scott too was beginning to understand what 'naked existence' meant: survival in the most basic sense. To get there, though, required something else again. Just what this was represented the fundamental question confronting Scott Heywood and Viktor Frankl. Before each man lay the greatest challenge he would ever know.

9

The Photo

Scott was badly shaken. Less than 200 metres from where he was on parade, an Australian POW had just been executed. Bob Goulden, a 24-year-old private, had seen an opportunity to escape the aerodrome prison camp at Victoria Point on the night of 7 July 1942. Four days later, a Burmese guide leading an armed Japanese patrol found him, exhausted, hiding in a coconut grove 25 kilometres away. Although he offered no resistance to his arrest, he did not give himself up. Held overnight, he was taken back to the camp at Victoria Point to be punished.

Goulden had only enlisted in the AIF's 2/9th Field Ambulance in May 1941, and had arrived in Singapore on 26 January 1942. Just twenty days later, he was a POW. A fencer by trade, he had left Australia knowing that his wife was pregnant, with the baby due in March. Now, with his life about to end, he still did not know his wife had given birth to his son four months earlier.

Before Goulden made his break, the Japanese had warned of the consequences for escapees. Major Green knew Goulden had been unhappy, but he had not told anyone about his plan to escape. Pleading his case at short notice at a summary trial, Green explained that Goulden was worried about his wife and he was, ill-advisedly, trying to get to her. Green's defence was to no avail. Insisting Goulden knew the penalty for escape was death, the Japanese commander had already ordered ten Australians to dig a grave.

Shortly before midday, the Australians were assembled on the parade ground and Goulden, hands tied behind his back, was taken from the guardhouse. A Japanese officer formally read the sentence: he was to be shot at midday. Accompanied by a firing squad, Goulden was led off towards a hill, past his mates. Here was a comrade being marched to his execution, and they were powerless to stop an unfolding horror.

Scott steeled himself for the volley that followed a few minutes later. In a gesture of respect, the squad honoured Goulden by presenting arms to his lifeless body before marching off.

The execution stunned the Australians, and the camp went quiet. They felt a helpless anger. While there was nothing to be done about it, there was one thing that Scott, in his distress, *could* do: pick up a pen to write to Marge, even if his letter could not be posted. The fall of Singapore five months earlier had stirred up a mix of anger, humiliation and inertia that had made writing difficult. Scott was no longer his own master. Faced with degradation on a daily basis, giving up would have been easy. Slowly, he began to adapt to this alien life; his helplessness gave way to a discovery that there were things he could control. It was Bob Goulden's execution that jolted him back. He had to write to Marge, and he went straight to the point.

At last here I am. Perhaps Sunday's affair has hurried me
up after reading the last letter written by Bob Goulden
to his wife. Poor devil, I don't think he realised even then
he was going to be shot. Not that I'm getting morbid or
anything, but one never knows …

Scott was facing up to the reality of being a POW. There were
no assurances that he would be treated fairly, or even humanely.
He may just die, perhaps by disease or even maltreatment.
But Scott felt he needed to reconnect with Marge, to feel her
presence, a presence that anchored him.

He needed to steady his thoughts. Officially recording
what had happened to Bob Goulden was one of his duties
as the newly appointed regimental sergeant major (RSM).
'Who would have said this time twelve months ago that I'd
have finished up as RSM of 700 men in a prison camp?' Scott
wondered. 'Still, there it is.' The role of RSM gave him access to
the most precious of commodities – paper. Officially, this was
for his administrative work; unofficially, a few pages would
not be missed. Even though the Japanese forbade all writing of
letters and diaries, he would put this windfall to good use. By
writing to Marge, he could debrief: 'Spent the morning typing
out Goulden's Court of Inquiry … a very bad show that. More
could have been done to save him. He was murdered if ever a
man was.'

As Scott pored over the letter, the old feelings he had
pushed down since the surrender returned: once more he
longed for that sense of Marge being close. He had brought
the photos and the four tattered letters from Singapore that
had survived the hellship – those images and words that kept
the vital thread of connection alive. And there was one photo

that spoke loudest. 'You are looking at me as I write, still with the gate open. I like that snap the best … and one of these days you are going to close the gate behind me.'

A faded copy of that same photo has survived the years, and shows a slim, dark-haired Marge in the front garden of her parents' house at Dandenong. In the background, a girl pushes an old pram while a fashionable young woman approaches with a stroller. Wearing a crisp floral dress, Marge is standing at the front fence, leaning nonchalantly on the wire gate with her right arm resting along the top. She is holding it open: it is a welcoming scene of suburban tranquillity, frozen in time, daisies lining the straight concrete path to the street.

It was a scene in stark contrast to Scott's circumstances. Something he could long to return to. One thing, however, stood out above everything else: Marge's enigmatic smile. Into this Scott fell every night.

The transcendental power of love was something they had long established: two minutes at 9 pm were sacrosanct, wherever Scott was. Their separation necessarily added another dimension to their connection, which to Scott was a spiritual experience. This was something he felt most strongly at church, in whatever form church took.

Viktor Frankl, incarcerated at Auschwitz, felt that same power, declaring that love goes far beyond the physical person. Providentially, he believed the physical presence of the beloved was not essential – that love found its deepest meaning in the inner self. Inherently, Scott sensed this.

Marge, meanwhile, was in a vacuum. There was nothing but silence – no word about Scott's whereabouts or fate. The Japanese allowed no correspondence or information about their POWs. A letter from the Military Records Office on 25 June

The image of Marge standing at the open gate held so much meaning for Scott. He gave it 'three [kisses] every night'. Each day he looked at the photo, he thought Marge grew 'more beautiful'.

1942 advised Marge that Scott would be listed as 'Missing'. The minister conveyed 'his sincere sympathy' and recognised Marge's 'natural anxiety'.

Three weeks later, the Melbourne *Sun* reported that there were 674 Victorian soldiers missing. Staring out at Marge was Scott's photo. He somehow looked different in a newspaper photo under the heading 'MISSING'. The black-and-white photo was achingly familiar, yet somehow otherworldly. A few days later, the *Dandenong Journal* noted that Scott was the son-in-law of the local sergeant and his wife: 'May they and their daughter soon receive happier tidings.' Reporting Scott as missing later that month, the *Weekly Times* noted that he was prominent in football as a member of the Stawell Warriors team, and well known in tennis circles too. His fate was now in the public arena, ensuring recognition of Marge's stress and anticipatory grief – if it was to come to that.

All Marge could do was pray – as did Scott. At church he allowed himself to sense her close. 'I could feel you there,' he said. 'Maybe you were at church. We will go as often as we can when I come home.' He read her letters when he was lonely and despondent. Each night he looked at Marge's photo, until she gradually faded from sight as the light went out. 'I get down in the dumps frequently these days,' wrote Scott. 'Sometimes it all seems so hopeless and you seem further away than ever. I quite often curse the day I left you, then I think that I've done my duty and paid my debt to society.'

For Tilly Frankl, there was also silence. The Nazis allowed no correspondence for the entire war. Although at Auschwitz for some months, she had no way of contacting Viktor – he was so close and yet so very far away. Similarly, he knew neither where she was nor even if she were still alive. The last time he'd seen her was when they'd been separated into male and female groups at the Auschwitz-Birkenau train station. The last thing he'd said to her was, 'Stay alive at any price. At any price!' She knew what he meant.

In Poland, as in Burma, disease was rife among the prisoners. At Auschwitz, 1942 saw raging epidemics, especially typhus, which claimed the greatest number of lives. Many prisoners suffered from tuberculosis, malaria, meningitis and dysentery. In Burma in 1942, malaria, dysentery, beriberi and tropical ulcers were rife. More worrying, from time to time there would be an outbreak of cholera.

Scott had already endured a tough time with dysentery at Victoria Point – he'd been hardly able to 'crawl up from the latrines', as he wrote. 'It was awful to sit there and hear the poor devils – a lot were much worse than me.' He had been so ill he doubted he would recover. But recover he did, and he reported that he was now 'a ball of muscle'.

At first, the conditions for prisoners were adequate, if basic. The Japanese control was fairly lax at Victoria Point, and the Australian commander of 'A' Force, Brigadier Arthur Varley, established a relatively good working relationship with the Japanese gaolers. Varley had gained a reputation for having a strong personality, and for his vigorous and fearless championship of the troops – which would be tested. John Garran even noted that one of the guards 'thanked men for working so well'. When an AIF officer died, the Japanese sent a floral tribute and a tray of fruit. One Japanese sergeant, nicknamed Henry, even took an interest in the welfare of the sick.

Henry mingled with the Australians often, and Scott took a liking to him. 'Henry is asleep on my bed,' he wrote. 'He is not a bad stick and is very like a lad in lots of ways. The little sergeant is a very happy chap, can't speak very much English but always has a grin on his face.'

The Japanese in charge of the camp were friendly enough, even handing out cigarettes. They kept assuring the POWs that they would soon be going home. 'If only they were right,' Scott mused. 'Still, someday it must happen, and I am sure of it coming.' This Scott reaffirmed as much for himself as for Marge. He promised her that although they had lost twelve months together, he would make it up to her when he returned. He could see himself 'sitting by the fire and listening to the wireless. And the satisfaction of knowing I have done my little bit when lots who should have did not.' He 'boiled' when he thought of those who had refused to serve. So many others had stayed behind, letting others like Bob Goulden carry the responsibility – and the price. Bob was not a shirker, but he was dead.

Despite the early harmony, it soon became clear that the Japanese were philosophically and logistically unprepared for dealing with massive numbers of POWs. Having been trained in a military culture that saw death as the only honourable alternative to surrender, they felt little concern for the welfare of those who were now their prisoners. At that time, for the Japanese military, surrender meant shame. This attitude determined the environment in which the POWs went about their daily lives, impacting everything from the food supply to their health care and living conditions.

The camps were under the control of a Japanese officer, who had a staff of guards and a quartermaster. An AIF combatant officer was the officer in charge of the POWs, assisted by an adjutant, quartermaster and medical officers. As RSM, Scott was the link between the officers and the men. This role also involved helping his mate Doug 'Baldy' McFadyen with his work as quartermaster, which included organising rations and meals. Meat days were considered red-letter days. On the off days, there were vegetables and 'jungle stew' with rice.

Food was now a preoccupation for every prisoner, as Scott summed up: 'If only we had a change from the eternal rice plus the grubs. We have our bad and good days on them ... A lot are missed but what the eye doesn't see the heart doesn't grieve over, and we have to eat something.' Their rations were supplemented when they could capture 'anything that crawled, flew or swam'. At Auschwitz, Viktor Frankl prayed that the person serving the soup would ladle it from the bottom of the pot, so he might score a scrap of meat. Scott made the same prayer.

Preparations for the railway got underway in September, and Scott suspected that life was about to get a lot harder. The POWs' individual rice ration had been cut again, down to 7 ounces a day – about 200 grams. Vitamin deficiency quickly became evident. Beriberi was increasing, as was fever. 'Our medical stores are done,' he noted, adding that doctors would have to end treatment any day. Skin complaints were bad, with more than seventy men affected. And it was not just the men's health:

It is interesting to stand and look around at the faces, some with heavy beards, some with only rags, some with no boots and the bum out of their trousers and torn shirts. Things are going to be very tough before long. We have no replacements, so when things wear out it is going to be just too bad.

At the start of August, after helping clear debris at the airfield, 'A' Force prepared to leave Victoria Point for Tavoy. Henry and another guard, Ishakawa, were sad to see the POWs go, and organised a farewell party for the Orderly Room staff. Scott appreciated the gesture, and described the feast:

> We had two biscuits, two bananas each, and about six tins of pineapple between ten of us, plus a packet of smokes and tea. Then they came to light with three bottles of beer. Can you imagine it – beer after all these weeks? It tasted like the nectar of the gods – it was beautiful.

Scott made a speech and toasted their health, with Henry translating the remarks to Ishakawa, who was 'tickled pink'. Scott thought it a good sign that both guards thought of the bedraggled POWs in this kindly way. He wanted to get a photo of Henry to bring home, as he had been a good friend. 'They have treated us very well since we have been here and have done what they could for us, particularly the sick fellows,' he wrote. When the war was over, Scott planned to write to him. 'He was decent to us while we were there, and did what he could to make our life bearable.'

In truth, Scott and his mates had been lucky to strike Henry, Ishakawa and the guards at Victoria Point. These men had been the exceptions that prove the rule.

*

Back home in Stawell, Keith Murdoch's account of the fall of Singapore, published in *The Herald* in mid-August 1942, would have caught Marge's attention – and one paragraph in particular: '[T]here were noble stands. At one time the Army Service Corps drivers and clerks and the headquarters personnel held a line and counter-attacked with great bravery.'

Scott had told her in his final letter from Singapore that he was 'going back to the infantry ... as a standby in case of fire'. Marge wondered if Murdoch's piece was referring to Scott's unit. Worryingly, Murdoch had gone on to say that there was no list of the living. Neither was there a list of the dead, and Murdoch concluded that the Japanese 'wish to play upon our feelings'.

Marge, along with other wives and families, felt her feelings too were being played upon. It was all very well for Murdoch to assert that the diggers would be 'helped by their proud spirit and their unquenchable Australianism', but Marge had a more fundamental question: was Scott alive or dead? There was no answer to this. Her sense of dread only increased.

In Burma, all Scott could do was write, as if the situation were normal, and hope that the letters he addressed almost daily to Marge could at some stage be posted. Maybe it would be when they reached the next camp, or maybe the one after. He could not, and would not, give up hope.

Before leaving Victoria Point, Scott – ever the observer – described how he looked out across the paddy fields to the hills, watching the local villagers ploughing with a mob of buffalo, and the women in their multicoloured sarongs planting rice. 'It is good to wander through the jungle scrub and be met at the door of the happy home by mum wearing a very elaborate brassiere and sarong with three or four naked kids running around,' he reflected.

Such interludes had fascinated Scott since he'd first disembarked in Singapore. He told Marge he and his mates were 'certainly seeing the world', even if it was as POWs. Bob Goulden's execution aside, Victoria Point had been tolerable – a 'bright spot', as Scott put it. How long this would last was another question altogether.

10

Unforgiving

If it was a hellship that took Scott from Singapore to Victoria Point, then the voyage to Tavoy evoked in him a vision of hell. Sometime in the past he had seen a painting of Dante's *Inferno* – all naked bodies and flailing limbs – and in the experience of sailing from Victoria Point he saw it in reality. The metaphor could not have been more fitting.

He was among more than 280 POWs – including troops from the 2/4th Machine Gun Battalion – who on 6 August 1942 boarded two ships, each smaller than a Manly ferry. They were dirty and foul-smelling; one was the *Tatu Maru*, and the other was only ever identified as *No. 593*. As they had left their huts with their gear, the Australians had also grabbed whatever cooking utensils they could for the next camp – frying pans, tins and drums. Scott noted that the hold of his ship was a cramped 20 metres by 6 metres, with just one ladder up to the deck above. Ventilation was a single opening of just 50 centimetres by 20 centimetres – about the size of a briefcase. A sole lamp lit the fetid, crowded area, and the men jostled to find space to lie down.

The ship left port at daybreak in fine weather that soon gave way to rain. With a tarpaulin pulled over the opening to the deck, the hold became a hellhole. 'The tub pitched, tossed and rolled all in one, and the race for the stairs began,' Scott recorded. Seasick men pushed for space along the crowded deck rail. Those who couldn't elbow their way through made 'a noble effort to throw it over the heads of those who could'. Scott's own stomach was turning somersaults. Below, men unable to make it on deck were 'heaving the anchor', adding to the general putrescence.

The wind lifted the tarp and down came the water. The men were soaked and lying in water, too miserable to move. By the time night fell, the heat and stench struck like a blow. 'Try and picture the scene,' Scott wrote. 'A kerosene light flickering over the occupants, legs, arms and bodies, glistening with sweat and packed like sardines in all attitudes.'

Off the boat after three days at sea, Scott caught a reflection of himself and was staggered at the sight: he was filthy, his face black and with a growth of beard. On arrival at Tavoy, the men, including the sick, were forced to march 40 kilometres to the new camp. The consequences of the British scorched-earth policy when withdrawing from the town were soon evident: dozens of large brick buildings lay in ruins, gutted.

Conditions in the camp did nothing to lift the men's spirits. Those with fever were left unattended, some for thirty-six hours, while the healthy men were ordered into an old hall. This was to be their cramped living space for their time in Tavoy. Nearly 200 men began 'living, eating and sleeping in a floor space not as big as a dancing space in the Stawell Town Hall', as Scott put it.

Scott and his mates were able to set themselves up near a window, and soon the hall was crisscrossed with makeshift clotheslines, with odds and ends hanging from them. 'You dare not take a chance to hang them outside to dry – too many tea leaves [thieves] about,' he explained. Their new surroundings allowed for little privacy, and curiosity drew the locals to the POWs. Scott saw the situation with a deal of whimsy:

We wash and shower in water that smells to high heaven, while the dusky ladies study our form and whatnot. I am afraid some of my habits are going to be hard to lose. Don't be surprised if you catch me on the lawn in front having a shower under the hose, while the folk passing by wonder if I'm crazy or not. Modesty is a thing of the past, I fancy.

The atmosphere was particularly putrid at night. In the cramped conditions, dysentery spread fast, with about 100 men hospitalised within days. 'It is pitiful to see the walking skeletons about the place,' Scott wrote. 'Some of the poor devils can hardly crawl around.' A few fine days were enough to bring out the mosquitoes, creating ideal conditions for cholera and typhoid to break out.

Scott couldn't get Lofty out of his mind. Not knowing what had happened to him was hard to bear. Scraps of information had suggested he'd survived the fighting at Muar but might have been wounded – and then nothing. Lofty was almost family. Scott recalled one drunken night at Seymour, when Lofty and some others had woken Marge, 'shouting out that they had brought Scotty home'. They didn't come any better than Lofty. In a letter to Marge, he reminisced about Lofty, at

Warrant Officer 'Lofty' Waters was not just Scott's great mate, but also godfather to Doug Heywood.

the same time assuring her that he thought the world of her and the family. 'What a reunion we'll have when this is all over.'

Then he chanced upon Lofty's batman – with news! There was a chance he was still alive. Having got away, Lofty had wandered about in the rubber trees for two days after the fighting at Muar. He had a shrapnel wound but was not badly hurt. In the fray, he had become separated from his batman. Then Lofty had been captured, and nothing had been heard of him since.

A month later word came that Lofty was safe in Padang; apart from a wound in the arm, he was in good health. Scott was overjoyed. 'If it is correct, my prayers for his safety have been answered and I may yet see him again,' he wrote. But if there was encouraging news about Lofty, an underlying frustration remained. 'All we want is news of our loved ones and a chance for another crack at these blokes.'

In the absence of news, Scott often looked at the card Marge had sent the previous year, along with his wedding ring, and the signet ring and medallion she had also sent. The card stayed in his wallet and he strongly believed these keepsakes had kept him safe.

> Have not lost much condition. I think you would know
> me if I walked in unexpectedly. That is how I would like
> to come home, just walk in some evening about teatime
> and watch you and the bairns for a few minutes before
> making my presence known. How I'd love to see your face
> if it could be so.

In his dreams, the surprised delight on their faces warmed his heart. But there was a stark reality he had to reluctantly acknowledge, and it filled him with sadness.

The days are slipping by, and they grow older and I miss another stage of their childhood. I will never have had the opportunity of seeing them grow from babyhood to early childhood, something you, my darling, have on your own. Their Daddy will be a strange being to them when they eventually do see him.

*

Although Japan had suffered a setback in the Pacific, its domination of Burma was almost complete and now its pressure on India was intensifying. Scott noticed a troubling change in attitude among the Japanese guards at Tavoy, compared with those at Victoria Point. 'Quite a few of the lads have been done up,' he wrote. 'They are bash merchants up here.' There had been liberal use of rifle butts, boots and heavy sticks.

Already the guards had begun to exercise the brutality that would make the Burma Railway infamous. An early muster parade exemplified this. Men in the Regimental Aid Post (RAP), most stricken with fever and dysentery and hardly able to walk, were ordered on parade, where they were made to stand for an hour. Scott wondered just how many more items would be metaphorically written on 'the ledger' against the Japanese.

The list was growing rapidly, and Victoria Point began to seem more like a rest camp – especially when the news of the execution of more Australians at Tavoy filtered through. As it had been with the execution of Bob Goulden, the circumstances deeply alarmed Scott. Yet again he had no doubt it was murder.

The so-called 'Tavoy Eight' were members of the 4th Anti-Tank Regiment who had escaped from the Tavoy aerodrome camp to the nearby hills on the night of 2 June 1942. Three days later, they were recaptured. By next day, the escapees had been tried in secret and condemned to death. They had been found guilty of breaking a proclamation issued by Major Hiroshi Itsui, the regional commander, that 'those who escape or plan to escape shall be shot dead'. The Japanese were unforgiving and gave just four hours' notice to Brigadier Varley that the eight men would be shot shortly before sunset at a spot near the aerodrome.

With time at a premium, Varley immediately wrote and delivered a letter of protest to the camp commandant, Captain Hirayasu Shina. When Shina rejected his approach, Varley demanded to see Major Itsui. According to the chaplain Fred Bashford, Itsui treated Varley with contempt and ordered him out of his office.

On leaving, Varley saw the eight men in the distance and shouted out to them, 'You are for it, lads.' Bashford and the Catholic chaplain Harry Smith approached Shina and asked to speak to the men. Shina refused, saying, 'After dead, you may see them.' This, he explained, was laid down by the Imperial Japanese Army. Already, a working party of forty men had been detailed to dig graves. Bashford, Smith and Varley were ordered to make their way to the execution site, where Shina again refused permission for them to speak to the condemned men.

As Varley, Bashford and Smith looked on on, the eight had their hands tied behind their backs and were blindfolded, before being forced to sit down, their legs splayed in front of them, and were then tied to posts. The firing party of sixteen Japanese, according to Bashford, 'seemed to treat the matter as a joke or a picnic'. Again Bashford sought to speak to the men, and again he was refused permission.

According to Varley, 'Just before death the spirit of these eight Australians was wonderful. They all spoke cheerio and good luck messages to one another and never showed any sign of fear. A truly courageous end.'

Shina gave the order. The men died instantly. After the execution, the firing squad presented arms and the entire assembled company of Japanese saluted.

Bashford described how 'Shina then smiled to me and condescendingly said, "Now you may see them."' According to Bashford, Varley had done everything in his power to save the men, and had shouted to Major Itsui, 'Whoever ordered this execution will pay for it after the war.' Shina, Bashford added, had acted in 'a callous manner throughout the entire proceedings'.

Officially recording these 'gruesome and ghastly' events helped Scott relieve some of the outrage he felt. He was determined 'to get the details down', to ensure that justice would be done after the war for these men, whose bodies had been 'kicked into the grave' by the Japanese. 'One day we will square the account for all they've done to us, and those they have murdered,' Scott wrote.

The war correspondent and POW Rohan Rivett summed up the chances of escape when he arrived at Tavoy not long after the executions: 'Distances, the jungles, the sea and the native population were more effective custodians than stone walls and iron bars.'

If Scott had ever been tempted, the Japanese response was persuasive. What made life more tolerable was the presence of mates. 'The gang has stuck together and shared everything that has come along, good and bad,' he noted.

On the Burma Railway, mateship was critical – the lives of men depended on it. The opportunity to debrief with each other about the day's events, to curse the guards' latest brutal insults and to plan revenge helped them integrate the events and check their resentment. Humour at the expense of the brutal guards never went astray. They all had nicknames – 'the Boy Bastard', 'the Snake', 'Dogface', 'Dopey', 'Stupid', 'Pig's Head' – to which they all answered. 'It is funny at work,' Scott said. 'Someone calls out "Dopey" and he comes running.'

Scott's gang included men from the AASC such as Alan Donaldson, Baldy McFadyen and Laurie Osmand, 'Wimpy' Edwards, Murray Knight and Murray Cheyne. Having all been through the fighting in Malaya and Singapore, they stuck together tightly and watched over each other's health. They would lie awake at night and talk of home and family, often wondering out loud what things would be like when the war was over.

When Laurie came down with dysentery, the gang's concern grew. His progress seemed too slow; he had been going downhill for a few weeks. He'd been 'skin and bone' when he'd left Victoria Point, but Scott thought he was progressing slowly at Tavoy. But a week later word came that Laurie had died. Scott was grief-stricken. 'Poor old fellow,' he wrote. 'He put up a very gallant fight until near the finish, when he had continuous diarrhoea and gave up hope.'

Despite Scott's entreaties, he and the rest of Laurie's mates were not allowed to see his grave. This was hard – Laurie was one of them. Scott felt for Laurie's wife and children, waiting in vain for him to come home, who couldn't be informed of his death. In Scott's view, that so many men had needlessly died since they'd left Changi was enough to damn the Japanese 'forever in the eyes of the civilised world'.

Already the conditions of their existence were getting everyone down. Scott admitted to having the blues. 'Even a look at my photos didn't brighten me up like it usually does,' he wrote. He knew he needed to pull himself out of despondency, as it was dangerous to remain there too long. So he conjured up the image of sitting in front of a roaring fire, with Marge on his knee, listening to the radio. This was a recurring theme. 'Those days seem very far away now, though each night I see you still waiting at the gate for me, wearing the frock that Lofty and I had so much fun buying.'

That image of Marge was so powerful that it helped counter the pain of the new reality Scott had to confront each day. It would take a long time to wipe away the memories of the ever-increasing insults and bashings. 'If you lift a hand, it's a bayonet for you,' he lamented. So different from the fun of buying a frock.

11

A Safe Space

The dreams, when they came, were vivid. Scott had been a POW for more than six months, and in his sleep he began to relive his war experiences. 'Sometimes I dream that I'm telling people all the things that have happened here and in Malaya: the blue is on again and we are dodging bombs and shells,' he wrote. He dreamt his mother was dying, then his father, then Marge's mother and he couldn't get to Marge to console her. He felt he was letting her down. His sense of shame around the surrender, and of powerlessness concerning Marge, was playing out as he slept.

Scott recognised that a malaise was beginning to grip the men at Tavoy. So many factors were contributing to their gloom and misery, and many fell into moping about their existence. At the root of it, for Scott, was his battle with the reality that Marge was so far away, and uncontactable.

If only I knew how you were, life would be bearable at least. I just bit Jock's head off a while ago. This existence is getting us all down. We are all stagnating here. It is

time we moved on, even if we put up with worse than this.
All we do is lounge around and eat our miserable pittance.

Scott intuitively knew that his thoughts of Marge were his
pathway to regaining equilibrium. Dreaming of her could keep
the nightmares at bay.

> I was trying to sleep, not very successfully, and lying with
> my eyes closed, there seemed to be a light shining which
> gradually focused itself into a small circle, and I could see
> your face, just your head. It was very vivid, kept recurring
> for quite a while.

He cursed the fact that he could not get a letter through to
her, a liberty he heard had been granted the POWs at Mergui.
'What we would have given for the same privilege,' he said. 'I'd
give half the money in the pay book if I could. If only I knew
how you and the bairns were.' In the meantime, Marge's letters,
along with the few photos, had to suffice. 'They are my greatest
treasure at present. Without them I don't know how I'd get on.'
Scott did not hide his feelings for Marge from his mates.
They were in awe of the power of the relationship, and they all
wanted to meet her after the war.

> We look like having a few parties when we come home –
> everyone wants to come to Dandenong to meet you.
> Accommodation won't worry us, as all we'll want is a
> couple of blankets. As Alan [Campbell] said the other
> night, 'If ever you and I go home blotto and Marge goes
> crook, we can curl up on the floor.' If you won't feed us,
> all we will want is a pound of rice.

Sergeant Alan Campbell (right) was one of the mates with whom Scott envisaged having a continuing post-war friendship. Writing of this image, Scott urged Marge to appreciate just 'how slim I've got'.

If thoughts of home anchored him, conversations with his mates reflected Scott's yearning for get-togethers post-war, where alcohol would flow and there would be food aplenty and much merriment. All the things the gang missed so much. Their wishes to meet each other's families spread the spirit of camaraderie they valued so highly.

Scott wanted Marge to choose a holiday location for a few weeks when the war was over. They were 'all going to gather at Healesville for a start', he told her; there would be Alan Campbell's family, along with Jack Heathwood, Bob Skilton and Laurie Phillips and their families. Baldy McFadyen would be there 'to keep us in order'.

He enjoyed foreshadowing a future he was determined to make happen – it would be a return to normality. Like Lofty, his new mates would also be like family to Marge. He knew she would welcome them, and enjoy seeing them together, even when they 'tied one on'. The thought of sitting 'in a nice, cosy beer parlour having a few jugs' brought Scott wistful hope, as did 'doing the rounds of the pubs with Pop and then getting abused when we come home'.

The past and the future had become the present. Such dreams of the future served another purpose: they inoculated the men against thoughts of giving up. They were a brotherhood. Their shared experiences were something that only they would understand. Even now he could see it, even if the images in his dreams didn't always end quite the way they started.

I had a very vivid dream of you and home last night. We were up in Stawell having a great old time. It was just getting interesting when one of the chaps fell downstairs in the dark and woke the hall. You should have heard the

abuse. I couldn't take my thoughts back into it again, and
Jock's knees annoyed me for the rest of the night.

Small things became momentous. He and his mates, he told
Marge, had just enjoyed the rare pleasure of afternoon tea
three days in a row. Sweet potatoes, curry and dhal patties
with a cup of tea. 'We are living pretty well,' he wrote. 'Every
night we have our feed of dhal and that gives us vitamins A, B
and C.' Nonetheless, he would have relished the opportunity
to have a nice ham sandwich.

The locals were willing to help supply food to the POWs,
Scott explained. 'The Burmese were round the fence last night
throwing over parcels of food for us. Their generosity and
kindness is beyond description. They would willingly feed all
the POWs here, but Nip would not allow it.'

In one of Marge's letters to him in Malaya, she had described
her mother cooking 'a nice cold chicken and duckling for
lunch today ... with a lovely cool salad. How you would have
enjoyed it.' He was not so sure:

> If you remember, I passed very caustic comments on it
> when I answered your letter at the time, and I still think
> of it as I sit down with my spoon to a mess tin containing
> ⅓ lb of indifferently cooked rice and some greasy
> vegetable stew. No meat; we hastily add some salt and
> curry powder and then tear in, trying to imagine we are
> having roast beef and Yorkshire pudding. Still, those days
> will come again.

He had now spent eight months as a prisoner, and Scott mused
that perhaps the war would soon be over – perhaps even by

Christmas – and they would be released. Everyone could still hope. But in early October 1942 that hope turned to alarm when word came that an American submarine, the USS *Grouper*, had torpedoed a Japanese transport carrying POWs. There had been a heavy loss of life.

The news sent shockwaves through the families of POWs. Marge was unnerved. *The Age* on 9 October 1942 carried a report out of New York under the heading 'ALLEGED SINKING OF PRISON SHIP'. The story said the *Lisbon Maru* had been torpedoed on 1 October in the South China Sea and that 1800 British and Australian prisoners had been aboard, en route to Japan. More than 800 men had been lost.

When Scott heard the news, his first thoughts were for Marge. She did not know where he was, and he feared she might think he was on the doomed transport. 'I can imagine how you have been all day today, worried out of your mind,' he wrote. He wondered too if the names of the 3000 Australians who formed 'A' Force had reached Australia – the men who made up the contingent that had sailed from Singapore for Burma in May.

This would likely have been the case if Captain Charles Cousens, an officer attached to 2/19th Battalion, had returned home with the list. An anguished Scott hoped Cousens had – but, alas, he hadn't. Just why was about to become one of the great Australian military conundrums of the war. It was also one of those intersections of fate whose ramifications affected both Scott and Marge, each imagining what the consequences of the sinking meant for the other.

Through no wish of his own, Cousens was in Tokyo when the sinking happened. Just why he was there was a consequence of the surrender in Singapore, when AIF headquarters in Malaya had inadvertently revealed key details about Cousens: that before the war he had been a Sydney radio announcer. While at Changi, Cousens had refused to broadcast for the Japanese and was sent to Burma with 'A' Force. In early August, Scott heard rumours that Cousens had left Burma, and this led him to hope that somehow he might have been returned to Australia. But in fact the Japanese had sent Cousens to Tokyo, from where he had at least hoped that he might be able to broadcast the names of POWs to Australian families anxiously awaiting news. Instead, under threat of torture and death, Cousens wrote propaganda scripts, 'coached' English-speaking Japanese announcers and made short-wave broadcasts over Radio Tokyo.

The lack of information about the sinking of the *Lisbon Maru* left Scott angry and helpless. 'Oh, if only I could reach you with news in some way,' he wrote; all he wanted was to let Marge know he was 'as good as gold and safe as houses'. But he couldn't.

Nor could he get the sinking out of his mind, imagining the horror the POWs on the 7000-tonne transport had experienced. Battened into three cargo holds, they were unable to climb to safety as the ship went down. The torpedoes would have killed hundreds. 'Poor devils, they wouldn't have a hope,' Scott lamented. He was incensed that not only did the Japanese vastly overload their transport ships, but they also failed to give them distinguishing marks to signify that POWs were part of the cargo. 'We are hoping none of our chaps were on board, but that is a forlorn one.'

Behind the danger that the sinking highlighted was a loophole in the 1929 Geneva Convention on the treatment of POWs. The convention contained no articles relating to the transfer of POWs by sea, and all warring nations were reluctant to address the problem, fearing it would advantage the enemy.

Before the *Lisbon Maru* there had been another sinking of an unmarked POW transport, the *Montevideo Maru*, torpedoed by a US submarine on 1 July 1942 off the Philippines. It resulted in the loss of 1053 Australian lives, making it the greatest maritime disaster in Australian history.

The *Lisbon Maru* tragedy punctured the refuge that Scott had created for himself, the space he shared with Marge in his mind. This was a space that was safe, where he could imagine Marge as being close, talk to her and look at her photo, to the point that he felt he was with her and could begin writing. But now, when there was an urgent need to reassure her, he was powerless. The information he knew Marge would read back in Australia destabilised his sense of security. There was nothing he could do, and it tormented him.

In the event, no Australians were on board the *Lisbon Maru*. The POWs were British, and of the 1816 on board, 842 died. Not knowing this, Scott just fervently hoped that the names would be published in Australia soon. 'Then you will know I am safe.'

For both him and Marge, it was the lack of information about the other that was so cruel.

12

Inner Life

It took just a few moments: immersing himself in the beauty of nature offered Scott an almost reverential feeling of wonder. Viktor Frankl could feel it too. As a psychiatrist, spending three years in captivity gave Frankl the opportunity to witness first-hand the various means internees used to cope with the rigours of captivity. Those who could find even a shred of meaning in their lives at least had something to hang onto. Their survival depended on it. Frankl saw it in others, and he saw it in himself.

The nineteenth-century philosopher Henri-Frédéric Amiel wrote: 'A man who has no inner life is a slave to his surroundings.' This could hardly be more apt than for those in captivity. The more intense the inner life, the more intense the experience of nature and art. Scott was one of the lucky ones: he had an inner life. He could retreat from the grotesqueness of his immediate surroundings to his 'talks' with Marge. 'Although it wasn't Sunday, I was keeping you company,' he wrote on one occasion. 'Do you ever stop when you are doing something during the day as if I was with you? I often do, darling. I sometimes find myself on the point of speaking aloud to you.'

Viktor Frankl, too, yearned for his wife, Tilly. She could have been just a hundred or so metres away, in another part of Auschwitz, but how could he know? Still he could reach her in other ways. In the deathly grey of Auschwitz, encircled by a wall of barbed wire, there was limited opportunity to take in the natural beauty of the surrounding landscape. There was more opportunity while working on railway lines in the nearby countryside. But to take that opportunity brought risk. In their dawn march to a worksite, those not marching smartly enough over the icy ground were yelled at threateningly, bashed with a rifle butt or sharply kicked by guards. But Viktor could talk silently to Tilly.

At work one morning, he was again struggling with the hopelessness of his situation and the ever-present threat of death when, out of nowhere, he felt his spirit soar through the gloom – and just at that moment a light came on in a distant farmhouse. This was a sign. Yes, there was an ultimate purpose. He was alive to the symbolism.

Scott, too, was marched with other POWs to worksites on the railway they were building through the jungle. Likewise, he snatched moments when the guards were not so attentive, mesmerised by country so different from the flatlands of Victoria's Wimmera region. He was alive to it all, and it took his breath away.

Looking back across the mountains, the sight was even more splendid. The smoke of village fires rising against the heavy green of the mountain ranges. Behind the range a deep green strip of sky merging into the clouds. Purple and heliotrope were predominant in the lower strata, then came the beautiful rose and pink colours with a background of deep scarlet. The bright green gaps merged into the golden red and light gold clouds as the eye moved further up the sky. Gradually they faded out into the leaden grey sky, the reflection faintly seen on the rippling surface of the sea. As the darkness of the twilight descended, one was left with a sense that something beautiful had left the world and had left behind it a feeling of peace.

That Scott was left with 'a feeling of peace' highlighted his ability to immerse himself in the vision before him. It would have been easier for him to feel that his life was out of control, that fate had dealt him an unfair hand. To counter this, he sought experiences in which he was transfixed by nature and the beauty of the environment around him. He may not even have been aware of doing this, but nature suffused him with a stillness of mind, however momentary, and through this nurtured his determination to survive.

He understood that he had to hang on to his sanity at any cost. Hope can be agonising, but instinctively he knew how to nurture it. Viktor Frankl, too, at a very conscious level, knew this well.

The two men were unalike in many ways, but what they did share was greater than their differences. Both could be transported by wonder and awe, swept away by a spectacular sunset or the momentary flight of a bird. Scott would relive the feeling later that evening when describing it in a letter. They found in the daily grind of their captivity small pleasures and celebrated them. Both could retreat into an inner life that could transport them as easily to the past, reliving longed-for memories, or to an envisioned future. They weren't entrapped by these memories or fantasies; rather, they helped them endure the present. Their strategy was to reach out beyond themselves, for something other than themselves.

The medical officer at Tavoy, Rowley Richards, also understood the value of stopping to take in the natural environment. 'Our darker thoughts were tempered with recollections of the sheer beauty of Burma: her rosy red dawns, shadowy hills of all shades of green, gigantic teak trees and the loveliness of a freshly picked orchid,' he later wrote. While Dr Richards clearly appreciated the beauty of Burma, Scott devoured it.

The chance to read provided another means by which Scott could lose himself. Books were a rare commodity, but treasured by the men. For this they had Brigadier Varley to thank. While at the camp at Tavoy, he became aware of a well-stocked library of English-language books at the Tavoy Club, recently abandoned by the British. Not unreasonably, Varley asked the Japanese officer in charge of the POWs at that time, Lieutenant Tanaka, for at least some books. The lieutenant's response was blunt: 'I cannot read – why should you prisoners?' Repeated requests brought no further joy. Varley changed his tactics. 'I then asked for latrine paper and the books were produced,' he noted dryly.

John Garran wrote that 'books just now seem available in plenty. A batch of good ones came in from Tavoy Club Library, where a party was cleaning it up for the Japs to occupy the building. Have in view "Lenin" and "Rats, Lice and History". Still reading "Akbar". Interesting.'

One of the psychological dangers threatening the men in captivity was the feeling that imprisonment meant a complete break with the past and disconnection with their future. The mental discipline of reading was thought to keep alive the flame of intellectual curiosity, and to provide a ready means of escapism, if not escape.

The range at Tavoy included mostly well-known authors of the day. Among them were Rudyard Kipling, Sinclair Lewis, John Steinbeck, Arthur Conan Doyle, Ernest Hemingway, Janet Taylor Caldwell, James Hilton and Miles Franklin. Books changed hands frequently and were read and reread, becoming increasingly tattered. Informal libraries were created where possible. The men tended to cling to books; once read, they could be bartered for the next book, or the pages used for rolling cigarettes, or even for writing diaries.

Dr Richards remembered how each man had three or four books, and this stock became a mobile library.

> We'd read our books and pass them around. We'd have a
> little session before lights out discussing the merits of the
> book. Initially the popular books were *Lady Chatterley's
> Lover* and they soon get worn out. The books that were
> the most popular were the Bibles. Bible paper was very
> thin and very good for rolling cigarettes, which they made
> from chopped up cigars. The books that became very
> popular were the encyclopedias, the *Golden Treasury of
> English Verse*, and philosophy books.

Scott always had a book to tell Marge about. Fiction encouraged him to be carried off into the story, feeling with, and for, the characters. Of course, every book he read seemed to mention at least one heavenly sounding meal; his eyes always lit upon any mention of food. In a clear allusion to

Lady Chatterley's Lover, he added that there were some very fine books about, 'and some not so hot. A lot of them banned at home, rightly so.'

Some indeed conjured up images he likened to himself – even the notorious cannibal prisoner Matt Gabbett, who escaped from Port Arthur in Marcus Clark's novel *For the Term of His Natural Life*. 'I have lost a fair bit of weight last month or so. I look like Matt Gabbett now in my Shanghai shorts,' he wrote, recalling the 1927 film of the book. The similarity of the conditions at the convict-era prisons of Tasmania and the railway camps of Burma clearly sparked the comparison. What also would not have gone unnoticed by Scott was that the story depicts both the ugliness and the resilience of man. Like the hero of the book, Rufus Dawes, he could now relate to maintaining resilience in the face of ugliness.

Scott was mesmerised by the power of words, and writing came naturally to him. Fortuitously, when the British hurriedly quit Tavoy they left behind supplies of pens, ink and paper marked 'naval message'. As RSM, he had access to these materials, and on this naval message paper he wrote his letters to Marge – letters he knew may never be sent. Perhaps writing put him in a frame of mind to sleep, affording him some level of peace, rather than the nightmares that often beset his mates. He was not immune from nightmares, but at least he could share them with Marge, on paper, rather than suppressing feelings that needed an outlet.

Viktor Frankl also knew the positive impact of writing. He was convinced that a key factor in his survival was reconstructing the manuscript that he had sewn into his overcoat but on entering Auschwitz had been forced to give up. A fellow inmate gave him a pencil stub for his fortieth birthday, along with a few SS forms that he had 'miraculously' filched. On the backs of these forms Frankl was able to scribble notes.

In Japanese and Nazi camps alike, paper was scarce, but as both Frankl and Scott knew, what was written on these pages was precious. Both men were aware that swift punishment would follow if their writings, whether manuscript or letter, were found by the guards. Neither doubted this was a risk worth taking.

13

Doctor's Orders

Like all the other POWs, Scott was now a number. He took it in his stride. 'We now wear a wooden block with it painted on,' he recorded; '2642 is mine.' Viktor Frankl suffered the indignity of having the number 119104 tattooed on his left arm – a more efficient form of identification perhaps, but also more dehumanising in its effect.

The allocation of numbers for POWs coincided with a speech by Lieutenant Colonel Yoshitada Nagatomo, Chief of the War Prisoners, Number 3 Branch, Thanbyuzayat. Small in stature but large in self-importance, and with a high-pitched, singsong voice, Nagatomo 'read us the riot act and we got our new numbers', as Scott described it.

> We waited an hour for his highness and then he mounted
> the table and told us just what we were. It was very funny.
> We are a rabble, and Nippon is almighty. We were to
> think ourselves honoured that we were given the chance,
> and privilege, of helping to build the railway line through
> to Bangkok.

There was a chilling conclusion to Nagatomo's speech: there would be many POWs who would not see their homes again. The railroad would be built, the Japanese officer said, 'if we have to build it over the white man's body'.

This was the objective, of course, of their journey from Singapore: the construction of the Burma Railway. Thanbyuzayat was the starting point on the Burmese side, and known as 0 Kilo.

It soon became apparent how much of an honour it was for Scott to work for the Japanese Emperor when he arrived at the 14 Kilo camp, at Thetkaw, on 24 October 1942, after a voyage from Tavoy. Unlike the previous voyages, this one had been made in conditions better than anyone expected. They had travelled by barge downriver to the Andaman Sea, where they boarded a boat for the journey up the coast to Moulmein, a staging post on the way to Thetkaw.

The launch was about forty feet with the cutest little outboard latrine over the stern. Both banks of the river were lined with paddy fields, and occasionally a small native kampong would appear in sight. A very muddy and filthy stream widening as we approached the sea to about three-quarters of a mile, with mud banks and fish traps. As the tide ran out you could see the bamboo poles of the fish traps shaking as a fish tried to escape. We sailed downstream for hours. As evening approached, the smoke of fires ascended like a blue pall against the dark green of the jungle-covered mountains. The old bargee spoke a bit of English and we had a yarn to him. Thirty rupees a month the Nips paid him, but would not do any repairs for him.

Once at Thetkaw, they set up camp in a rubber plantation, sleeping in huts that were well spaced apart. Lice in the camps at night were so bad that many POWs left their narrow bamboo beds and slept outside. However, once the heat of the day was gone, the nights and early mornings were bitterly cold. Few had blankets, and those who had a rice bag to cover themselves were lucky.

They began work on the railway almost immediately. Each POW was required to shift 1.2 cubic metres of earth per day, in dry and dusty conditions. It was the start of the dry season, and the heat from the sun became intense. For the many men who did not have water bottles, staying hydrated became an additional daily problem.

After just a day or two 'on the shovel' under a scorching tropical sun, Scott proudly announced to Marge: 'I haven't even raised a blister, so your old pot and pan is not in bad nick after all, sweetheart. We toil all day and come home at night to a lovely swim in a creek 200 yards away, and it is beautiful.'

Besides finding a positive rationale in the labour, Scott had settled on his method of coping. He had his rituals around photos and letters, and he had his lucky charms. Along with the signet ring, Marge had sent him a medallion, which he was sure had kept him doubly safe in the battle for Singapore. Now it was lost – lost while working. He searched and searched, fearing his luck would change without it. 'I wouldn't have lost it for the world,' he said. 'Feel very miserable about it now.'

In this mood, he wrote of his despair, of things being 'so hopeless' for his fellow Australian servicemen – 'poor deluded patriots' – caught up in the war. They were sweating their souls out for their Japanese captors, 'all because our country sold us into slavery ... pardon my whingeing, but I wish I had some of our pot-bellied politicians here.'

A vein of resentment was running through Scott's letters – and not only for the treatment meted out by the guards. At a deeper level was the shame of the surrender, and this continued to rankle. He felt the need to write about it, yet while doing so, it was as though he suddenly remembered it was Marge he was writing to, and his tone changed abruptly – he softened and addressed her directly, reassuring her, and thereby himself.

Nearly a year had passed since he'd had news of Marge, and Scott found this almost unbearable. He felt helpless and frustrated in his attempts to get word to her. He knew how worried she would be. He prayed that someone, somehow had contacted Marge. He focused intensely on his 9 pm pact. 'I try to reach you at nights, but don't know whether or not I am successful,' he wrote. With an unusually forlorn tone, Scott finished his letter with: 'Better days are ahead, aren't they, and keep smiling.'

*

With a deadline of just eighteen months to construct the railway connecting Thanbyuzayat with Ban Pong, the Thai distribution point for POWs sent from Changi to work on the railway, the work took on a new urgency. The Japanese rarely allowed time for recreation, let alone for church on Sundays. Every day was a work day, except on the whim of the guards, who occasionally allowed a day off – including holidays to commemorate the memory of some past emperor or other. But there was no regularity, and this meant that Scott's ritual of being at church 'with Marge' was random at best.

To keep the construction on schedule, the guards – most of whom were now Koreans – doubled down on discipline. Small infractions were pounced upon. In early November 1942, Scott's bridge-building team was paraded and it was bluntly explained to them that they were prisoners, not guests, and would be shot on sight if they resisted their captors. 'They humiliate us in every way and use us as beasts of burden,' he noted. 'If Australia ever wants to resume relations with them, there are a few thousand of us who will have a say. When one thinks of the many who have died needlessly since we moved from Changi, it is sufficient to damn them forever.'

The men were paid a pittance for their work: 15 cents for NCOs, and 10 cents (about two pence in Australian currency) for privates. In theory, officers were paid the Japanese equivalent of their army pay, but a large sum was banked on their behalf by the Japanese and board and lodgings were deducted. The result was that although officers received less than a quarter of their entitlement, this was still far above what the lower ranks would receive and did not fluctuate in proportion to the number of days worked.

For Scott, the ruthlessness of the Japanese attitude was exemplified by the eighty-seven 'House Rules for War Prisoners' that Nagatomo had drawn up. These preposterous rules, often harsh and sometimes petty, began by stipulating that POWs should follow the rules of the Imperial Japanese Army and obey orders from officers. POWs 'should never try to escape', and those who did not intend to escape should submit a declaration. Anyone who did not submit a declaration would be locked up. Escape would be punished by death – 'shot dead on the spot'. Meetings without approval were prohibited, POWs should salute officers, they should stand to attention when an officer approached their rooms, and they were banned from singing or talking aloud. 'Smoking should be done at a fixed place where ash-tray is placed', and the men should 'not speak, smoke or rest on the ground during the working hours excluding interval time'.

When he saw the rules in early October, Major Green refused to sign them because of the requirement that POWs would not attempt to escape. His refusal followed an order from Brigadier Varley that he should not sign. Nagatomo ordered Green into solitary confinement, where he was held in a dark, airless room, just 1 metre by 1.5 metres, with no blanket or bedding. He was given a starvation diet of salted rice and water, pushed through a hole in the door to him twice daily.

Varley wrote a letter of protest. In response, Nagatomo threatened to starve all the troops until they signed. Varley made it plain to Nagatomo that it was every Australian's duty to escape, and referred him to articles of the Hague Convention whereby POWs could not be asked or compelled to sign such a demand. Varley's strategy was to demonstrate that the use of compulsion in having POWs sign the letter was illegal. His focus was on after the war, and potential charges of war crimes.

Nagatomo was unmoved, asserting he had the right to imprison POWs, or shoot them for disobedience if necessary. He ordered Varley be locked up. He and Green would be held in confinement until they signed – regardless of their health. Varley reiterated that signing would be illegal, but knew he had no option. 'Under these conditions I will sign.' Green also signed under duress.

Released, Varley addressed the Australians, saying he was satisfied that 'force' was used for the whole AIF contingent. In signing, he had set a precedent. It was his advice that 'no good purpose' would be served by refusing to sign. Officers and men alike backed him. Scott had little doubt that Green would have been left to die if he hadn't signed. 'There is a long score to settle when the tide turns,' he noted.

But, as number 2642, Scott had no option, solemnly swearing on his honour that he would not 'under any circumstances attempt to escape'. He signed it with his name, nationality and new number, giving his rank as Warrant Officer Class 1.

*

The stand-off served as a dispiriting diversion from the worsening situation at the camp. The sanitary conditions were bad; the latrines were open to flies. A daily fly quota for each man was introduced – the number he had to deliver to 'the fly catcher'. The men soon found it was less stressful to begin a recycling program and substitute each day's catch for the next day's quota.

Septic sores and tropical ulcers quickly became widespread. Rats and bugs made the situation worse. Men in the 'hospital' – a building worse than a fowl house, according to Varley – had no blankets, no bandages and no medicines. The number of sick men rose from 8 per cent of the POW population to 30 per cent. 'This is a battle for life,' Varley concluded.

Much of the illness was due to the prolonged inadequate diet and subsequent vitamin deficiency. The men spoke of food, dreamt of food and planned menus for when they returned home. Given that their expectations were so low, Curly, the cook, cemented his importance by being able to turn very little into a sumptuous feast. Scott was especially pleased when eggs were available because of their protein – and adequate protein was only available infrequently. He needed it if he was to shift his 1.2 cubic metres of black loam each day. Scott even gave up smoking in order to put his money into eggs. 'Two per day will keep me going well,' he wrote. 'The eggs here are beauties, big fresh duck eggs. All we lack is the steak to slap them on.' He was in no doubt that maintaining his health was crucial. 'If I can hang on to my health I will be satisfied. I am looking after myself – I have such a lot to come home to.'

Disease spread quickly through the camp, through contagion and through vitamin deficiency. Outbreaks of beriberi became frequent, due to thiamine deficiency, causing men's feet, ankles and face to swell up, puffy like a mound of dough. The jungles of Burma and Thailand were also hyperendemic for malaria. For those unlucky to come down with both beriberi and malaria, the outcome was often fatal.

And then there were the tropical ulcers. A scratch on the leg would inevitably grow bigger, day by day, and fester, sometimes starting at the ankle and ending at the knee. Doctors would gouge out the putrid flesh with a spoon because they had no other means of treatment. Many men begged them to amputate.

From just such a scratch on his leg, Baldy McFadyen developed an ulcer that would lay him up for two months. The sight of dozens of men bedridden with suppurating leg ulcers was frightening, as healing in the tropics, with almost no medical supplies, was a long and painful process.

Finally there was the dysentery, which 'dragged the poor fellows down', Scott wrote. For this he blamed the 'mucky rice' they were given for breakfast.

He took hope from the arrival of the 2/4th Machine Gun Battalion's medical officer, Captain Claude 'Pills' Anderson.

'He's a wonder, the finest MO I've ever seen,' said Scott. Anderson would work at the RAP from 8 am until 9 pm, dressing wounds. The story quickly spread that after an enemy shell exploded in Malaya, Anderson had sustained shrapnel in his thigh but refused to let anyone touch it until he had attended to fifteen or so wounded men around him.

Scott took exception to the failure of men to come forward to assist Captain Anderson when he appealed for just four volunteers from the 300-odd on sick parade one morning. 'He cursed and swore, for the first time on record, so I'm told,' Scott wrote.

Anderson, like all the MOs, quickly realised that besides the medical care of the men, there was a need to give them the hope that they would survive. Dr Rowley Richards agreed, noting in his diary, 'We're not without purpose, we're not beaten ... We can live in spite of the Japs and this bloody jungle. Just live, day by day by day.'

Living for a purpose and with hope was doctor's orders.

*

Scott could handle the physical labour, but the conditions under which they worked added another level of difficulty. On days with no wind, the heat intensified. 'You toil there under a cloudless sky, with a pitiless sun blazing down, burning the lights out of you,' he told Marge. Down in the cuttings, the work was particularly gruelling, and the air stifling. 'It was a killer down there,' Scott said. 'I'll give the temperature at about 150 degrees. We had ten collapse today and there will be more tomorrow.'

Scott was selected as a *kumicho* – an officer in charge of fifty POW workers, and responsible for carrying out Japanese orders. To signify his position, he wore a yellow armband and kept a workbook in which he had to record each man's work, noting 'their diligence or idleness'.

Being in charge did not stop him from labouring alongside his men – or from standing up for them. Major George Harris told Scott the guards had raised hell about him, saying he wasn't to be a *kumicho* any longer. Harris gave the guards as good as he got, as Scott later reported: 'He said that if the Japs didn't stop interfering, our officers would leave them to it and let them do their own supervising. Result, I am still a "Kumi" boss, but got sacked off my job.'

For the men, Scott was a preferred *kumicho*; one group approached Major Green to ask that they be allowed to work under him. 'I must be doing okay,' Scott wrote. Around him, men worked in their underwear, or with rags around their waists. The Japanese provided clothing that amounted to little more than a G-string, coupled with cheap boots. The sun did not let up and they were all developing a deep, sunburnt tan. 'The sun certainly burns you up and dries you out,' Scott said. 'You can feel it drawing the sweat out of you.' His boots were soon worn through and he was forced to work in bare feet.

Most of the men 'worked like hell', making their daily metreage, but there were those who couldn't keep up and had to be helped out. This added to Scott's workload, leaving him 'done to a frazzle' at the end of the day. He couldn't abide those who shirked their workload. In a volunteer army, formed on an ethos of Anzac egalitarianism, such actions cut deep. Scott loathed bludgers, a term that covered a range of offending. 'The old AIF spirit is not there,' he lamented on one occasion.

Thieving between the men or unfairness in the distribution of goods also riled him. A corporal had been caught going through the tobacco leaves, putting his small ones in the men's pile and taking big ones. It was a small thing in itself, but when prized goods were pilfered, mateship suffered. These were the factors that now determined their survival as a group. And the group needed to function smoothly as they struggled with the work and the brutal enforcement.

But there were moments when the presence of the others receded, and Scott was alone. Such times sometimes happened when he rose early to use the latrines. One morning in mid-November, he was struck by the sight he took in as the day began.

> The sun was up, the rays striking the mountain ranges. They looked like threads of spun gold from the sky to earth, striking the mountaintops and into the valleys. The hills in the distance were dark green blending into deep purple, the rays just striking the tops, the valley dark green with the blue smoke of countless fires rising to the sky. As one looked at it, something inside seemed to say that the world was not such a bad place.

Scott drew nourishment from such scenes, reminding himself that his present predicament would end at some unknown time. A few days later, he wrote to Marge saying that he felt 'strangely happy today, for no apparent reason. Found myself whistling on the way for my wash this morning and a curious feeling in the old ticker, as if something momentous was about to happen.'

There were straws in the wind that led Scott to believe there were signs of progress in a world at war. He had heard from a clandestine radio a news bulletin that the Axis forces were being routed in North Africa and encircled in the Battle of Stalingrad. In the Pacific, Australian troops in New Guinea were pushing the Japanese back, while in the Solomon Islands US forces had sunk two Japanese battleships, some cruisers and several transports, with the loss of 30,000 troops. 'It looks as if the heat will be on Musso and Adolf very shortly,' Scott wrote. He dared to hope that Imperial Japan would be next.

14

The Last of the Human Freedoms

In the months since the fall of Singapore, Scott had become consumed by two fundamental questions: what made men go to war, and was the ultimate sacrifice of life worth it? And now the consequences of that defeat plagued him. It was a defeat the AIF had not seen coming, and the ramifications were playing out in numerous POW camps in South-east Asia that imprisoned more than 22,000 diggers. Scott had been certain of victory at the height of the fighting, and the bitterness he felt about the capitulation lingered. Labouring all day, he had time for introspection. He reflected on the brave men he had encountered in Singapore, heedless of danger.

He thought about the British sergeant major in charge of the anti-aircraft battery who kept his men going by sheer example. As the bombs were falling, he spurred on the crew: 'Come on, you bastards, keep your heads up and your guns going, we'll see where they are when the bastards land, that's right, stay with 'em.' With bombs falling all around them, the men kept firing, even when just fifteen metres away their mates were blown to hell. This took commitment and courage in the face of looming defeat. 'Was it worth anything, I wonder?' Scott asked.

He remembered too the officer from the Plymouth Argylls, a British infantry regiment so tough they were nicknamed 'the Jungle Beasts'. The officer, despite being hit, had fought all the way from Bukit Timah Road with eight of his troops. Scott had stayed with him as he died at Tanglin Barracks. His men were in tears, saying goodbye. His last words were: 'I'll soon be back, lads. Remember the regiment and fight on to the last.'

Scott had memories of incidents perpetrated by the Japanese in Malaya that he just couldn't erase from his mind: wounded men tied to trees and used as bayonet dummies; four men captured in a truck, two of whom were shot dead and the other two, both wounded, left to die. 'Was it worthwhile when we finish like this?' Scott wondered on 4 December 1942. 'Toiling harder than coolies for a miserable 4d [pence] a day for an illiterate, barbarous, uncivilised race?'

The images of ordinary men dying were overwhelming. But in what was now a well-established practice, Scott found increasingly that describing these images in words made them less vivid in his mind. He could then turn his focus to life with Marge.

> I long for the day to come when I can come home to you and settle down with our family. The future is the only thing to look forward to. We'll have our home and life together, precious one, and never mind the world. Let it roll by.

Scott's emotions were big. Whether it was anger and resentment at his current predicament, or wonder and love at things that brought him joy, he felt it all intensely. After twenty days working on the railway without a break, he sought comfort in his idealised future with Marge. All he had to do was bring out her photos. 'I had a look at my photos before going to sleep today,' he wrote, 'and you are still as beautiful as ever. Hardly a night goes by that I don't dream of you and home.'

He missed Marge deeply, and just wanted to be home with her, and his resentment grew towards those at home who had not enlisted. Even family members were not exempt from his disgruntlement – including Marge's brother Russ. 'I often wonder how Russ would have fared, had he been here without your mother doing everything for him,' Scott related. 'I fancy it would have broken him; he couldn't battle for himself.' His resentment even manifested in a dream in which Scott was castigating Russ for not doing his bit. Unbeknown to Scott, Russ had enlisted in the army on 12 August 1942 and was indeed 'doing his bit'.

The events that were unfolding challenged the men's equilibrium. How could they not? The death rate, on average, was about two men every three days, usually from dysentery. Burials virtually became a daily ritual. Torture was standard practice. 'Our wounded [are] hung up by the thumbs or nailed to trees and tied to ant beds,' Scott wrote. This was pure barbarism, and would challenge anyone's grip on sanity.

Then there was the matter of what the Japanese called the 'extreme penalty'. The fate of three Dutch POWs who had escaped exemplified this. When they were recaptured, Varley, along with the Dutch officers, argued that they should not be shot. To do so would be in contravention of Japan's signature to the Hague Convention, they said. Nagatomo was unmoved. The POWs had signed the declaration that they would not escape, and then the three Dutchmen had made their break. Therefore, Nagatomo responded, Japan was entitled to execute them.

Varley said they had signed under duress, but Nagatomo rejected this. He argued that Varley had no right to claim this, as he too had signed the declaration, and if he had not done this of his own free will, he would go back to the guardhouse. 'And he did not care if I died there,' Varley noted. Six days later, the Dutch were taken to the cemetery and shot.

That was not the end of it. Private George Whitfield, of the 8th Division's Petrol Company, had given himself up after escaping on 10 November 1942, and was in custody at the camp. Scott had been impressed by his courage in making a break for it. 'One can't help hoping in a way that he succeeds,' he wrote, even though it meant extra guards at night to discourage others. Scott thought Whitfield looked like getting away. Just over a month later, though, Whitfield's freedom ended. He walked into the camp, saying he had no chance of escape. The Japanese had offered the Burmese a reward of 100 rupees for each man they captured. The Burmese, of course, had been watching his movements.

The Australians tried desperately to save his life, the MOs arguing that he was 'slightly deficient mentally, and a moral imbecile, not responsible for his actions'. Whitfield was put into hospital, with one Japanese officer saying he would not be shot, and that in view of his mental condition he would be kept in the hospital for ten days, after which he would be returned to the camp. On a whim, however, the guards decided he was mentally sound and, without warning, the next day Whitfield was taken from the hospital to the cemetery and shot.

Shocked, Scott wrote to Marge:

Well, they shot Whitfield on Sunday morning, honey. He was frying an egg near the RAP when they drove up in a truck, jumped out, grabbed him, tied his hands and put him in the truck. Away they went to the cemetery and shot him. Came back and got the Brigadier and Padre to go out and identify the body. Bad luck if they'd got the wrong man. No trial or anything for him.

Whitfield had been 'one of us', Scott said. He felt for the man's wife and family. With the three Dutch, that made four now who had been shot in the camp, to go with the eight at Tavoy, the three at Mergui and Bob Goulden at Victoria Point. 'Sixteen murders,' Scott noted. 'We'll square the ledger some day, I hope.'

And there was much to square. Even leaving aside these murders, a pattern of gross brutality governed camp life. Getting some degree of immediate justice was rare. Because they were scared of Colonel Nagatomo, the Japanese and Korean guards covered up any complaints the POWs made, and lied to minimise those that got through.

But there was the odd exception, including one occasion in early December 1942 when four POWs were accused of buying goods from locals. They were lined up and bashed by a guard. When one of the four claimed he was innocent, and Major Green protested on his behalf, the camp commandant listened – and ordered the guard to be punished.

Scott was amused: 'Nippo gets an awful doing with sticks for hitting an innocent man. The chap concerned is made to stand at the guardhouse till he admits it.' The guard refused to admit his culpability and was ordered to stand there until he did. Attempting to ensure this did not go beyond a rare loss of face for the guards, the POWs were warned that they would be shot if they were seen trading with the locals or breaking the camp rules. 'All the makings of a first-class melodrama,' Scott thought.

However, it was an issue not involving the guards that threatened to impede the ability of the men to labour all day in the tropical sun. The camp's supply of salt ran out. Scott understood the seriousness of the consequences. 'The sun tears the tripe out of you all day, and talk about sweat – [you] must lose pints a day,' he wrote. What angered him was that their own officers were not doing anything to organise the supplies that would resolve the problem.

> What care they for the welfare of the men? They sit in camp all day and don't even deign to appear out on the job. I am very disappointed with the Padre. He doesn't go near the sick, and he should at least go out and cheer up the men a bit, but like the rest, spends his time spine bashing. It gets me down sometimes, sweetheart, but what can you do? The game stinks. Wish I was home with you, out of it all, living our lives together and trying to forget I was in the AIF.

Such was his bitterness that Scott cursed and abused the guards while labouring. He expected a bashing. Contributing to his anger and frustration was the decision to make the POWs work longer hours on the railway. The work day did not end until evening, and they were only allowed one day off in every ten. The men were now desperately short of clothes, theirs being rotted by sweat. Scott and his team were digging 1.4 cubic metres a day up top, 1.1 metres lower down and a metre on the bottom – and sometimes the work had to be redone. For John Garran, that meant pulling down a bridge that had only been built the day before. 'Pulled out all the piles,' he wrote. 'Some only 3 feet in the ground.'

Shovelling toughened Scott's hands until they were rough with corns, and his feet were as 'hard as goat's knees'. Barefoot though he was, stones no longer worried him, and nor did red-hot coals. 'I must be improving with the shovel as I had a job to convince one chap today that I wasn't a navvy in civvy life,' he wrote with amusement. But his exhaustion did eventually exact a physical cost. 'My writing is a bit unsteady tonight, treasure, [but] I haven't been drinking,' he wrote. 'It is the result of tossing dirt up seven feet odd onto the top of the cutting. Only one complaint up there, the gravel is hard on the bare feet.'

The work was more than a physical challenge. The conditions digging two to three metres down in a cutting were akin to working in an oven. Scott lost 'gallons of sweat'. But he contented himself that he was getting into 'great nick', and everyone told him how fit he looked. He was taking back a modicum of control by casting the work in a different light.

As Viktor Frankl reflected about his time at Auschwitz, it was attitude that mattered: man can be stripped of everything except for one thing, 'the last of the human freedoms – to choose one's attitude in any set of circumstances'.

Given the circumstances Scott found himself in, he intuitively knew he had to make that choice, if only to increase his chances of survival.

15

Eyes Right

As Marge opened *The Herald* in early December 1942, she desperately hoped there would be news of Scott. In the paper was the first list of 221 Australian soldiers officially reported as POWs in Japanese hands. Nothing had been heard of Scott since the fall of Singapore, ten months earlier. Marge was not alone: many families read that first official list hoping to see a name that would give them something to cling on to. With heart in mouth, Marge went straight to page 3, scanning the surnames beginning with 'H'. But Scott's name was not there.

In releasing the information, the Minister for the Army, Frank Forde, pointed to the despair being felt across the country about the fate of the POWs. Any further names received, he said, would be communicated to the next of kin by telegram before release. He urged relatives and friends to refrain from seeking information from District Records officers, 'who were being hampered in their work by having to deal with large numbers of inquiries'. The workload of Records officers was unlikely to have been front-of-mind for relatives aching for news.

By now Marge had moved to the Murray River town of Mildura, where her father had taken over as the sergeant in charge of the police station. Christmas was approaching – her second without Scott – and she yearned to find out information about him.

Two days after the list was published, she again wrote to the Australian Red Cross, in Melbourne, asking if they could help her send a cable or parcel to Scott, as she had heard a Radio Tokyo announcement that raised this as a possibility. A week before Christmas, a letter from the Red Cross arrived, signed by Mrs T.W. 'Vera' White, Director of the Red Cross Bureau for Wounded Missing and Prisoners of War. She was already familiar with Marge's circumstances, as they had corresponded several months earlier when it had seemed that Scott and so many 8th Division men had just vanished after Singapore capitulated.

Vera White felt for all these women, as she knew the despair they felt. Before marrying, Mrs White was Vera Deakin, daughter of a former Australian prime minister, Alfred Deakin. During World War I she had opened the Australian Wounded and Missing Inquiry Bureau, first in Cairo and then in London, gathering information about the fate of Australian soldiers in the Gallipoli campaign and then the Western Front. In one year alone, the bureau wrote more than 25,000 letters in response to inquiries from relatives. In London she had met and married a young officer, Thomas White, who had recently escaped from Turkey, where he had been a POW. Now, in World War II, he had resigned as a federal MP and rejoined the RAAF, seeing service in Australia and Britain. Vera was now running the Victorian Division of the Red Cross, undertaking the same heartbreaking role.

In her letter to Marge, Vera wrote that, at present, it was not possible for her to send either a cable or parcel to Scott. The Radio Tokyo announcement that Marge had heard regarding cables could only be considered as propaganda. The Japanese had not yet given the International Red Cross any official indication that they would accept either cables or parcels for prisoners. Everything possible was being done to open up some channel of communication.

However, Marge was perhaps heartened that the Australian Red Cross had learned its first shipment of food and medical supplies had been distributed, and that a further shipment of warm winter clothing for POWs in the Far East was on its way. Vera added: 'With our sincere sympathy in your great anxiety and our hope that reassuring news of your husband may soon reach you.'

'Anxiety' – Vera had written that word tens of thousands of times across two world wars, replying to mothers, wives and fiancées filled with fear of the unknown.

There was an intriguing link between Vera and Marge, of which neither was aware. In Burma, one of the books that Scott devoured was Thomas White's account of his time as a POW in Turkey, *Guests of the Unspeakable: The Odyssey of an Australian Airman – Being a Record of Captivity and Escape in Turkey*. The book inspired Scott to ponder writing his own account of life as a POW when the war was over. He told Marge of his idea, even coming up with the title: *Guests of the Uncivilised*. 'I could use these letters for notes. An idea, eh? Our fortune is made now.'

In Mildura, evidence of the war was daily around Marge: RAAF fighter pilots were completing training at No. 2 Operational Training Unit, which had opened near the town that year. Already there had been several deaths after aircraft being flown by trainee pilots plummeted to the ground. There could be no sense of ease as to what the war effort entailed for families. And for Marge, this meant only one thing: although Scott had willingly become part of that effort, as a family they were all paying a price.

In Burma, as Christmas neared, Scott sensed this too. But still he tried to make the best of the situation. 'Four weeks tomorrow till Xmas, darling,' he wrote. 'I'll be with you playing Santa Claus. Maybe next year we'll do it together.' And if that miraculously came to pass, he went on, he would tell her about the beautiful shrine he had marvelled at while walking home from the day's labouring. The shrine was 'perched on a hilltop, its four spires and the centre one gold tipped, with its sky-blue entrance facing east. Very pretty these shrines. You find them overlooking the paddy fields, supposed to protect them.'

These were sights that made Scott's heart sing. But then there was always the thud of reality hitting, on return to camp. There was the lousy food – 'hardly fit for pigs, grubs galore in the rice'. And then there were the lines of more than 400 men on sick parade in the days before Christmas, many with ulcers, dysentery and sore throats. What made the atmosphere worse was the attitude of the guards. The issue in itself might be small, but given the volatile atmosphere ever-present in the camp, Scott knew it could blow right out of proportion, often with dire outcomes.

Nippon is becoming almost unbearable in the camp now. You have to salute all the time. As we came in tonight one of them was waiting for us, and those that didn't salute were wheeled into the jug. I had a log on one shoulder and the billy in my other hand, so favoured him with a nod. I fancy that all is not going well with them. All these little pinpricks, and there are dozens of them these days, seem to point to something.

What that was could only be conjectured, but the fact that Allied planes were being sighted seemed to Scott 'a good sign'. He thought this was why the guards were uptight.

> Nippo is bunging it on. All *kumichos* were called up at lights-out last night and had to tell the men to salute and bow to every Jap they see. He has started and looks like continuing. An irritation campaign in the hope of providing incidents to have a go at us. We are cooperating by making them sick of returning the compliments.

The diggers relished turning the tables on what was meant to be a punishment. A *tenko* – a parade – finished with an order for an hour of saluting in the Japanese manner, by bowing, in preparation for an expected visit by a general. Scott could hardly hide his amusement as the men turned the occasion into a farcical performance.

> I've seen some funny things in my time, but it beat anything. I was in front watching while Nippo put the lads through their paces – I nearly collapsed at times. Once had to turn away so that Nip couldn't see me, he must have tumbled as I got a slap on the back. If you could have seen them bowing from the waist, 'Long John' Garran, 6' 4", old Doug with his neck stretched out like an ostrich. It was an act. Nip singing out *'Kashira migi'*

[Eyes right!] and heads going right, the dancing up and down.

Scott grasped moments when the need to be on guard was not so great. As time wore on, he lived these moments more and more. 'I often plan our home at nights, how much we will spend on furniture, how much in the bank, where we will go for Xmas and Easter each year,' he told Marge.

The boys were growing fast, he knew, and he couldn't be there for them. He felt badly about this, but to compensate he would imagine helping them with their schoolwork. 'That will be the cry soon, I suppose – "Daddy, how do you do this?" I have a lot of time to make up for with our two.' These were not mere idle thoughts. 'If there wasn't any future to plan, things would be pretty hopeless here, I'm afraid,' he observed.

There was one thing he was not especially happy about, and he dreamt about it: 'Was home again with you, darling. John and Doug were there, but no daughter. We'll argue about her when I come home.' That was an argument Scott was looking forward to.

The family was never far from his mind, not least when he saw a month-old baby elephant, no more than a metre high, that was following its mother everywhere. 'The baby is the cutest little fellow,' he wrote. 'Would make a lovely pet for the bairns if he'd stay this size.'

What was so hard to abide was not knowing when the captivity would end. At home, prisoners knew the length of their sentence and could adjust themselves to a release date. For a POW, there was no set time laid down to count off the days to freedom. There were plenty of rumours, but Scott was losing faith in these. He had been hopeful of an early release at Tavoy. The Burmese workers had insisted the Japanese had vacated Thailand for Singapore, and that the offensive in Burma would start any day. It didn't happen. Nevertheless, as Scott wrote, 'One can't help hoping a bit.'

He knew Marge would be doing her Christmas shopping and playing Santa Claus to the boys. John would be old enough now to appreciate Christmas, and he could just see the glee of a small boy opening his stocking on Christmas morning. He knew it would be a miserable Christmas for many Australian families, and he spared a thought for the wives and families who had suffered the 'terrific blow' of hearing the news that their loved one had survived all the terrors of the war, only to die as a POW.

Twelve months earlier, Scott remembered, he had been under a rubber tree with Lofty in Malaya and they had drunk to Marge's health for Christmas. He'd been fed up at the time, a feeling that bore no comparison with what he was experiencing now as a POW. The coming Christmas would be 'not a very happy one for any of us', he told Marge. 'I'd never have believed we'd be here in twelve months' time. Nearly twelve months a POW.' Summoning up some optimism, he assured himself it would not be for much longer.

But for now there were just the family photos, even if they were the worse for wear. He gave the photo of Marge waiting at the gate three kisses. Next year would be different, he resolved: the war would be over, and he could enjoy a few beers with Pop before lunch and dinner. And they would be doing their Christmas shopping together.

Thoughts of home were everywhere in the camp that night as the men gathered for a Christmas Eve concert, held on an impromptu stage with a 'V for victory' sign on the front.

Scott was among thirty voices in a newly formed choir. The carols and hymns, sung with the emotion of men kept far from their families, made the occasion memorable. 'That was a great night, to see the faces of about 500 men grouped round the platform in the darkness, partly relieved by the light of candles,' he wrote.

There was something liberating about singing in a group, and on this night it seemed to have been cathartic, cutting through the low spirits everyone felt at not being home for Christmas. The show went so well that the choir was later formalised with a committee, and with practice to be held twice weekly. Scott was now giving full voice to his singing, discovering anew not only the natural exuberance it evoked in him, but hope.

Try as he might, Scott did not sleep well that night. He worried about Marge. Lying awake and restless on his bamboo bed, he wondered what she was doing. He pictured her in bed asleep, curled up with young John for company. He could also picture John and Doug playing in the backyard. His thoughts settled on his return. What a day it would be, getting off the train, walking home and seeing them waiting for him. The images of Marge and the boys were worth waiting for. It would happen – of that he had no doubt – but there was still the reality of the present, and the knowledge that Marge didn't know where he was, or even if he was alive. That void now controlled their lives.

'If only I could be certain that you had some news of us,' Scott wrote. 'Even if I can't hear from you, life would be more bearable.' It was such a small thing to ask on Christmas Day.

16

The Ring

The beard was off, and Scott looked ten years younger, according to his mates. 'Am thinner in the face but look remarkably well, everyone says,' he told Marge. That was his most important news on Christmas Day, 1942. He felt 'in the pink', and was sure that if she could see him, all her fears would be put to rest. 'I had a look at myself in a big mirror today and look a picture. Brown and solid-looking, no fat at all.' He valued his health and wanted to 'look a picture' for Marge.

Christmas Day dawned for the 1000 men in the camp, and instead of the usual pap, there was rice and stew for breakfast, plus some fried rice as a treat. *Tenko* had been at 9 am, and church parade an hour later. For Christmas lunch they had managed to acquire two pigs to augment the usual rice and stew. 'The stew was a beauty and plenty of it,' Scott reported. 'The pork gave it a lovely taste.'

On this day especially, Scott wanted Marge close. 'I have been with you all day, particularly at church this morning,' he told her. 'There were a great many of the lads there and it was a nice service. Maybe you were at Communion. I could visualise you there.'

Although this wasn't his happiest Christmas, Scott took heart from believing 'our homes are safe from harm' as the worst of the Japanese threat of invasion of Australia appeared over. The news that Lofty had been transferred from Padang to Changi was like a Christmas gift. 'Only one thing could have been more welcome than that, and that is news of you,' Scott wrote.

As the day wore on, the mood among the men lightened, and this led to a singsong being arranged for two nights later. Scott enjoyed being part of the newly formed choir. The evening service had sparked a vivid comparison in his mind with church at home. When the congregation of men was asked to sing a hymn, they responded exuberantly. 'Did they let it go!' Such was their gusto, Scott noted, that it contrasted well with 'the feeble efforts put up at home'.

That same day, Scott was 'happy as a sand boy' for another reason: he had been able to write a lettercard to Marge that the Japanese would post. The news helped lift the festive mood. Filling in the brief lettercard was the first chance the POWs had of breaking the near year-long silence with their families. Scott had only two lines in which to say everything, and he thought all day about what he would write. The words did not come easily. Finally, within the template laid down by the Japanese, he settled on a prosaic message: he was all right, and he urged Marge to keep smiling and not to worry.

After penning the note, Scott wrote his customary diary letter to Marge, in which he promised to devote the rest of his life to making up to her for the long months of worry and anxiety. 'May my letter take wings and fly home to you,' he added. He enjoyed imagining the postman arriving at the house with the Japanese lettercard in hand, bringing word of him at last, and the excitement and the phone calls that would follow.

Scott was in a positive mood, with so much happening at once. After hearing of Lofty, and getting news that the Japanese were evacuating Rangoon, Scott thought the situation looked 'pretty hunky-dory'. But any spirit of goodwill was shattered by news from the nearby camp at the 18-kilometre mark. What had happened underlined the unpredictability and volatility of the camps, and once more left Scott enraged.

Sergeant Ron O'Donnell, of the 2/10th Field Regiment, had been drawn into an incident involving the purchase of a cigarette case on Christmas Eve. O'Donnell had intervened in the dispute, but the situation turned ugly when the guards arrived with rifles and machine guns. 'Our blokes took them off the yellow hounds,' Scott wrote. 'Gave them back later in the day.'

Two days later, on Boxing Day, O'Donnell was a member of a work party under the control of a guard who had a violent reputation. O'Donnell sought permission to relieve himself. The guard followed him and shot him in the chest at point-blank range, claiming he was attempting to escape. Colonel Anderson rejected the claim as preposterous. Scott had no doubt that this was cold-blooded murder. Again, he visualised retribution, singling out Nagatomo for execution for war crimes at the end of the war.

Scott hoped that New Year's Eve at Thetkaw camp would herald a year that would end the war and allow him to return home. The previous New Year's Eve, in Malaya, he had sung 'Home Sweet Home' to finish a concert in the dark. It had been a night filled with the soaring emotions of men at war, and away from home, and was seared into his memory.

There would be another concert to see out 1942. For this, he somehow managed to cobble together enough tattered clothing that he could pass as wearing a kilt and glengarry cap for a Scottish-themed evening. 'You should have seen me, my pipe major's jacket, kilt, sporran, socks, spats and glengarry, the real McKie,' he told Marge. 'John and Doug will be able to dress up in the Gordon Highlander's uniform that Daddy brought home from the war.'

The concert opened to a full house and featured a play. Scott described how, as the climax was reached, the heroine, 'little Eva', was in the clutches of the villain and was about to be rescued by 'Arnold Arsepaper', the hero. At that moment, one of the Japanese guards 'flew on to the stage from the audience and rescued the fair damsel'. It brought the house down.

John Garran thought the event a highlight too, and noted that, as the Japanese had been drinking, they relaxed their hard-line protocols and made efforts to be friendly. 'They were very friendly in their cups, which surely shows no unconscious antipathy,' he wrote.

As midnight approached, Scott was on stage, mesmerised by the sight of the audience before him. The faces of unkempt and ill-clad men, sitting on the ground in rapt silence, were lit up in the firelight. In the play of light and shadows, a voice suddenly rang out, singing the Scottish ballad 'My Ain Folk'. At this makeshift camp in the middle of a jungle, Scott was stunned by the moment. The other men, also spending their second New Year's Eve away from their families, were left spellbound. Then they all joined in for the second verse. 'As I looked at the faces, I was very near tears,' Scott said. 'There was a lump in my throat. Every man, no matter what his life may have been or where he was from, was "Back in Aussie with his ain folks".' As the twelve strokes of midnight sounded, they sang 'Auld Lang Syne' and welcomed in 1943.

Scott finished the night by walking around the camp and wishing everyone a happy New Year. There was a drop of homebrew with Curly and Tom, a rissole supper and a yarn with Jock, Tiny and Uncle. Scott climbed into his narrow sleeping space in the palm-roofed hut at about 1.30 am. 'I lay awake for a long time thinking of home and you,' he told Marge. 'I saw the old out and new in without you. I was with you, standing alongside, with your hand in mine. Did you feel me?' He wondered what the year ahead would bring.

New Year's Day ushered in a brief pausing of hostilities in the camp. Brigadier Varley was among the officers invited to Japanese headquarters to watch sumo wrestling and to dine with the Japanese officers to celebrate New Year's Day. The brandy flowed as the Japanese attempted to get the Australians drunk, without success. Varley noted that three prostitutes helped to serve at the table. One Australian officer sang 'Home Sweet Home' in English, accompanied by a Japanese lieutenant in Japanese. 'It was a classic,' Varley wrote.

*

Momentary though it may have been, Scott experienced a new lightness with the dawning of 1943. He felt a sense of peace, inspired by the beauty of the jungle hills. He drank in the cooling sea breezes.

As I write this, the sun is going down in a blaze of red, a molten ball of fire. The sunrise comes each day as we are nearly out to work. The big red ball [is] so close it seems to be sitting on top of the hills – the hills that seem to beckon us, saying: 'Come, beyond me lies freedom.' If only one could be sure of that.

The hills were alive with birds and wildlife. 'Have just been admiring a beautiful bird, some type of honeyeater by the look of him,' Scott added. 'Some of the parrots here are absolutely beyond description.' When a 2-metre cobra appeared near the camp, an elephant working with the men saw it. 'Suddenly it rushed at us (we didn't wait for anything) and planted its foot on the snake and ground it into the dust,' he noted with awe. 'I tell you that beasts are nearly human.'

Scott believed the Japanese were beginning, if grudgingly, to respect his work ethic. He had just finished after a day 'under a killing sun' and had no doubt that he was very fit, even though the work left him weary. As he reflected on the day and prepared for his family time with a letter to Marge, he was confident that a night's rest would put him right. 'Funny today again, I went to work as if I was treading on air,' he told her. 'You seem to be with me, and I could see your face shimmering before me. I often get those feelings.'

Scott was not alone. Viktor Frankl experienced the same phenomenon as he likewise swung a shovel on a railway near Auschwitz. Labouring in a gang in the early morning, Frankl looked up at the fading stars and noticed that the pink light of the sun was struggling through. Quite suddenly, he saw, with uncanny clarity, an image of Tilly. 'I heard her answering me, saw her smile, her frank and encouraging look,' he wrote. 'Real or not, her look was then more luminous than the sun.'

Both men had a capacity to retreat into themselves, to experience a powerful moment of joy that transcended their reality and would somehow reset their equilibrium. In essence, they were dissociating, even for a few moments, from the awfulness of their respective worlds. This, in turn, allowed them to cope with camp life more easily than was possible for many others.

At the same time, Scott would not allow himself to be carried away by rumours of Allied successes as 1943 began, even when his officers were optimistic. 'I feel hopeful but will not be broken-hearted if nothing happens,' he noted. 'Have developed rather a fatalistic attitude towards things – what is to be will be.' Yet Scott was not so accepting that he didn't feel aggrieved when a guard perpetrated some random atrocity. Inherently, he knew that to remain alert to what was happening in his immediate environment was essential to his safety and that of the men, but at the same time he was learning to distinguish between that which could be let go, and that which called for a strong reaction.

Scott also took care to attend to the details of his life. It gave him a reassuring sense of familiarity and control, when in reality there was so little. Inevitably, there were times when seemingly small things challenged him and a strong reaction followed.

Besides the signet ring, Scott's wedding ring was critical to his sense of equanimity – it was a direct link to Marge. To lose it was unthinkable, but in mid-January he nearly did. He was washing when he found the ring was missing. In the half-light of day, he made a frantic search of the quarters but couldn't find it. He asked his mate Curly to help him look in the creek. Perhaps his weight loss had increased the chances of it slipping off his finger. As he told Marge:

> Was showing him where I was washing when we both
> said together, 'There it is,' and sure enough it was. What
> a relief! I'd have gone silly had I lost it. Am going to bind
> it again tonight, losing my medallion was bad enough, but
> the ring is my most treasured possession.

Scott's discipline in writing to Marge did not go unnoticed. Others began keeping diaries. Just how many surprised him, and some kept him company at night, writing. But his letters to Marge remained unique. 'Some of them are quite envious of me and my letters to you,' he wrote. Scott's dreams about Marge became more frequent and graphic. Sometimes he imagined waking in the morning with Marge's head on his shoulder, kissing her awake.

> Had two beautiful dreams about you last night. We were
> having great fun together in some city, I remember you
> catching your stocking in some barbed wire and ripping
> it, you started to cry, and I kissed you and told you not to
> worry. We'd go home and get another pair.

As hard as it must have been for him to rouse from such dreams, he treasured them and would focus on them for some time afterwards, ensuring the after-effect lingered.

If the New Year had begun with a renewed sense of hope for Scott, by the end of January the mood was changing. The death of Private Charles Johnson contributed to this. A popular driver with the 2/4th Reserve Motor Transport Company, 'Johnno' died from the effects of malnutrition, dysentery and finally heart failure on 24 January 1943. He was thirty-nine.

Scott was present for his service the night before Johnno was buried in the jungle near their camp.

> As we sat on the stage, we had as accompaniment the
> noise of the hammers as they made his coffin for him. We
> lined the roads afterwards as they carried him through to
> a hut where a guard was mounted for the night. The Jap
> boss made a funeral oration and paid his respects. It's very
> easy for them to put on a show but we will never forget
> our hosts when the tide turns.

This was a situation from which Scott couldn't detach. Thoughts of Marge sustained him, but the death of mates tore at him.

17

Hope

Somehow, Marge made it through Christmas and the New Year, deprived of any news about Scott. She had John and Doug to care for, alone. For all she knew, and despite all her efforts to find out what had happened to him after the fall of Singapore, Scott could be dead. The best she could hope for was that he was a POW. Somewhere.

She was at her wits' end as she coped with the heat and dust of midsummer in Mildura, unaware that Scott had written a lettercard to her – it would take months to arrive. In the grip of despair, Marge wrote to Doris Parry, the wife of Major Jack Parry, Scott's commanding officer. Marge knew that Jack Parry was a friend to Scott, and that he regarded the boys of the Army Service Corps as one big family.

On the same day that Scott mourned Johnno's death in the Burmese jungle, Doris Parry wrote back to Marge. She understood her worry. Doris said that some time ago she had visited a sergeant from the Army Service Corps who had been invalided home three days before Singapore fell. He had assured her that, up to that date, there had been no casualties

To return home from the war to establish a home with Marge and their family was for Scott such a powerful motivation that not even the inhumanity of the Burma Railway could defeat it.

in the unit. 'I am telling you this as it might help, being later news than you had from your husband,' Doris wrote. 'I have been notified that my husband is in a camp in Malaya, and I sincerely hope that all his men are there also.'

Every family in Australia that had not heard from a husband, son or brother was experiencing the same sense of helplessness that engulfed Marge. After an agonising eleven months, they could do nothing but wait.

That same week, in his hut in the camp at Thetkaw, Scott was, in turn, concerned for Marge. 'As the days go by, I think that each day brings my letter[card] nearer to you,' he told her. 'That is if they ever send them on. Each day also brings us nearer home.' Would the Japanese even post his letter? How could he know? His worry affected his singing at choir practice. 'We are coming along very well. Got chipped again for hanging on, can't help it. I was far away thinking of you.' The Japanese could 'keep the food and comforts if only I can hear from you that you are well'. In his letters, Scott spoke of hope. As he endeavoured to sustain Marge in her hope for their future, he was simultaneously convincing himself.

Again and again Scott sought to maintain equanimity by pausing to take in the surrounding natural environment, and more and more the world around him was a source of wonder to him. 'The nights here at present are beautiful, the moon is full and the heavens ablaze with stars,' he wrote. 'Each morning early we see the Southern Cross low down in the sky. I often stand and admire the beautiful sunsets; they turn the hills blood-red in colour.' He could never look at these sunsets without thinking of Marge at home, wondering what she was doing at that very moment.

Scott took joy from the sight of birds, and what meaning he

might derive from their sudden presence, as did Viktor Frankl. While labouring on the rail line near Auschwitz, Frankl again beheld an image of Tilly, and in that instant a bird flew towards him, perched right in front of him on his newly dug pile of soil, 'and looked steadily at me', he related.

Similarly, Scott left his worksite one day seeking water, and climbed down a narrow gully, cool with abundant ferns. He reached a tiny stream of spring water. With birds of brilliant plumage, large and small, flying and calling overhead, he immediately felt at peace with the world. 'I thought, if only I could bring Marge here to see this.'

The sight of birds in their natural setting riveted Scott and Frankl alike. Each derived his own meaning relating to his wife, and each his own solace before the spell was inevitably broken. Scott filled his bucket and went back 'to the noise and cursing as the lads put the railroad through'.

Just as the old adage describes how two prisoners looking out of their cell window see different things – bars for one, stars for the other – Scott, like Viktor Frankl, had a dream for the future that no bars could contain. In the concentration camp, Frankl noticed that prisoners who had lost faith in the future also lost their spiritual hold, and this led to mental and, inevitably, physical decay. This might happen slowly, or it might be a sudden giving-up. But in an effort to encourage fellow prisoners around him to hang on, he spurred them to find a sense of purpose. Some did; many did not.

Dr Rowley Richards wrote that 'men who genuinely believed they would get well had a much better chance of making it than those who became negative or lost hope'. From what he witnessed, he believed there were two essential factors as to whether a man would survive or not as a POW. Important above all was the ability to maintain hope. Secondly, but also vital, was the degree to which he was able to adapt. Both of these characteristics Scott had in abundance.

The more Scott wrote, the more his personality emerged. His motivation for life was strong, and he felt a sense of obligation to others. He had high personal standards, which he constantly strove to preserve. This was a time for self-reflection, to consider past behaviour, and how, after the war was over and he was back home, he would change.

Sitting around the fire one night while he rested an injured foot, Scott had a long yarn with one of his mates, Sam Attwell. They discussed generalities, which included what their attitude to life would be when they returned home. 'We have decided that we will not be half as inconsiderate as we were formerly,' he told Marge. 'When I reflect on my past sins, I could have behaved better on occasions, couldn't I? Still, you won't know me when I come home.'

Scott's calm demeanour and integrity, together with his organisational skills, did not go unnoticed by the AIF officers. The 2/29th Battalion's Captain David West called Scott and two other warrant officers together to tell them the plan of action if there was an air raid. He had given them 'the good oil' about organisation in the camp. 'In the event of anything happening I am a Platoon Commander,' Scott noted on 9 January 1943. Just what Captain West had in mind was not clear, but if it ever came to pass, he saw Scott playing a key role in its success.

That aside, Curly and Doug were already planning post-war careers for themselves, and for Scott. Once home, they would stay in the army, and they reckoned Scott should become the RSM of a Melbourne unit. Scott thought they would make a great combination. All this gave him something else to dream about.

Scott had earned his stripes literally, while in the militia, and metaphorically, while at war and as a POW. Dr Richards reckoned that his own years in the militia had prepared him for the challenges he faced in Burma with 'A' Force. This was undoubtedly the case with Scott too. He took his responsibilities as a warrant officer seriously. His years of training before the war were paying off, albeit adjusted to fit these very different circumstances.

The situation inside the camps was a natural example of the psychologist Abraham Maslow's 'hierarchy of needs', under which the physiological needs of food, shelter and safety were noted as the essentials for life. Survival in the camps called for resourcefulness and not a little cunning, especially in order to satisfy the core need of hunger. Judicious pilfering from the Japanese stores was seen as fair enough. Trading with the Thetkaw locals was more clandestine than it had been at Tavoy, but it added some protein and fresh vegetables to the POWs' diet of rice and watery soup. Without this supplementation, it was often the grubs in the rice that provided the protein, as Baldy McFadyen found one evening. 'Doug got the grandfather of them last night,' Scott noted. 'About one inch long.'

Scott saw himself as 'terribly lucky' to be in such good health, and knew he had to remain disease-free. He was aware of vitamin deficiency and the havoc it played with men's bodies. For this reason, he was in the habit – daily, when he could – of taking brewed-up yeast or grass extracts as a source of vitamin B, to stave off beriberi. Yet the men's overall intake of food was barely adequate to sustain life, and intestinal illnesses were becoming virtually endemic.

A lecture by the camp doctor shook the men up, as was his intention. He warned that they were facing a dysentery epidemic, and that cholera was probably unavoidable. He further warned that, if it hit, 50 per cent of the men would die. Scott bemoaned the fact that the doctor had been right when he upbraided them for not looking after themselves properly. 'At least some of us,' he wrote. 'You have no idea the way some of them carry on. They don't worry about dishes. We are most careful, scald ours, night and morning.' Scott's hygiene standards had become a critical aspect of his survival skills.

To Scott, the easiest way to keep fit was through work. Each day he would put in, and often more than most. At this stage of the railway construction, digging was the norm. 'Spent the day on the banjo [long-handled shovel] again,' he told Marge. 'Am in good form now – the potato patch will present no difficulties to me when I come home.' In his own mind, he was already there.

Having had only one day off sick since arriving in Burma made Scott rather proud. Baldy McFadyen, however, chipped him for having kept working all these months without a day in camp. 'I'll keep going, though,' Scott said. 'It fills the day in, all right, makes the day go quickly.' Inevitably, he pushed his luck too far. 'At last the old war horse has broken down,' he ruefully admitted to Marge at the end of January. He had split open his toe on a stump and was designated 'NO DUTY' for a week. 'A beautiful gash, and here am I, cooling my heels in camp. Needless to say, Curly and Doug are highly delighted at my enforced holiday.'

To mark the occasion, Scott went on, 'we were invited out to supper last night. "Mrs Campbell" entertained, rice rissoles and coffee.' Hosting a meal that, in the context of a POW camp, was special, Alan Campbell had outdone himself – hence the 'Mrs Campbell' moniker. This was high praise indeed.

18

What Will Be Will Be

Major Alan Mull had had enough. After breakfast on 11 February 1943, the 46-year-old and two mates, Gunner Keith Dickinson, thirty-nine, and Private Alex Bell, twenty-nine, broke camp and faded into the jungle. They took with them three weeks' rations and sarongs for disguise. The final straw was a beating that three Japanese privates had inflicted on Mull for daring to buy bananas from local Burmese. Now their goal was to walk to India.

Scott had been aware for weeks that Mull – 'the Skipper', as he called him – was seriously considering escape. They had known each other since Bonegilla, and Scott thought Mull, a Service Corps officer, had done a great job during the last frenzied days in Singapore, when he had been appointed OC (Officer Commanding) of a newly created AASC Company. Mull had told Scott a week before Christmas 1942 that if nothing happened soon, he was going to make a break for it. 'Better to be shot escaping than die in the wet season,' he told Scott. Having been a rubber planter, and having spent eight years in Burma with the Indian Army, Mull knew the Burmese wet season well.

Most POWs, at some point in their captivity, toyed with the idea of escape. No doubt Scott did, but he felt such love for and responsibility towards Marge and his children that he discarded any thoughts of breaking free as far too risky. As hard as it was, staying put meant he was more likely to make it home.

Dickinson was a Bendigo mine surveyor in civilian life and spoke Malay, while Bell was a metallurgist who had been working in Malaya. With Mull, they had survival skills and experience, and figured that if they couldn't get out, no one could. Before the guards knew that the three men were missing, word spread among the POWs that they had quietly left 14 Kilo camp at Thetkaw. Scott knew the dangers they faced, but also the payoff if they succeeded in making it to safety.

> Nippo doesn't know as yet. Wait till he does, then things
> will move. I saw the Skipper just before he went, shook
> hands and wished him all the best. The two with him
> are surveyors with long experience in the jungle so they
> have a great chance. I hope they are successful, for their
> sakes and for ours. The repercussions will be very severe, I
> imagine, but we can put up with them. All we can do now
> is pray for their safety.

Scott's hope for their successful bid for freedom had an element of self-interest. He calculated that if the three were to reach the outside world, word would spread and Marge may get to hear that he was safe and well.

When 'the balloon went up', the repercussions were immediate. POW officers were beaten and tight restrictions on movement implemented. On 17 February 1943, without warning, the men were ordered on parade and made to bring with them all their belongings. The order struck alarm for Scott. His letters to Marge were in his hut, and at grave risk of discovery. He fought to keep his rising panic under control. 'My letters. What will I do with them?' he later wrote. 'I put them in my shorts pocket, no chance to plant a thing. The Nip is right on my ginger.'

Filled with trepidation, Scott walked to the parade ground to find the guards carrying out a mass looting campaign, confiscating not just knives and watches but also photos of wives and families. Some of the items that were tipped out surprised him – but also confirmed the Australian bent for larrikinism.

> Out of one of the chap's gear came a pair of chrome
> headlights, brand new; a pair of sidelights; [and a] bike
> lamp and generator. Everyone was amused. Another fellow
> who has been getting around in shorts which just covered
> the essential parts (or should I say he has tatters over
> them) produced two brand new shorts. Two pair of shorts,
> pyjamas, etc., and his cobbers have been feeding him.

Self-interest was never far away in a POW camp. A guard walking along the line of men with their gear piled in front of them finally stopped in front of Scott, who said his prayers. But the guard went easy. Scott thought this was because he had worked hard under his command the previous day. He wrote to Marge: 'Still have my precious letters to you, though when I saw the bulk of them, I wondered if you will be bothered reading them all. My letters are safe now, buried out of harm's way.' Digging a hole and burying the letters was the safest way to keep them hidden from the guards.

Scott may have been relieved, but the experience was also unsettling. Nightly parades lasting up to four hours were ordered around this time, and guards went on nightly rampages. A concert at the camp helped restore his spirits. He took in the night sky as it fell over the landscape around him, but, seven weeks into the new year that had begun with so much hope, it now took effort to be cheerful. Worry for Marge preoccupied him. 'Just to know you are safe and well would make this existence tolerable,' he told her. This was becoming a familiar refrain in his letters.

Scott's next letter to Marge was written on 'very dirty and very crinkled' paper. Not that the crackdown deterred him from writing. 'Wimpy has just been down. He complains that whenever he comes down, he finds me writing,' he related. With tensions in the camp heightened by the three POWs' escape, and with health conditions deteriorating, the mood was heavy and everyone was on alert.

Fourteen days after he escaped, Keith Dickinson was caught, 80 kilometres from Thetkaw. He told the Japanese that after crossing hills and steep ridges, and moving through heavy scrub with Mull and Bell on the day they had escaped, exhaustion had forced them to rest as they headed towards the Thai border. The next day, Dickinson had been unable to press on, and told Mull and Bell to continue without him. They left him with food and water, and fifteen rupees.

Dickinson had attempted to reach water in a gully but slipped and fell, landing on a ledge, where he spent the next two days, before he climbed out and discovered a pump house. Taking shelter and resting there, he finally signalled to some

Burmese boys, who led him to a mangrove thicket, where he hid. By now he was very weak, having survived only on bananas and sugar, and he hoped that another Burmese would take him downriver by boat. Instead, he was led to a house where he was arrested – a consequence of the bounty paid to Burmese for handing over escapees.

The Japanese now subjected Dickinson to torture, hanging him up by his thumbs. Scott was fatalistic. 'I keep thinking of poor old Keith,' he lamented. 'Still, he knew the risks before he went.' Four days later, on 2 March 1943, Dickinson was executed. 'They led him out from the guardhouse to the cemetery, made him kneel down and shot him.' There had been no trial. To Scott, Dickinson's murder was yet another outrage to add to his list, which was growing daily. A sense of resignation was descending upon Scott – and he was not alone. 'Everyone has adopted a fatalistic attitude – what is to be will be, and we can't stop it.'

Two weeks after he had buried his letters, Scott dug them up and looked at the pile they made. 'They are bulky, sweetheart, you'll never get through them,' he told Marge. Orders had come from the guards to be prepared to move to the next camp, so Scott took the letters back to his hut.

Something else was playing on Scott's mind as he thought of the future – not just his and Marge's, but the children's. Would all the sacrifice of the war be for naught, as was the case with World War I? Would John and Doug 'have to fight to keep an invader from our doorsteps for another twenty-five years'? Scott's fear was not uncommon among soldiers, particularly POWs. This level of suffering could not, they felt, be for nothing.

Scott's ruminations were cut short by the news that, after five weeks of freedom, Alex Bell and Alan Mull were dead.

After they had parted from Dickinson, they had become lost in the mountains for nearly a week. Unarmed, they travelled at night, swimming rivers and making their way through the jungle. Unexpectedly, pro-Japanese Burmese police appeared who, after firing warning shots, demanded they surrender. As the Australians attempted to escape, Bell was shot through his right arm; Mull was killed in the gunfire and his body tied to a bullock wagon. They had travelled 160 kilometres from the camp.

Bell was locked up in a village guardhouse, before being handed over to the Japanese. They took him to Thanbyuzayat, where he was tortured. On 16 March he was taken from the guardhouse to the back of the town's cemetery, where a firing squad stood ready. After shaking hands with the officer in charge, he calmly refused to kneel, saying he would die on his feet. He was said to have walked slowly to his grave, looked into it and shrugged his broad shoulders. Then he was shot.

In his diary, Varley described Bell's behaviour as 'most gallant'. Scott noted that even the Japanese regarded Bell as a credit to the Australian Army. 'Alex refused to have his hands tied, stood to attention and faced it like a man,' he noted. At church, the boys were in full voice when singing a hymn in Bell's memory, their anger at his murder ringing out. 'We sang "Rock of Ages". It was Alex Bell's last request that the choir sing this. I wonder if he heard us.'

Scott had well known the dangers Mull, Dickinson and Bell had faced, and the slim chance they had of survival. But they had left their families at home to fight for their country, he recognised, and had deserved the chance to escape.

There was something else Scott did not know. Padre Bashford, who spent time with Alex Bell the day before he was executed, explained later that there were 'deliberate' differences in the details of his statement compared with Keith Dickinson's. This was 'in order that no reprisals would be taken against other POWs by the Japanese on discovery of an organised escape'. Scott was one of those who had known.

19

The Tree

Time was up at Thetkaw. Finally. The job was done and it was time to head to a new camp. Clambering aboard a truck, Scott joined a convoy of POWs for 'one more pleasure trip as guests of Nippon'. They were headed for Meilo, the 75 Kilo camp. Trucks rumbled over a deeply rutted track, throwing the men against each other. Sitting on the tailboard seat, Scott contemplated how best to position himself among thirty other jostling bodies, all trying to keep clouds of dust at bay as they covered their mouths and noses with handkerchiefs.

Amid plenty of curses from his fellow POWs, Scott's irritation at the discomfort softened as the dust subsided just enough for him to take in the countryside, which became hillier the further they went. As was his wont, he saw far more than was actually there. Sheer rock faces and rugged escarpments rose up sharply; in Scott's mind these became castles and keeps from olden times, 'ready to repel all invaders'. They seemed to say: 'Attempt me if you dare!'

Approaching the foothills of a range, Scott saw 'gigantic trees, creepers winding round them like huge pythons, or hanging from the branches; bamboos cut off about twelve feet up and left hanging, so it's watch your head'. There were hundreds of bullock carts carrying timber for bridges over precipitous gorges. 'We see what we are in for here,' Scott commented.

Stiff, dusty and fed up after several hours on the road, they finally arrived at Meilo, Scott's fourth camp. 'A sorrier looking lot you'd see nowhere,' he observed. 'We fell in, were counted and then I staggered to our hut.' Located in a valley near the Mezali River, Meilo was where the mountains began. He soon caught up with Baldy McFadyen, who'd arrived earlier and now directed him to a pool to clean up. 'Down I went to find a beautiful, swift-flowing river, with crystal-clear water. In I went and came out clean and feeling pretty good. Then a meal, and a ripper too.'

Revived, the next morning, 9 March 1943, Scott was up early to take in his new environment, climbing a steep hill, from where he gazed out across the valley and settled his mind and body. Smoke haze obscured the view, so this time his sensations were more auditory.

The monkeys are calling in the hills behind me and roosters are heralding the dawn of a new day. The sun comes up and I begin to understand why the ancient races made the sun their god. Up it came, throwing the hills and valleys into relief, the sky a rosy glow and the deep ever-changing greens of the hills and valleys seeming to be the beginnings of a new world. The monkey chorus rises to a crescendo as if a pagan choir were chanting to their god.

Along with the chants of monkeys were sounds, not far away, that reminded him of war. All day and night he felt he could hear the crack of machine guns, rifles and mortars as the heat burst the bamboo.

There was a tree at this camp known as the Pride of Burma; it was regarded as the most majestic of flowering tropical trees. Resplendent in red flowers, it was off-limits to the POWs. On no account was it to be touched. It was the favourite tree of a Japanese lieutenant, who took great pleasure in its beauty. For the Australians who had just moved into the camp, however, it proved too great a temptation.

The fate of the tree caused a 'big blue', unfolding in an environment where to contravene the strict rules enforced by the Japanese military was to invite serious punishment. Scott captured the saga with wry, triumphant humour. He painted it as a scene in a play for Marge, where all was calm within the valley camp – except for the thud of axes, which could be heard reverberating through the jungle.

Suddenly a cry of 'timber!' and a rending crash as a forest giant comes crashing down. Silence. A distracted adjutant rushes on the scene. 'Christ Almighty, who cut that bloody tree down?' The woodcutter's chorus, 'We did, sir' ...

Adjutant (in a frantic tone): 'Holy Jesus, you've cut down the Jap lieutenant's favourite tree.'

Reply: 'Bugger the Jap lieutenant, we want firewood.'

The curtain falls with the adjutant staggering away, murmuring, 'What am I to tell him?'

This was, Scott wrote at the end of March 1943, a pathetic little tale, but 'we have a few such incidents to brighten our existence'. When they happened, Scott was not going to let them pass unnoticed – particularly as he was now resigned to being in Burma come the next Christmas. The weather was as 'hot as the hobs of Hades', and it was getting him down already. He realised he could slip into nostalgia if he spent too much time poring over his photos and letters; for his own peace of mind, he needed to avoid this.

Scott recognised that an incident such as the felling of the tree provided a diversion and allowed the POWs a minor triumph, if only in their own minds. And Scott's spirits needed lifting.

As Viktor Frankl found, humour in a concentration camp was another of the soul's weapons in the fight for self-preservation. With his tight group of mates, Scott was determined to give truth to this, reassuring Marge: 'Wish you could be looking in at suppertime and see us tearing in by candlelight. We ain't got much money but we manage to knock out a fair bit of fun.'

One joke doing the rounds appealed to Scott as 'a beauty': an Englishman, a Frenchman and a Japanese were in an aircraft that suddenly lost altitude. Fearing the worst, the pilot turned and asked one to pay the supreme sacrifice to lighten the load. The Frenchman volunteered, saying, 'Vive la France!' and jumped out. But the plane continued to lose altitude, causing the pilot to make yet another appeal. The Englishman jumped up, shouting, 'There'll always be an England' – and hurled the Japanese overboard. At least it went a little way towards quenching a universal thirst for revenge.

Sometimes, in a camp full of the sick and the damned, the humour could be poignant in Scott's eyes. This was the effect on him on 22 August 1943, he explained to Marge, when he went to the latrines at daylight.

I was immediately struck with the resemblance between the twenty-odd fellows squatting there and a mob of swallows perched on a telephone line. As I came away, I met a chap coming along in his birthday suit, his trousers in one hand and a disgusted look on his face. He hadn't made it. I had to laugh, he looked so comical.

Finally, too, he'd become used to the knotty bamboo beds, and was sleeping well. He mused that he could establish a company to manufacture the beds when he returned to Australia – they would be known as Bamboo Bliss. A jingle would sell them: 'When better beds are built, we'll build 'em, enjoy bamboo bliss on our Burma Beds.'

At Meilo Camp, Lieutenant Colonel Ramsay and Black Force joined with Green Force, with Ramsay appointed the commander. On 1 April 1943, the last of the sick from 26 Kilo camp arrived; Meilo Camp was already home to more than 1800 men. It was April Fools' Day and Scott was struck by an irony. 'The more one considers things, the more certain one is that we were fools all right,' he mused. 'Still, we volunteered for it, so quit grousing, Heywood.'

As if he didn't already have a thousand reasons to grouse, Scott was battling a malaria relapse. Malaria was rife in the camp: his mates Laurie and Baldy were down with it and he was on quinine daily. The side effects could be grim. He had tossed and turned all night, which he put down to the quinine, supplies of which at that stage were still adequate. 'Twenty-four grains of that a day makes one feel a bit wonky,' he observed. 'The bells ring in the old ears all day.' Malaria was one thing, but cholera was quite another. It too had broken out in the camp.

Although the ringing in his ears was annoying, it didn't stop Scott from writing his letters to Marge. But he was concerned when he got wind of another unannounced search of the camp, where men were living in huts with three-tier beds crammed inside, and he lost no time in burying the letters once again. It had been too close a shave the last time a search was sprung.

But burying paper comes with risk, and Scott could have cried when he dug them up later that month. 'The white ants had got in and chewed lumps out of them,' he reported. 'I have not got over it yet. Parts of them no longer exist so I'll just have to try to fill in the blank spaces from memory. I was heartbroken.' A day later he concluded that while important parts had been eaten, he mostly could reconstruct the twenty pages that had been destroyed.

If it wasn't white ants, it was mosquitoes and sandflies that infested the new camp. Insect-borne disease was now endemic. As shoes wore out, bare feet meant many of the men were suffering skin lesions and cuts. Foot infections could be catastrophic.

The condition of one dysentery case whom Scott had helped stretcher to the RAP left him shocked. The POW had become a virtual skeleton in four days and looked like a dead man when they carried him in. 'It is tragic to see what some of the men have come to,' Scott wrote. 'Big strong fellows, walking bags of skin and bone.'

Witnessing men in such condition in mid-1943 made Scott all the more determined to keep himself as well as possible physically. He had learned a thing or two about nutrition, and this was now paying off. He knew plants could provide supplementary vitamins, and through trial and error picked up bits of knowledge wherever he could. 'A fair tea tonight, rice and onions and potato water,' he reported one day. 'Plus, the result of my cooking snake plant, elephant ear, bamboo shoots, lily stalk and three boiled onions. I am as full as a tick at present.'

And so, feeling good, he settled down to write. The only problem was that he was down to powdered ink, and it wasn't running too well. Still, it enabled him to lose himself in composing his thoughts for Marge, recording his observations of camp life and the countryside.

Scott was often struck by the beauty of the night when the moon was full and the heavens ablaze with stars. He would pause to take it in. In the early mornings he would look for the Southern Cross low down in the sky. But it was the sunsets that would stop him in his tracks. 'Old Doug is an admirer of the sunset too,' he told Marge. 'It was funny a minute ago. A crow was cawing in the tree above us, one of the lads piped up, "Go away, you'll wait a bloody long time for me to die."'

In a reflective moment, Scott discussed the increasingly despondent mood in the camp with Lance Corporal Alf Strempel. Alf was one of the mates with whom he enjoyed ruminating about life. 'He was saying how the young chaps were getting a bit silly, and the old ones getting morose,' Scott wrote. He worried about just how many men would actually make it home, but he assured Marge that he'd be one of them: she should never fear that he would not get home.

20

Dying Is Part of Your Job

A foreboding gripped Scott about the challenges the POWs would face at Meilo. He watched with deepening concern as a convoy of 200 bullock carts brought timber for the railway. Running downhill with no brakes, the carts went full speed to the bottom and across a bridge, before the rise on the other side pulled them up. If the conditions, equipment and infrastructure were as primitive as this, then the working environment would be difficult to tame. 'We will be some time here, I fancy, as there is tons of work,' he wrote to Marge. 'Big trees – 8 feet through – to be felled and got away. Bamboo forests to be cut and dug out.'

If there was a benefit to the new camp, it was that construction was initially slow. 'They only take about 150 out to work and I have decided to go out when I feel like it,' he explained. 'A funny camp, this – we have no fence up and just wander anywhere.' For Scott, this was a welcome breather. 'I am getting lazy these days. Just lounge around all day, sleep most of the afternoon.' He had time for supper with a close mate, Warrant Officer Keith Burrill of the RAAF: the two men enjoyed a 'good brew of rissoles with coffee to wash them down'. Keith was a nightly call.

John Garran had a similar attitude to Scott. 'A party of seven of us get together, and when the work is being located three go bush, and we get a four-man job between the seven of us.' Despite the lack of work, the worry was that fevers were raging among the men, while the furnace-like heat of the day created conditions of extreme discomfort.

The men took advantage of the rest – the first they'd had for some months. The lack of a coherent Japanese plan for building the railroad through the difficult terrain at 75 Kilo bemused Scott. 'There is a colossal quantity of work to be done and Nip has no idea of how to do it,' he told Marge. 'He is in a hopeless mess, new levels and new ideas every day.' To make it worse, the wet season was approaching. 'We are bridging a river at present. A long bridge, 250 yards. I give it five minutes when the water rises,' he wrote on 24 March 1943.

Scott attributed the engineering incompetence to the fact the Japanese had departed from the original British survey line. Because of the lack of equipment, the construction was rough. Opposite the camp, an embankment was built a metre too high – it had to be lowered by shovel. There were no known levels and the line was going through by eye – which in the mountainous countryside meant levels were irregular and the track not straight. 'A creek runs through the valley between two mountains,' Scott described. 'They are filling it in with a twelve-foot embankment and making the creek change course. How it will be when the rain comes! Honestly, it's better than a comic opera, a ragtime railway line.' John Garran added to the picture of incompetence, citing skips from a cutting emptying dirt down a gully instead of using it to form an embankment.

The few weeks of comparative rest came to an abrupt end. However incompetently, the Japanese were ready to resume work on the railway. The first sign came one morning when the workers had left camp for the day's labour. The 'company bastard', as Scott described him, lined up all the No Duties men and examined them. 'Sent about sixty out to work,' Scott said. 'It is murder. Men just one day out of hospital with fever and dysentery are made to work in this terrific heat.'

Before long, more than 220 Light Duty and No Duty men were being sent out to work. Raging high temperatures were not deemed serious enough to keep someone in the RAP. As a concession, their daily metreage was reduced to 'only' 0.7 cubic metres. When an Australian officer protested on 9 April 1943 that the conditions would mean that men would die, the Japanese response was indifference: 'Well, let them, we have plenty more.' Nagatomo's warning was being put into practice as a new regime of 'Speedo! Speedo!' was enforced on the unwilling labourers.

As demands intensified, shifts lengthened. Work parties left camp at 8 am and did not return until well after midnight. The reason was soon clear to Scott:

> We have been informed that our part of the line here will be finished by 5th May, even if it is over our dead bodies. So that is that, and if we have to go on like this on the food we are getting, it will be over our corpses.

Work was now rigidly enforced as the men struggled in the difficult terrain. Such was the new level of brutality that even an elephant was shot after throwing its driver, who was also shot. 'They are both lying out near the bridge stinking to high heaven,' Scott wrote. 'Nice gentlemen.'

The Burmese and Thai labourers were put to work on the light, level stretches, while the excavation of the hard ground was saved for the POWs. Scott cursed when the daily metreage was suddenly increased to 2 cubic metres. From 6 metres down, the men dragged the dirt up a 30-degree slope, and then carried it another 30 metres to the dump.

The guards demanded a rhythmic work chant from the POW gangs assigned to the bridges. It was a monotonous job, and the pull and drop team were ordered to chant 'Ichi-nie-san-sie' as they pulled the rope taut, then raised the heavy iron or teak-log 'monkey' in the middle of a rough bamboo frame, before letting it drop from a height of about 3 metres. With a thud, a trimmed log would be driven into the ground. Scott was not sure of the exact words, but he wanted Marge to know, 'I have the tune off now.'

Wal Williams, a private in the 2/19th Battalion, was part of the pile-driving gangs at the time. 'There might be twenty to thirty blokes pulling this thing up, and it would be positioned over the pile and just let her go,' he recalled years later. 'Back you'd go again. They would drive in about twenty of these things a day. That was a shift. It was hard and dangerous work.'

On one such shift, on 29 April 1943, Scott reckoned that, with the aid of an elephant, they established 'an all-time Burma record. Twenty-two piles were driven for the day.'

The night shift was worse, with men working by the light of bamboo fires. Bridge work was particularly dangerous, with frequent bad accidents among men spiking trestles to the piles while balancing precariously on rickety scaffolding 15 metres and more above the river or gorge below. Some fell; others were buried under landslides.

Sickness was also on the rise. There were now more than a hundred sick men in the RAP daily. Since they'd arrived, more than 300 cases of fever had been reported. Alarmed at the deteriorating health situation, with the number reaching 500 No Duties men out of a camp of 1800 men, Brigadier Varley spoke to Major General Akira Sasa, group commander of the POW railroad construction camps, who bluntly told him that a sickness rate of more than 20 per cent would not be tolerated. POWs were soldiers and 'dying is part of your job ... You have sick only because you don't try ... If you are sick you only lie down all day and if you lie down you don't need food. In future the sick will not get food, even rice – the workers only will be fed.' Varley was warned that this regime would be enforced in a week's time.

The Japanese regarded sickness as a contemptible weakness, and believed that if the sick were starved, they would be motivated to work harder. The railway had to be completed in four months. Major Green told the men they had tough times ahead, that the sick would have to work and that men would probably die.

The regular hospital visits left Varley feeling depressed as he came face to face with emaciated men: men weakened by prolonged dietary deficiency with little or no medication. Diarrhoea, skin diseases and malaria were by now endemic. Rats in the sleeping quarters were a constant reminder of the possibility of plague. Men whose clothing had worn out were reduced to working in a 'G' and no shoes. What made it worse for Varley was that the Japanese medical officer, Lieutenant Tomizo Higuchi, prevented direct approaches to Nagatomo for more medical supplies. Higuchi would make vague promises but they were seldom met. 'Through all this one must maintain calm and optimism,' Varley concluded.

If Varley knew the power of understatement, then Scott worried about the prophecy by the Minister for the Army, Frank Forde, which had filtered through, that the war could last for years. If he was correct, 'then many of us will be staying here permanently'. With hundreds of Japanese soldiers in trucks passing through the camp daily, Scott realised, the war would not be ending anytime soon and there was no chance of early release. All the while, the POWs were being worked 'just like slaves. All we lack is the whip.'

Anzac Day 1943 came as Scott marked his sixty-second week as a POW. It could not pass without a dawn service. Hundreds of men stood before a white cross driven into a roadside dirt heap, bedecked with wreaths. Scott was among them, and described the sombre mood for Marge to read one day:

As the dawn heightened the sky, the old chaps marched off, led by the band. If you could have seen it: a long line of men lining both sides of the road; the sky grey and stark; jungle-covered hills to the east; the shuffling of feet; the noise of dozens of men coughing; a dead silence of two minutes, then the sombre sky lightening with the dawn; the bugle sounds the opening of '[The] Last Post'. The dawn is on us. The band strikes up and disappears, leading the old diggers. We fall out to huts and eat our morning pap. So, another Anzac Day begins.

The service left Scott deep in reflection: a year ago, at the Anzac Day service in Changi, he had not expected that he would still be a POW a year later. All day his thoughts were with Marge as he leant on a rail, directing the levelling of the bearers for the next staging of the line. As he gazed out across a valley to the dark green hills, he admired the wild rugged beauty of the view and contented himself with the thought that, 'after all, things might be worse'. He was in good health, and had Marge and the boys to go back to. Like everyone, by May 1943, he had lost weight, but at 65 kilograms he was pleased to be lighter than the solid 82.5 kilos he had been when he left for active service.

Now he just wanted to go home. He was sick of being a POW. The photos of Marge remained his escape and salvation. 'Each night, last thing, I see you standing at the gate waiting for me. Never mind, treasure, one of these days you'll slam it shut behind me.'

As construction at the 75 Kilo camp neared completion, the demands on the men became even more extreme, the metreage they had to dig dramatically increasing. The toll on the men and the conditions under which they worked were the worst Scott had experienced to date.

We had a day of hell yesterday. All day long they stood over the men. Last night was like a slave scene from a picture. Imagine looking down from a height of twelve feet onto a series of holes. Toiling away are white men, their sweat-covered bodies glistening in the light of numerous flickering bamboo fires. Out of the hole and up the bank come two men at a time, carrying a bag and a pole along the bank. Tip the load, and down into the pit they go. Through the flickering light skulks a Nip. A scream and whack, he has caught someone resting.

They had worked all night, under the light of bamboo and pitch torches, finally stopping at 1 am, with the men worn out. They had pulled out 4.2 cubic metres a man – only to have to do it all over again the following day. Yet again, this was a scene for Scott reminiscent of Dante's *Inferno*, men reduced to shadows and guards yelling out, 'Speedo! Speedo!'

Yet there were exceptions among the guards, a few of whom understood that the work gangs could give just so much if the work was to be completed with reasonable efficiency. A guard on one shift not long after Anzac Day realised this after Scott and his team had worked all morning at the 71 Kilo site, before moving to the site at the 68 Kilo mark after lunch and staying there until late into the night. Then they walked 7 kilometres back to camp.

> We were absolutely done when we staggered in at
> 1.30 am. Had it not been for the guard, we would have
> been there all night. He knocked us off at 10.30 approx.
> and then the fun started. The engineers went for him.
> He whacked one with the butt of his rifle and came 'On
> guard' at them. Things looked nasty for a while, but he
> won the day and we came home.

Despite the brutality, in mid-May 1943 Scott had time to reflect on the results of the work as they finally prepared to leave the 75 Kilo camp. He was impressed by their achievements working through 'colossal embankments, 30 feet high and a mile long'. One cutting he worked on was 8 metres deep and nearly a kilometre in length. 'Tremendous, when you consider it was all done by hand,' he noted. 'Under different circumstances [it] would be magnificent.'

The consequence was a wholesale deterioration of the health of the POWs. This pushed the doctors to the limit. Among them was Captain Anderson, whose dedication deeply impressed Scott. 'Doc Anderson is looking washed out. What a man he is! Day after day he carries on, all day long.' Anderson wrote to Lieutenant Colonel Ramsay, the POW Commanding Officer at Meilo, expressing his alarm. Diarrhoea was causing men to lose weight so quickly that they could scarcely walk; many became so weakened that they were unfit even for light work.

Anderson objected to the indiscriminate grading of men for work by medically inexpert Japanese guards. Sending ill men to such backbreaking work not only ensured a relapse but lowered working efficiency. Surely, he thought, this was a consideration that should have greatly concerned the Japanese? But when Ramsay raised it with the guards, they took no notice.

Men continued to fall ill and continued to die. One was Corporal Jim Mooney, whose death particularly disturbed Scott. At the funeral, he stood near the grave, hearing the padre admonish those who might say this was God's doing. God had had no hand in his death; rather, it was the inhuman and barbaric treatment by their captors, the padre had said. Scott wrote to Marge: 'A thunderstorm was about as we buried poor Jim. The lightning was terrific, as were the thunderclaps. It seemed as if the heavens were angry at the inhumanity.'

Three more of Scott's mates died, and because there was now a shortage of wood for coffins, two were sewn into their blankets and carried to their graves on bamboo trestles. Scott stood watching. 'I wondered why it all had to be,' he mused. 'Why mankind should be so inhumane to man.'

This was the unanswerable question of the war, not just in Asia and the Pacific but also in Europe.

21

Tall Tales

To deal with rumours, lies and propaganda is a challenge at the best of times, but in Burma during World War II there was one overriding certainty: the speculation, claims and outright falsehoods played with the sanity of every POW. As part of a community that had been unwillingly thrown together, Scott was alert to the hopes and disappointments that spread through the camps.

In the early days after Singapore fell, every POW wanted to believe the Japanese were withdrawing, and that the war would soon be over. A rumour that seemed to be revived every couple of weeks was that Germany had capitulated. Dates came and dates went, and still they were here, being ground down by an unforgiving enemy in an unforgiving jungle. At Auschwitz, it was a similar story: rumours about the war's end abounded, raising hopes, only to dash them, which worsened the internees' war of nerves.

Rumours of the imminent arrival of letters that failed to materialise seemed particularly cruel to Scott, who hungered for news from home. In mid-June 1943, there were rumours of letters being burned, of cholera outbreaks further up the line, of escapes that occurred and others that did not, and of moving camp, even back to Changi. 'All sorts of wild rumours about again,' Scott told Marge. 'Changi is favourite, but I know different, they won't send us there.'

Word that circulated seemingly on the wind in the camps could be much more prosaic than the hoped-for end of labour on the railroad. And so it was three months later, when there were '[r]umours of a cigarette issue and one tin of milk to eleven men. If this is correct, things are looking up.'

Scott sensed that believing the nightmare was about to end soon was essential for so many men. 'It gives them hope from becoming too down in the dumps,' he'd commented a year earlier, in September 1942. Scott knew what it was like to feel down: he had been there, and had told Marge about it in his letters. His purpose in doing so, however, was not to garner her sympathy but to encourage her to believe that he was perfectly all right. She was not to get down in the dumps because of him.

As Scott wrote his letters that could not be posted, he envisioned something that was beyond rumour: it was a certainty that he and Marge would share a future together when the war was over. In the scheme of things, as he saw it, his prolonged absence from Marge was just a hiccup. It would end and their life together would resume, just as it was meant to. Scott's certainty could keep him out of 'the dumps', and he knew that if he allowed himself to go there, it would be disastrous. The evidence was all around him.

Scott could negotiate the rumours and work out and reject the lies, but Japanese propaganda was another matter altogether. As with any propaganda, it aimed to alter perceptions of the war and, in particular, of the daily lives of POWs. Behind their arrogance and general lack of concern for the welfare of the POWs, the Japanese military felt a need to show their domestic audience that they were exercising power and control in the nation's newly won dominions in a just and civilised manner. Film was the obvious way to create the impression that the POWs were living happily and working cheerfully under kind and benevolent rule.

John Garran quickly worked out that this 'sentimental tosh' was for home consumption. He was included in one such propaganda film made at Thanbyuzayat, where he had been transported from 75 Kilo in late April 1943 to take part in a concert for the emperor's birthday. In preparation, the band and concert party were all issued with tunics, shorts, hats and boots – 'so that we will look well in the film', as he noted. No one was photographed unless he was completely dressed. Men were shown taking fruit, smokes and bottles from the canteen – with the suggestion that it was bottled beer. All the goods were taken back as soon as the men were out of camera range. While amused by the flagrant hypocrisy, they couldn't help but feel manipulated.

Naturally, no such film could fail to include the benevolent medical care offered to the POWs. To underline this message, the film showed a hospital with about 700 men as patients. The ward was cleaned up, equipped with extra medicine bottles and the beds provided with clean white sheets for the occasion. Japanese orderlies were shown caring for the weak and disabled, while white-coated doctors 'operated' on the sick.

Lieutenant Colonel Tom Hamilton, a senior medical officer with 'A' Force, described appearing in a film having a 'fake consultation with Dr Higuchi over a POW's chest. This patient was suffering with piles.' In a quick change of scene and role, the men were then shown in the back of a truck, singing happily as they were driven to work on the railway. This was, as Scott noted, the only occasion that prisoners were driven to work – and then the truck went only as far as the camp gate. They had also handed around blank sheets of paper, and photographed men reading 'letters from home'. Scott supposed Marge might see the film some day; if she did, he knew, the stunts would amuse her. But the cynicism of the subterfuge repelled him. 'If they would only look after the sick it would be something.'

The Japanese efforts to present their camps in a positive light saw Scott chosen with other POWs in early June 1943 to be actors in yet another propaganda film. Dressed in borrowed clothes to replace their G-strings, they were to march past the camera in fours, singing happily as they went to work. Men without boots and clothing – about 30 per cent of the total number – were put on the inside ranks, and the fitter men on the outside.

Then, wrote Scott, the fun started. 'Would the boys sing? Not they.' On a count of three, they remained mute. 'The Japs are raving, the band playing "Pack Up Your Troubles" and we won't sing.' The Japanese then threatened to bring the sick out of hospital and make them stand in the sun. Finally, the Australians consented to sing 'Bless 'Em All' – but the end result was a ribald parody at the expense of guards they knew all too well.

Well, away we go, and as they pass the mike you can hear them roaring, 'Bless all the Pongoes and their bastard sons. Bless the Boy Bastard, etc.', only bless wasn't a word used. The Japs must have taken a tumble because later on they had about thirty lined up singing 'Pack Up Your Troubles'. Out we then go to do our stone breaking.

The sound engineer's face lit up with pleasure: he clearly thought he had obtained a propaganda scoop. If the Japanese at home bought it, those on the railroad who were forced to take part in the making of such films did not.

Although it was not meant to be amusing, Japanese propaganda did provide some light relief for the POWs, especially when it came in the form of ripping yarns of the fantastical successes of the Japanese military. Much of it appeared in the Japanese weekly newspaper *Greater Asia*, published in Rangoon and circulated among the POW camps in Burma. There were about thirty copies for a thousand men, and the prisoners rushed them because they were the only English-language news they could get – and the only humour.

Scott noted one comical story after the paper arrived at 105 Kilo camp in early June 1943: there was 'an amusing tale of a Nip pilot capturing a plane with a pistol. It is propaganda and then some.' The story went like this: a Japanese pilot ran out of ammunition when in combat with a Lockheed Lightning P-38, which also ran out. With great presence of mind, the Japanese pilot drew a pistol and forced the enemy to land and surrender. Yet another told of a Japanese pilot who, while attacking a British convoy, flew so low that, in swashbuckling style, he was able to cut off the captain's head with a sword as he passed. 'The paper is full of this sort of stuff,' Scott observed.

As intended, *Greater Asia*'s propaganda did boost the morale of the Japanese officers and guards, who were encouraged to believe they were winning the war. To Scott, it was 'the usual propaganda', one aim of which was to try to 'cause trouble between Britain and Yankee lads' in the POW camps. But it was also meant to convey a warning that Australians should be scared of the mighty Japanese air force, not least because

Japan had wondrously occupied Darwin and Sydney, had taken Adelaide after a bayonet charge, and their forces were mopping up elsewhere in Australia.

With this in mind, Brigadier Varley reported a conversation with a Japanese officer about the bombing of Australian cities. Asked if Townsville had been bombed, the Japanese officer replied: 'Bomb bomb.' What about Brisbane? Japanese officer: 'Bomb bomb.' And Sydney? Japanese: 'Bomb bomb.' What about Canberra? Japanese: 'Bomb bomb.' And Bullshit? Japanese: 'Bomb bomb.'

Amid the tall tales, even 'home by Christmas' was now met with a bitter laugh or a wry smile. Survival to Christmas was the only goal that mattered.

22

Fighting Despondency

Scott was malnourished, with recurring malaria and blurry vision. After eighteen months in captivity in the middle of the jungle, he realised he was not immune to the rampant illness and disease around him. He was now at 105 Kilo camp, Aungganaung, amid a health crisis that was worsening by the day.

The life-and-death situation he now found himself in had begun before leaving 75 Kilo camp at Meilo. For almost ten weeks the Japanese had forced the POWs to work at a furious pace to finish that section of the railway. On his final day there, Scott painted one last, vivid picture for Marge. 'As we came in last night, we could see the sky lit up. Came upon the "bridgies" working by floodlights run off a big generator. Can you imagine it, in the depth of the jungle?' There was a 30-foot bank lined against the skyline, with two huge fires blazing at its base.

Out of the dark bowels of the earth come pairs of men, toiling with a bag and pole. Up they go, a long line, the sweat glistening on their bodies. Down a track again to disappear again into the bowels of the earth, and so in the flickering firelight they go, up and down.

They had marched out of 75 Kilo on 17 May 1943, past the graves of dead comrades, on a two-day journey that seemed never-ending, the guards hounding the stragglers at the point of a bayonet. Scott had kept a close eye on those who showed signs of wilting, to help them through.

> Away we go, up hill and down dale, the mountain range on our left, the road cut out of it. I gave Murray [Cheyne] a lift with his gear second smoko out. He was euchred, had been helping a sick chap along. The spell did him good. Old Doug [Baldy] was battling on up in front. He looked half dead, but I'd see him each smoko. My method was to let them get ahead each start, then go through the field till spell time.

When they finally arrived, they 'slept like dead men on the hard knots on the bamboo'. The camp was situated on a slope, with filthy, vermin-infested attap huts.

When Scott woke and walked around the camp, all his senses were assailed – from the appearance of barely clad walking skeletons to the nauseating stench from suppurating wounds and the guttural sounds of men screaming in pain. And then there were the dead 'coolies', or local labourers. There were about sixty of them who had died of cholera. The POWs had to remove and bury them. In the jungle they found many more dead bodies. Surely this was what hell on earth looked like.

Scott tried to come to terms with existential conundrums that filled his mind in mid-June. 'I wonder what the meaning of it all is ... if God has turned his face against us,' he wrote. For weeks he had questioned just why humans were so cruel to their fellow men; now he began to question his faith, struggling with unanswerable questions.

The hardest part was not knowing when all this would end. And the death of mates who should have lived. 'We lost another today, a dysentery case again,' he wrote. 'The pity of it is that they could all be saved if we had the stuff to treat it, and [the] Japs have plenty.' The funeral for his fellow POW was being held as Scott wrote, and he could hear the hymn, 'Lead, Kindly Light'. The tune, he thought, would 'always bring back tragic memories in the future'.

Not long after, the most emaciated man he had ever seen hobbled past, a private. 'Poor devil, he was only skin and bone'. Sick as he was, the man had still saluted Scott: formalities still mattered for these men, even as death beckoned.

The funerals continued as amoebic dysentery spread. 'And two more, possibly four, will die within a week,' Scott told Marge. 'Something is wrong with the world when we can't get supplies. A few needles of emetine is all that is required.' But, as the medical officer Tom Hamilton had learned, Dr Higuchi would not allow it: he would lose face if he did.

The only heartening news was that heavy bombers had just dropped four tons of bombs on Thanbyuzayat, but the downside was that twenty POWs and eighty Burmese had been killed in the raid. Scott saw the madness of it all. 'As if we are not losing enough as it is,' he wrote in sadness. Nonetheless, as he told Marge, he was hearing positive things about the progress of the war, so perhaps it would only last a few months more.

Scott's despondency lifted when he noticed it was raining. It was the sort of night when he would have liked to sit down with Marge to hoe into steak and kidney pie, with cauliflower and white sauce, and then settle with her next to the fire. The boys would be asleep and they would listen to the radio. Those days would come again, he told himself. The thought of life with Marge steadied him.

It was night time, in those special minutes, when he could write to Marge and feel that closeness with her. Then he could review the day and set down his worries: how more and more tropical ulcers were appearing among the men, how a small cut or abrasion on the ankle could become infected and rapidly ulcerate into a gaping wound.

> Men in RAP with eyes eaten into the bone. As we continue to go downhill, they will get worse. I sometimes shudder when I look into the future and imagine how we'll be after six more months of this. Not many will be left … the Doc is talking of amputations. And all because we are undernourished.

Unsurprisingly, within the next few weeks the RAP lines grew longer and more desperate, the men looking more and more skeletal. 'The poor beggars cannot sleep for the pain and look just worn out,' Scott noted. A sharpened spoon was the usual rudimentary and painful method of sloughing out the ulcerated flesh, but other, more innovative treatments such as maggots or even river fish were also used. Men would immerse their legs in a river, and small fish would eat the slough, helping to clean the wound. Scott knew that a basic recognition by the Japanese of what was causing the crisis would help immeasurably. 'If the men had footwear there would not be half as many.'

As ulcers worsened, the sick were sent to Khonkan, the hospital at 55 Kilo. There, AIF surgeon Dr Bertie Coates worked in a bamboo lean-to, his only instruments being a knife, two pairs of artery forceps and a saw – one also used by the camp butchers and carpenters. For appendectomies he had razor blades. Coates was short and upright, with a trademark swagger, and spoke with a staccato flow of kindly, earthly wisdom. Those on the railway were left inspired when there was so little to inspire them. To many, Coates was a hero. Knowing that ulcers were progressive, and that without effective treatment they would lead to death, he realised that amputations were his best hope of saving lives – even though the mortality rate was bound to be high.

The lack of anaesthesia posed a serious problem, but with the help of a Dutch chemist, Captain C.J. Van Boxtel, a workable solution for use as a spinal anaesthetic was found. With Doc Anderson assisting, Coates was able to undertake amputations that at least gave the patient a chance of survival. Within a few weeks of his arrival at 55 Kilo, Coates had amputated 120 legs.

Wal Williams remembered witnessing an amputation performed in the open air. The patient was numb from the waist down. All the while Bertie Coates was smoking a cheroot.

He peeled back the skin just like a ladies' stocking, and then cut into the flesh and clamped the arteries before sawing through the bone. When he had finished, he told the orderly to take the saw back to the kitchen. A little while after, the fellow woke up and I remember him saying at some point, 'Excuse me, sir, you're smoking,' to which the doc replied, 'Son, there are no germs in ash.'

Occasionally the Japanese killed a yak for the POWs, and when they did Coates was allowed to remove strips from the outer surface of intestines. These were then washed and placed in a bottle of iodine. After seven days they were thought suitable to use as catgut for sutures.

Scott had first come across Coates at Tavoy, not long after the Australians arrived there, when the Japanese had need of his surgical skills. A Japanese doctor had bungled the removal of a soldier's appendix and urgently needed a surgeon to save his life. 'Couldn't get the bowel back so left the victim on the table and rushed out to the Drome for Colonel Coates, who came in, fixed up the damage and received one tin of milk as payment,' Scott noted.

On hearing that Coates was predicting that 60 per cent of the amputation cases would die within three months, Scott panicked. He had reason to: the doctors were considering amputating Baldy McFadyen's ulcerated leg. Scott did what he could for him. As luck would have it, the conservative treatment kicked in and Baldy's leg began to heal in the nick of time. Two of their mates, however, were not so lucky, Bruce Chapman and Alf Child did not survive their surgeries. Those who did hobbled around on crude wooden legs made from bamboo.

By mid-September 1943, so many deaths were tearing at Scott: 'You can imagine how I feel. Forty-four amputations have been done and fifty-one are waiting. Bruce Chapman and [Corporal] Jack Briggs have died. Stremp loses his leg. Men are dying, leaving young wives and kiddies they have never seen to face the world.' The same question plagued him: 'Why has it all got to be? As if they haven't enough to bear! I thank God every night for bringing me safely through another day.' Scott was one of the lucky ones who had managed to maintain a just adequate level of health. 'The end of sixty-nine weeks captivity, but I am still alive and kicking.'

If there was the glimmer of a bright side for Scott, it was the chance to fill in another lettercard to Marge. This was a nicely printed card, explaining the kindness with which the Japanese command was treating the POWs, not to mention the monthly picture shows. Two letters and one picture show in fourteen months were supposed to constitute kind treatment. But then, the Japanese interpreter had told Scott that a bomber had dropped the lettercards over Darwin. 'Isn't that a good one?' he wrote. 'I guess they are burnt by now.'

The wet season had begun with a vengeance in May. This meant working soaked to the skin and having to plough through mud up to the knees. The rivers became raging torrents that washed away sections of the new rail line. The men began constructing 'corduroy' – roads made of tree stumps laid across swamps. The camps, too, were a quagmire: huts surrounded by a sea of mud. A guard called Scott aside in the pouring rain on the way to work. 'This up to shit, no bloody good.'

Scott agreed, as he slipped and slithered in the mud, his bare feet suffering in the process. 'It is wicked watching the men with bad feet hobbling up the road or floundering in the mud,' he wrote. And to see the sick being dragged from their beds with raging temperatures to stand on parade for roll call was callous in the extreme. 'All goes under the heading of "kind and humane treatment". If we knew that their prisoners in Australia were getting the same treatment we wouldn't mind, but we know how well they are being looked after.'

The regular diet of rumours continued. Scott was momentarily buoyed by the suggestion that work was to be abandoned for the wet season as conditions worsened. So bad was the mud that, as he awaited confirmation of this, he detailed a work party to stand by in case they were needed to free bogged trucks. 'They are getting bogged in dozens now,' he told Marge. 'Two elephants are on full-time duty these days pulling them out. The road is inches deep in mud now. I give it a couple of weeks before it becomes impassable.'

Work was stopped, but the break did not last long. 'Their word, as usual was worth precisely nothing,' Scott observed drily. The rumours about returning to Changi persisted but Scott didn't believe those either. When the men heard that there were 60,000 letters in Burma for the POWs, they hoped against hope that this at least was true.

Fighting the despondency he felt because of these furphies, Scott arrived back at camp after yet another day on the rail line to be told there was a note waiting for him at the Orderly Room. Opening it, he found it was from Lofty Waters. 'I couldn't get to the kitchen and Curly quick enough, my fingers all thumbs as I tried to open it. He was okay.'

Lofty wrote that he had had a letter from Marge in March – four months earlier. The letter had been written in mid-1942, as Marge tried every possible avenue to try to find out what was happening with Scott. She had written, hopefully, to Lofty, and the letter eventually found him in Changi. 'All at Dandenong were well,' he said, adding that Marge was bearing up. This was Scott's greatest relief.

I can face the future now in a light heart, happy in the knowledge you are okay. Good old Lofty. Once again,

he has proved to be a friend in need. He is well, he says.
I have his letter. Will bring it home and frame it for all
time ... I can hardly realise it at all yet. Lofty really alive
and you safe and well ... He reckons it won't be long
before we are bashing the slops again.

Suddenly, everything was rosy. Scott was so happy he felt like
he could 'jump over the moon'. Knowing Marge and the boys
were well, and the prospect of a pub crawl with Lofty, revived
his spirits. As well, there was positive news about the war in
the Pacific. The Allies were definitely winning the war, even
if it was a battle of attrition. In a letter to Marge, he wrote:
'Things are moving down your way, and moving fast, I believe.
Once they get moving, they'll roll him [the enemy] up like a
window blind.'

All this made him think once more of the future. There
would be a big aviary in the yard, the boys would be taught to
play footy, tennis and cricket, and to do jobs around the house
and cut wood, just as Scott had done in his childhood. Those
experiences had prepared him for the hard labour he was now
doing. The war had convinced him that John and Doug must
become self-reliant: they must be able to cook and look after
and protect themselves. 'For this has proved that the man who
has battled a bit in life, and can fend for himself, is the one
who is standing up to this the best,' he noted.

Scott could see himself taking the boys to Saturday movie
matinees and telling them stories by the fire at night with Marge
on his knee. She was always in his dreams. 'I awoke and felt for
you, got your hand and you just turned over and snuggled into
my shoulder without waking, just as you used to,' he wrote one
evening. The years ahead would be happy ones.

23

The Gang

The jungle was alive with birdcalls and the sounds of myriad crickets and insects as Scott made his way to the river for his nightly wash. He stopped to watch butterflies flitting over the water and spotted the queen hovering near a pool, surrounded by dozens of colourful courtiers. The sun was setting on a warm and still day. He watched, his body stilled and at peace.

Marge might not have been there this night in October 1943, but it was as though she were. 'The sunsets of these nights are beautiful,' he wrote. 'You cannot imagine anything so magnificent. I would like to be standing with my arm around you watching them these nights, sweetheart.'

There was an exuberance about Scott at this time: although the brutal regime that now controlled his life could easily destroy the moment, he could quickly bounce back with a sunset, a cup of real tea, a chat with Curly – or Marge. From early on in his time as a POW on the railway, Scott had transcended the world of captivity deep in the jungle and communed with Marge as evening approached. 'At times you seem to come to me, and I get such a funny feeling, almost as if you were standing close to me and I could reach out and touch you,' he told her.

Around the same time in Auschwitz, Viktor Frankl experienced something uncannily similar: 'More and more I felt that she [Tilly] was present; that she was with me; I had the feeling that I was able to ... stretch out my hand and grasp hers.' The wonder and gentleness of these experiences stayed with both men, until the reality of everyday life shattered the moment.

The bottom line was, inevitably, death. It was a subject that could not be put to one side: it was all around, all the time. Scott acknowledged this: 'We were talking about the deaths last night. Not a cheerful subject, and we reckon that if one-third of us get home we will be fortunate.'

The word 'fortunate' held a deeper meaning in a POW camp, as life often came down to chance. Chance played its part: not saluting a guard, a piece of meat in the stew, news from home, or just getting through the day's labour. Construction was behind schedule, and a final burst to complete the railway was needed. In August 1943, Scott was among men ballasting and knapping stone for embankments. 'We have pushed the line through at a terrific pace and have now finished our end of it,' he noted. The men had been doing up to 4.6 cubic metres each, and were at the end of their tether. 'Four metres is a lot of dirt when you have to throw it all out and shovel it back – tossing up from one to two metres down is no joke.'

Back at camp, they were still subject to frequent unannounced searches. Scott again took the precaution of hiding his letters as the guards went through the huts for what he regarded as 'an organised looting campaign' in early October 1943. The 'boys got a thorough doing', with gear tipped everywhere. 'My letters were not as well hidden as usual, but they were okay,' he told Marge. 'All my snaps were emptied out but none were lost.'

By now, the tropical diseases decimating the POWs were reaching crisis point. Dysentery, malaria, pellagra and beriberi were a constant in their lives, along with the overriding fear of cholera. Then there were the bed bugs, fleas and scorpions – small by comparison but, as Scott could attest, maddeningly irritating. And lice. 'I had a delousing after my wash,' he wrote one day. 'Got about a dozen. So maybe I'll sleep a little better at nights. It's a horrible thing to be lousy, honey.'

Viktor Frankl was suffering the same annoyance. But, grateful for the smallest of mercies, he was happy when there was time before bed to delouse, even though it meant standing naked in frigid temperatures, picking off the lice; if not, it meant being kept awake half the night. Malnutrition and inhuman workloads ravaged the bodies of these men on both sides of the world.

In these dire conditions, it is often not the loners who survive, but those who form groups. This played out around Scott, as men pooled their skills to help meet their basic needs, supporting each other when sick and, importantly, buoying each other up. This satisfied a deep human need for belonging. Even stripped of everything else, they still had their mates. This made life more tolerable.

Not all the men had the benefit of these bonds, but those who did knew it. Able Seaman Frank McGovern, a survivor of the sinking of HMAS *Perth*, was one of those on the railroad who, like Scott, swore by mateship. He had no doubt it was stronger among the Australians than men of other nationalities. Frank knew Scott, but his mates were mostly those who had survived the sinking of the *Perth*. Years later, he spoke about the importance of mateship to POWs:

> If you didn't have a mate, you wouldn't get through. You just had to have somebody to lean on, somebody to help you along, otherwise it was pretty rough. They talk about the mateship being a bit hackneyed and all that, but it's not. It is real, absolutely, it's there. If you didn't have it, you'd find it tough going. No one's an island; you just had to have someone to talk to.

Wal Williams understood the importance of mateship too – even if it didn't always work out for him. 'Most of the blokes I cobbered up to never made it,' he recalled in September 2020.

That was the reality for so many of the men: their mates were dying. But everyone innately knew you could not risk being a loner. Having mates helped create a bulwark against being overwhelmed by brutality and disease. Fellow POW Harold Ramsey summed it up: 'The worst thing was if you got depressed. It was hard *not* to get depressed, but if you did, about ten days would be as long as you'd live.'

The myth of Australian mateship was part of the Anzac legend, as exemplified on the battlefields of World War I. Although post-war it became subject to arguable revisionism, on the Burma Railway mateship was critical: the sense of comradeship and the commitment to mutual dependence enhanced men's chances of survival. The opportunity to let off steam with each other about the day's events, curse the guards' latest brutality or plan revenge helped them cope – even as they lived, as Dr Rowley Richards put it, 'with the ugly anticipation that there were always likely to be worse days to come'.

Scott wrote about these bonds, formed over the months, almost daily in his stream-of-consciousness letters to Marge. His mates were 'all good coves' and stuck together. This was a major reason why they were generally healthy. The gang had shared everything that had come along, good and bad. An understanding within the group exemplified this: when one of them was sick, the others would look after him. Likewise, they gleefully shared any dubiously acquired food.

One of Scott's favourite moments, he told Marge, was the morning Alan Campbell woke him at 4 am at Victoria Point. 'Up we sneaked, pinched a tub of the Nips' fresh water and had a real wash with soap. Was it any good! When we told the rest in the morning, were we popular!' At Tavoy, under the threat of malaria, Scott was thankful for Doug having 'a [mosquito] net big enough for the three of us'. And when Doug fell ill in early March 1943, 'we wouldn't let him go out to work today as it was too hard and he got shoved off with the No Duties'.

Curly was another key member of Scott's circle, and he and Scott spent time over several months 'yarning about things'. The discussions riveted them both. 'Curly does some heavy thinking at times and opens up all sorts of subjects,' Scott told Marge. His presence lifted Scott's spirits, especially when Alan Campbell was present and able to add to the discussion. 'Having the lad along makes all the difference. We are together again. We can take all they can dish out.'

There was the memorable time when Curly had returned from Thanbyuzayat, bringing 'real tea' to Scott's hut when he was recovering from a fever. He had pilfered it from the Japanese. 'He blew in at about five, and you should have seen him caked with mud and dust, with rivulets of sweat trickling through,' Scott described. 'Gee, was I glad to see him. Seeing you would be the only greater joy. It seemed to buck me up no end.'

When Baldy McFadyen was struck down with a fever and a deteriorating leg ulcer, Curly and Scott knew he had to be moved to the hospital at 55 Kilo for treatment by Bertie Coates:

> We got old Doug away today. Curly and I had a talk last night and decided to pull some strings. He has been going downhill lately and wouldn't have lasted much longer. So, he goes back for a rest, leaving only two of the clan now to see it through. We'll battle on.

Inevitably, Scott fell ill with another bout of malaria. He was given yet more quinine tablets to treat his fever. Although Scott had little appetite, he noted appreciatively that 'Curly has fed me well today'. Another time Curly came down with fever, along with another of their mates, Don Tilley. 'I have two invalids on my hands,' Scott rued.

Within days there was a third when Wimpy Edwards, who had been with Scott from Singapore days, fell ill. This time, tough love was needed. 'I had occasion to get into Wimpy today,' Scott wrote. 'If he doesn't pull himself together, he'll be dead in three weeks. Has had the trots and has thrown in the towel properly, looks like nothing on earth. I stood over him and made him eat at lunchtime.' Scott's strong words did the trick. Within a few days, Wimpy was 'perky again and, although thin, is okay'.

Wimpy was not the only one to be motivated by Scott in this way. Despite dysentery, Murray Knight kept working, even though he was forced to go to the latrines for 'fifty-one evacuations inside twenty-two hours' – and Scott 'blitzed' him. By November 1943, such care was not fleeting but constant.

When the war was over, Scott wrote, those who survived would have a duty of care for the families of fallen comrades: 'We owe our dead and maimed a debt we can never repay, and it will be our job to see that their families do not want for anything when we come home.' If they were not properly looked after, it would be enough to sway any election, he vowed. Scott had seen enough as a soldier and POW to know the difference between good and bad leadership.

24

White Japs

Scott was a straight shooter. There were many things he felt strongly about, and it seemed he did not leave anyone in doubt as to his view. Among POWs, with the 'self' that was presented to the world stripped away, there was little room for dissembling, or shirking one's responsibilities. And there was no excuse for not standing up for another POW. Especially if you were an officer.

If the daily threat to survival tested friendships among POWs, it also tested the courage of their officers. Some readily stood up for their men, although this invited reprisal bashings from the guards. The stress of this was too much for some, who tended to take a back seat to avoid the unceasing confrontation. Taking a low profile led to an easier life. But the men viewed this poorly. In the extreme conditions of the Burma Railway, relationships between officers and other ranks soon became more consistently strained than in any other Australian theatre of the war.

The men, having been imbued with the Anzac legend, expected to encounter an egalitarian army in which officers treated the other ranks with respect and dignity – they expected to be led by an informal, rather than a formal, military discipline. Instead, they found that, from 1940, the officer class had become more elitist, playing a very different role from those in the Great War.

The extreme conditions of captivity, in which survival was at front of mind for all the men, officers and other ranks alike, exaggerated the division. Officers were seen as enjoying privileges and perks that were not available to the men. And in a fight for survival, this rankled.

From early on in Burma, Scott believed, some officers, particularly those in the more junior ranks of lieutenant or captain, hadn't pulled their weight. In his mind, the measure of a man in captivity was how he put in, the example he set and how he cared for the men when sickness hit. Under the pressures of captivity, disease and cruelty, he had no hesitation in criticising those he believed were not standing by their men. The obsequiousness some junior officers displayed towards the guards grated.

After the Singapore surrender, many of the other ranks were already critical of the officers when they arrived in Burma. They believed they had been sold out, especially by combatant officers. Scott was one of the many who felt a deep sense of grievance about the failure of the military hierarchy in the lost campaign. 'I am beginning to be certain now why we failed so badly when the blue was on, and the men bear only a small portion of the blame,' he wrote.

Medical officer Colonel Bertie Coates was vocal in criticising the leadership failure. He was, said Scott, very bitter about the defeat. 'You should hear him go to town on GOC Bennett. If ever they meet up, I should like to be present. Still, he was

only one; we were let down all along the line by our officers.'
A Royal Commission in 1945 would find that Bennett had not
been justified in leaving his men.

Amid these souring relations, an officer had added fuel to the
fire in Tavoy when he was discovered stealing from the men's
trust fund. 'Our trust fund is being tickled up again by one of
them,' Scott reported in disgust. 'We have him tabbed, though.'

Few transgressions went unnoticed as officers repeatedly
looked after themselves first. Scott railed to Marge that the
officers had 'put on another good act' when 2000 cigars came
in. 'Most of the men are without any and they swiped 500 for
themselves.' From early on, Scott 'did not think it possible that
grown men could behave as some of them are doing'. He noted
that men who were sick in the RAP got nothing extra to eat,
while the officers kept eggs for themselves. 'As long as they get
a lot, bugger anyone else. They are not the men's bootlaces,' he
concluded in March 1943.

It had not taken Scott long to observe that, in captivity,
officers were not setting the example the men required, putting
themselves first. Wary of what he could see happening, he
declined the offered opportunity to share with officers their
privileges in captivity:

> Officers! Far better for us had we been segregated from
> them. My remarks to our CO have turned out to be
> right when I told him I'd sooner stay with the men in the
> sergeants' mess and be one of them than go to the officers'
> mess among the prize lot he had there.

At camp in Seymour in February 1940, Scott had felt there
was a mutual understanding and respect between the officers

and other ranks: they respected each other's roles. He wrote to Marge describing 'a most enjoyable night doing night stunts. I have a decent bunch of fellows in my section, nearly all officers.' In Malacca in October 1941, before hostilities began, he had described 'four or five' officers who were 'the tops', although he added, in a sign that his eye for performance was becoming more critical, the rest were 'not worth two bob, the lot'.

Senior officers such as Brigadier Varley and Major Green had a crucial role, largely unseen by the men, in negotiating with Japanese officers around the general conditions in the camps, pleading for leniency for POWs' infractions and the like. Scott respected their efforts; rather, it was with the junior officers that tensions smouldered, and had done so since Singapore. In Scott's mind, these men set a bad example on the railway; 'Consequently, [I] have only contempt for them.' He and other NCOs were fed up.

> We have to stand as the buffer between men and officers
> and try to square off the things we know are rotten. No
> wonder the troops are hard to handle … I have no time
> for the lazy hounds. They stand and watch sick men
> sweating and labouring under the sun and never lift a
> hand.

It was the NCOs who took over the day-to-day running of the men, which included general organisation and rostering work parties. To many, these men were the real leaders – and the heroes. The NCOs such as Scott tended to live with the men, eating the same rations and leading them on their work parties.

Scott believed that junior officers, who did not have to work, abused their privileges. While he and other warrant officers led their groups on their work missions, the junior officers loafed around in camp. 'Not one of them lifts a pick or shovel all day long,' Scott noted. 'Just a pack of useless bludgers.' It was 'nothing to see twelve groups go out to work and not an officer with them – we cop it all', he wrote on 30 May 1943.

As a senior NCO, Scott only needed to be at a worksite in a supervisory capacity. That was what the Japanese guards expected. But he was determined to work at the same rate as the men – or better. If they were sick and couldn't work at the same rate as fitter men, he would help them out.

Some officers took a dim view of this, letting it be known they believed Scott was setting a bad example – for them. 'Was warned off work today,' Scott reported. '*Kumichos* do not work, I was told.' He resented this, putting it down to some officers fearing they would have to put in alongside the men. Undeterred, he continued – ignoring the metreage increase to 1.4 cubic metres per man.

More than anything, the sight of officers not working offended Scott's sense of fairness. At Thetkaw, in November 1942, he decided to take a stand. 'Tried to get the officers to take their turn on picket tonight but no avail,' he wrote. A few days later they did. Having embarrassed the officers into grudgingly considering their own contribution, he noted that this was 'a victory for Heywood W.S.'. With the men living so closely together, word spread quickly when anyone was seen not to have done the right thing, or behaved fairly. However small the misdemeanour, there was outrage, especially if it was an officer who had offended. At the 75 Kilo camp at Meilo, the allocation of new boots became what Scott described as a scandalous affair. 'The officers are nearly all wearing new boots, and the good ones,' he told Marge. 'The men who really need them, the workers, are still without.'

Scott noted with some satisfaction the day in January 1943 when Green Force's commander, Major Green, 'blitzed the officers and made them put in one and a half hours each on latrine digging'. A day earlier Scott had walked through their quarters to find most of the officers lying on their beds. 'The lazy, good-for-nothing loafers just lie on their backs while the WOs do their work,' he fumed.

As relations with the officers frayed, Scott felt he had become 'as popular as the rats under the house'. He also believed that too many officers had become friendly with the Japanese, socialising with them and sharing coffee and smokes, 'kowtowing to them and worrying not one iota about the welfare of the sick and well men under them'. The POWs, he commented in September 1942, labelled those officers 'white Japs'.

In this, Scott had the support of Major Ian Cameron of the 2/9th Field Ambulance. 'Major Cameron has wiped them off,' Scott wrote. 'Says that the Japs will soon be sleeping and eating with them in their quarters. No matter at what hour of the day you enter the quarters, you can find one or more Japs there yapping.'

In theory, the officers were entitled to privileged treatment, a slightly higher level of pay and, importantly, under the 1929 Geneva Convention, the right not to work. As with the 1907 Hague Convention, anyone above the rank of warrant officer was forbidden to work. While Japan had not ratified the Geneva Convention, on the Burma Railway there was a distinct disincentive for officers to volunteer for work: if they did so, they knew, their own chances of survival would worsen. Another perk was that officers were able to supplement an utterly inadequate diet with their extra pay, at least to a small degree. And just a small change in diet could make the difference between wellness and succumbing to disease or death. To Scott, this smacked not only of selfishness but of blatant disregard for the men.

Major Cameron was not the only officer who backed Scott's views. Dr Richards saw camps 'where some of the senior officers took privileges, got better food. Disgraceful conduct, and the only people in the camp willing to look after not only the sick, but also the well blokes, were the doctors.'

Scott's one wish was that Major Jack Parry could have been there 'to trim them into shape and set the example'. To Scott, Parry was one in a hundred as a commanding officer. Although Parry had been a taskmaster, he was tough but fair. In Scott's view, he was the benchmark.

*

Whatever Scott's feelings about the Australian officers, he saved his most intense anger for the Japanese and Korean guards. Their cruelty did not let up, and neither did his anger.

It worsened at 105 Kilo camp when, under pressure from their Japanese superiors, the Korean guards spurred the prisoners on with impossible metreage demands and brutal hours. All the while, the POWs lived in a camp located in a hollow where water would gush down and flood the camp, leaving the ground awash with mud. The work, under the threat of harsh discipline, left the men fatigued, while the camp conditions gave them little chance to recover.

Scott spelled out his thoughts about the need for retribution after the war over and over in his letters to Marge. Not least among his grievances was the time Baldy McFadyen was sent out to work with a high fever in late June 1943. 'It hurts to have to stand by and watch such things happen,' he wrote. 'One's blood boils yet we are helpless.'

What Scott saw each day was a disregard for human life that relentlessly, and often viciously, ground people down. At Auschwitz, Viktor Frankl too recognised that there was no longer any appreciation of human life or human dignity; rather, the internees were treated as animals, exterminated or worked to the point of death, with 'a small but dangerous pack watch[ing] them from all sides, well versed in the methods of torture'.

At the same time, however, in considering the human capacity for right and wrong, Frankl saw good and evil as running through all people, and that there were conditions that brought out indecency in decent people. Similarly, he believed human kindness could be found in all groups, even those which, as a whole, it would be easy to condemn. The boundaries between groups overlapped, and men could not be simplified as either angels or devils. No group was of 'pure race', and 'therefore one occasionally found a decent fellow among the camp guards'.

Scott recognised balance when he saw it, and noted several instances when the Japanese guards displayed humanity. There had been the young guards Henry and Ishakawa at Victoria Point, with whom he had formed friendships, and who were particularly generous with food and cigarettes; they had even given Scott and the Orderly Room staff a farewell party. In early October 1943, as the railway neared completion, Scott was critical of his work gang's behaviour towards one Japanese officer.

I was a bit disgusted with our chaps today. They won't give this Jap corporal a go at all, and he is a gentleman, as far as they can be. He was saying he has seven days to go and has a certain amount of work to get done. If it isn't, he is for it. I am all in favour of hindering them in any way, but I say if one of them gives us a go, it is up to us to play ball.

Scott thought too that some of the Japanese engineers at work on the railway were a very different proposition from the general run of guards. At 108 Kilo, he noted that a new group of engineers were 'not a bad crew. They want their pound of flesh but are not bash merchants.'

He had a long talk with the chief engineer, while working with him to determine embankments and cuttings along the line's final stage. The engineer, who spoke English, was generous with his knowledge, and Scott appreciated that he was teaching him as they surveyed the terrain. 'Gave me three cigs and we sat by the fire and talked for an hour or more. We discussed the war. He doesn't like it.' Both disapproved of the bombing of civilians, and talked about Japan and Australia, comparing them.

Scott found the discussion engrossing, and thought these particular engineers a good bunch who were more civilised than the majority he had dealt with. He enjoyed being out working with them, finding it a relief to be away 'from the screeching and yelling that generally goes on'. And he had something in common with the chief engineer: 'Has a wife in Japan and the baby he has not seen.'

Nothing could resonate more strongly with Scott.

25

No Cause to Celebrate

The message that Marge had hungered for took more than nine months to arrive. This was due in part to Scott's lettercard being delivered to the Heywood family home in Stawell, while Marge was now living in Mildura. Although delayed, his news could not have been more welcome.

> I am interned at the war prisoners' camp at Moulmein in Burma. My health is good, I have not had any illness. I am working for pay at 25 cents per day. I am with friends – Alan, Doug [Baldy], Jack, Laurie, Wimpy. Sorry I am a worry. Hope you, bairns and families OK. All my love, dearest. Keep smiling, don't worry. I am OK.

How typical of Scott, telling Marge to 'keep smiling' and not to worry. That's just what he would say. She could let the nightmare scenarios go – for now. Official confirmation followed within days, with a simple and straightforward telegram from Minister for the Army Frank Forde on 9 October 1943:

W.S. HEYWOOD PRISONER OF WAR. I HAVE TO INFORM YOU
THAT VX 39162 HEYWOOD W.S. PREVIOUSLY REPORTED
MISSING IS NOW REPORTED PRISONER OF WAR.

After twenty months of silence, suddenly Marge could utter a
sigh of relief – Scott was safe! The news spread quickly, with
a local Mildura newspaper running a story that 'friends of
Mrs Heywood rejoice with her and her family concerning the
good news received regarding her husband'. The news was also
carried in the Stawell paper. Scott was right in his prediction
nine months earlier when he wrote the lettercard – the phones
were indeed running hot.

Vera Deakin White had also been in touch, organising a
letter from Marge to Scott via the Red Cross. There could be
no reference to places, ports, business matters, the cost and
conditions of living, and the surnames of people. It was still
not possible to send food, clothing or personal items.

Telegrams from friends and family addressed to Marge
began arriving at her father's police station in Mildura. People
were thrilled to hear the news about Scott. Marge's Aunt Ella
wrote to her on 9 November 1943 that she was overjoyed to
know Marge had heard from Scott: 'It makes you feel that they
are no longer amongst the almost forgotten people, doesn't it.'

The Records Office was also in touch, informing Marge
that, from information received, Scott was 'Now interned
Thailand Camp'. A story in *The Herald* on 12 November
caught Marge's eye: 'Messages to Australian prisoners of war
in Japanese hands may now be sent through Papal channels.'
Through the Vatican's delegate in Australia, arrangements
could also be made for prisoners to send replies through the
Papal delegate at Tokyo and Vatican Radio.

Marge contacted the Vatican delegate with high hopes. She badly wanted to get a letter through to Scott. She could guess what a letter from her would mean to him. The response was not encouraging, pointing out, firstly, that the cost of telegrams was exorbitant – the equivalent of $27.50 per word today, according to the Reserve Bank of Australia. Furthermore, the telegrams could only be sent to POWs in Japan. Another dashed hope.

There was increasing concern among Allied nations regarding not only the 'lamentable situation' of POWs in Japanese hands, but also the failure to secure them protection and relief in accordance with the principles of the Prisoner of War Convention. But the International Red Cross concluded that Japan was not interested in their high humanitarian ideals. All they were getting from Japan was 'persistent and typical evasiveness'.

A month later, in November 1943, a printed card entitled 'Service des Prisoners [*sic*] de Guerre' was sent to Marge and other POW relatives. Headed 'Imperial Japanese Army', the message was the same for all recipients. It began 'I am still in a POW Camp near Moulmein, Burma' and assured families how well the men were being treated by their Japanese guards. They were labouring daily, quartered in plain huts and the climate was good. It continued:

Our life is now easier with regard to food, medicine and clothes. The Japanese Commander sincerely endeavours to treat prisoners kindly. Canteens are established where we can buy some extra foods and smokes. By courtesy of the Japanese Commander we conduct concerts in the camps, and a limited number go to a picture show about once a month.

Something at the bottom of the card jumped out at Marge: Scott had signed it. She could doubt the veracity of the benevolence of the Japanese towards the POWs, but his signature was real.

From Scott's perspective, the content of the message both amused and angered the men, but if it put the wives' minds at rest, then so be it. As long as Marge was getting *some* word from him, that was preferable to no news at all. Links with home, any which way, were the critical issue.

Coinciding with the arrival of the letter, the Burma Railway was completed when the two tracks met about 18 kilometres south of Three Pagodas Pass, at Kon Kuta, Thailand, on 16 October 1943. The Japanese marked the occasion with a ceremony, with the Australians watching on in amusement. A brass band played, and a film crew captured the moment a Japanese officer drove home a gold-painted spike. A concert was held that night, but Scott could muster little enthusiasm. 'Should be a fair show,' he remarked. 'If Curly feels like it, we'll be going along.'

Three days later, Scott was already noting 'a fair bit of steam train activity. The line is right through now.' But ballasting and stone knapping did not stop. 'We are to be the maintenance gangs,' he told Marge. The POWs continued ramming ballast, adjusting rails and tightening fish plates.

Scott wanted Marge to know that he was '100 per cent', but in reality he was worn out. He was still working hard with his drilling gang, six days a week, as chief offsider to the engineer in charge of rock blasting. They were blowing the holes together. 'Had the hammer and drill men,' he wrote one day. 'We put in seven shots, all pretty good.'

Not long after, the Japanese arranged celebrations to mark the completion of the line. Scott thought a memorial service a month later for those who had died was an impressive and moving affair. 'We fell in and marched to the cemetery,' he noted. 'A big cross came in from Thanbyuzayat and was dedicated by our padre.' Colonel Ramsay spoke, reiterating that the ceremony was held to commemorate the deaths of POWs who had died on the line. The cause of these deaths was not for him to determine, but would be the subject of investigation later on. The men marched off after 'The Last Post' was played; Scott's company returned later and laid a wreath on the cross.

Scott reflected that the completion of the railway was certainly an achievement, but it was not one to celebrate. Between the camp at 105 Kilo and Thanbyuzayat were the graves of some 1300 POWs. Between 105 Kilo and 133 Kilo there was one grave for every 200 metres. Eighteen months earlier, Brigadier Varley had predicted just this outcome: 'The Japanese will carry out [their] schedule and do not mind if the line is dotted with crosses.'

Scott thought back to Colonel Nagatomo's speech, and he bitterly recalled the colonel's words: 'As Nagatomo said, they are building the line over our dead bodies.' There had been so much death. One morning he saw a Burmese man lying gravely ill on the ground:

Prodded him and the poor devil was alive. I lifted back the wet shawl he had over him. He looked about done so I passed on. He was alive at lunchtime when the Medical Orderlies passed, and they gave him a feed. He was still there tonight and begged for a drink, so I gave him one. He'll be dead in the morning. I remarked to some of the lads how callous we had become, just walking on and leaving the poor devil to die. We can do nothing for them. If we tried it would probably mean a bashing.

But Scott had not become so inured to death that he could walk past a dying man unmoved. His compassion was alive and well.

26

A Promised Land

As the railway began operations, the Australians prepared for an event they did want to celebrate: the 1943 Melbourne Cup. As the first Tuesday in November approached, thoughts turned to staging a concert and broadcast of the race. The tradition was so powerful that, wherever they were, Australian troops would mark the event. The year before, at Tavoy, an adjutant had approached the Japanese sergeant with a request for a holiday to be decreed. To the men's great delight, it was granted, which set off a flurry of activity.

Nominations were received for the 'runners' in the Cup. Some men acted as owners, others as jockeys or horses. Weights were worked out, and a 75-yard circular track laid out. 'Racecourse police' were appointed to fine officers and men for any trivial offence. A larrikin spirit took over as the Australians set about trying to emulate the fun associated with the day back home. A mock court decided the fines, and the 115 rupees raised went to the Tavoy hospital.

When Cup time came, the Japanese sergeant was present, together with a Japanese officer, sitting in the judges' box. The

'Governor' arrived – the Chief Petty Officer from the sunken *Repulse*, his breast a mass of medals. Amid great hilarity, there were seventeen starters in what proved to be a close race. The winning horse by a nose was named Sweet Potato; the cup was presented to the owner and trainer, and the whip to the jockey. That night a 'Cup Ball' was held, with a prize for the best female impersonator – a private who came as the actress Greta Garbo.

A year on, the men were tired, physically weakened and sicker than the previous November. But they needed something to lift their spirits, to reconnect with the culture that had shaped their lives. What they didn't know was that the running of the Melbourne Cup in both 1942 and 1943 had been shifted from the traditional first Tuesday in November to a Saturday by federal government regulations that banned midweek racing, decreeing it a distraction from the war effort. Unaware of this, the diggers improvised the running of the Cup on the traditional first Tuesday in November.

On Cup eve, Scott was sure they would make the most of the occasion. 'We have a gigantic sweep running for the RAP, 4000 tickets sold at 10 cents each. We have a rupee sweep going, all horses. The big one is being run a la Tatts. All we need now is a rest day.'

The next day, there was a phantom call of the race with a 'wireless set rigged up'; the winner was Peter Pan. He was, in fact, the winner of the 1932 and 1934 Cups. In his letter the next day, Scott rated the event a success. 'We could imagine we were home,' he wanted Marge to know. A concert had followed in the evening. 'We had a good time and several good laughs. Thank goodness we can still raise a laugh.'

Not long after, the men managed a wry laugh when a locomotive went through. They all knew it had to cross

500 metres of wet and soft packed earth on a long curve, and they watched with a sense of anticipation. The inevitable happened and the train derailed amid great clashing and clanging. A mighty cheer went up – but it meant rebuilding the line. Scott and his team were ordered to re-lay 300 metres of line over the next five days.

This was frustrating but not uncommon. A cutting had to be lowered by 1.5 metres over a length of 300 metres. All through the heat of the day, Scott's team dug and carried out the surplus stone. 'An hour for tea and into it again,' he wrote. 'I have never seen the lads work better ... Out we went again yesterday and laid the rails again, she was open for traffic last night.' Even if this was work for the enemy, a by-product was the esprit de corps that Scott fostered among his men. On 11 November 1943, they stood as one in the cutting to mark Armistice Day. 'I wish we could have filmed it. Every man stood to attention where he stood, and the Nips couldn't make out what was wrong.'

In early December, as some of the men prepared to move to Kanchanaburi, the Red Cross finally managed to get supplies and letters through to the administrative centre, Thanbyuzayat, from where they were passed to the camps. There were multiple cases of peaches, jam, sauce, sardines, green peas, soap, biscuits and butter – and 275,000 cigarettes. No letter for Scott made it through. Brigadier Varley ordered that the most dangerously sick of all nationalities should benefit first. The men made short work of this rare bounty and a return to something like a normal existence.

Again, as Christmas approached, Scott was laid low with malaria, which hit him hard. 'The Doc kept me off quinine for four days and I suffered a temperature every night – couldn't eat,' he recorded. There would be little to celebrate – and little to celebrate with. Food stocks were again so low that Brigadier Varley protested in writing to the Japanese about the shortages. Additional canteen supplies were organised – only to be immediately snaffled by Japanese officers, leaving the POWs to survive on rice and radish or turmeric water.

There was nothing in the larder for Christmas 1943. An issue of three packets of rubbishy cigarettes a man hardly compensated for the lack of food – but at least they helped suppress the appetite. And there was nothing like the extra delicacies the cooks had managed to rustle up for previous Christmases. What made matters worse was that the Australian POWs from Java had just received mail, and the word quickly spread through the camp that American servicemen in Australia were moving in on their women. 'Girls and fiancées have thrown them over for Yanks,' Scott noted. This did nothing to lift the men's spirits for the festive season.

It was not until two days after Christmas that Scott felt well enough to write to Marge: the fever had persisted, and left him shaking and shivering. Although feeling low, Scott tried to lift his spirits, as he always did, by thinking of Marge. 'I am late with my Xmas greetings, darling, but perhaps you got them on Xmas Eve. I tried very hard to reach you,' he wrote. 'I was thinking of you all Friday night, picturing you filling the bairns' stockings.' This was Scott's third Christmas away from Marge and the boys, and he was feeling it keenly. 'Next year we will all be together, and Xmas will be happy. I won't mind having malaria with you to look after me … a month or two with you will soon put me right again.' Meanwhile, he would endeavour to build up his strength to be ready for his next bout, as the fever had 'ripped pounds off me'. The death rate in the camp was now three men a day.

As the men began moving to Kanchanaburi at year's end, Scott promised that he would be thinking of Marge and reliving many happier New Year's Eves. He wished for 1944 to be a happier year for all. But it was hard not to expect there would be more tough times, and that release would be 'in the dim distant future'.

As 1943 ended, Scott went to the camp's cemetery and stood among the forest of crosses. He thought of the ninety-four men who lay buried there, and of the wives and families waiting at home for news of them and their return. 'That's what was so heartbreaking, the number of families not yet knowing their husband, son or father would not be coming home,' he explained. Row upon row of them, and 90 per cent could have been avoided. Looking at the names and dates on crosses reminded him of the passing of time. There had been so many friends who had died during the past year. 'So many needless lives sacrificed.' This was a very different New Year's Eve.

*

January brought a new job for Scott: acting camp sergeant-major. It involved organising the departure of hundreds of men, and meant long hours of nonstop work, with just enough time for meals. 'At last, I have things running smoothly and all the work of reorganising done,' he wrote ten days later, adding that he hoped he would keep his job after all the work he had done. It would take another two months to finish.

On picket duty Scott witnessed yet another incident involving a notorious guard known as 'the Bull', who rushed shirtless around the camp in a frenzy looking for victims to bash. 'The rotten reptile got two fellows smoking in bed just after bugle and gave one a frightful doing-up not twenty yards from where I was,' Scott wrote. 'He knocked the poor devil down and then got into him with boots and all.'

Frustratingly, canteen supplies arrived just as they prepared to leave the camp. Boxed meat, beans, fish, oil and 2000 melons, and sugar and cigars were suddenly in abundance. Another thirty boxes of meat arrived, and for a period they kept arriving at the rate of five boxes a day. It was unbelievable after so long. 'Meals have improved 100 per cent this week,' Scott noted. The bread Curly baked was an added bonus.

They were soon back to the status quo, however, as the food supplies dried up just as suddenly as they had appeared. Scott knew the impact on the men's health would be disastrous. They had been malnourished for too long; one-off food bounties made little difference. 'We are going to be very lucky to come out of this alive,' he wrote to Marge. 'We get absolutely no vitamin or fat content in our food and men are dying for want of them.'

By mid-February 1944, everyone was affected, including Scott, who was experiencing blurred vision. Other men were going blind because of the lack of vitamins – and were being beaten because they couldn't see the guards to salute. Many had to be led around. 'It is pitiful to see them walking, or rather groping, their way about the camp,' Scott wrote.

After one roll call, Scott stopped to read a notice for a camp concert. A POW standing alongside him asked, 'What does it say, Dig?' Scott read it to him. 'Poor beggar,' he thought. Scott expected the man's sight would come back, but felt for him. Some took matters into their own hands. Men were eating anything they could get their hands on – rats, unborn calves, even dogs. 'Bludger' the pup was eaten by six men. 'Some of them have sunk very low, I fear.'

Stories trickled through of the good living at Kanchanaburi – and these were reinforced when Murray returned from 'Kanchan' and reported it was possible to buy anything there, from roast duck to strawberry jam. The town sounded like the promised land. Scott wondered when their turn would come. When it did, the simpler foods and things of life would be all he would want.

27

Three Good Years Lost

One hundred and four weeks a slave. Scott hated the two-year anniversary of his having become a POW, 15 February 1944. Sold into slavery, he wrote bitterly, recalling the refrain: 'Rule, Britannia! Britannia, rule the waves. Britons never, never, never shall be slaves.' This anniversary hurt, challenging preconceptions and hopes that were central to Scott's beliefs and world view. 'Never did we think that it could be proven wrong,' he reflected. 'Yet here we are ordered around, spoken to like dogs by a pack of yellow hounds and bashed if we don't jump to it.'

Inherent in Scott's thinking was an attitude to race that held cultural sway in Australia, and had done so since European settlement in 1788 and the dispossession of the lands that Indigenous Australians had occupied for more than 60,000 years. Federation and the White Australia policy had cemented an anti-Asian attitude. Since before the Great War, an emerging Japan had been seen as a potential threat to Australia's national security, and the fear had grown in the years before World War II broke out.

As a result, Scott espoused a similar view of the Japanese to most Australians, whether at home or on the front line. But it was not an all-encompassing view. The official Australian historian of the Great War, Charles Bean, had criticised the government's racist vilification of the Japanese from the early years of World War II. He believed that to use extremist propaganda while engaged in a war against a vicious racist ideology was to court moral defeat.

Scott's anger was not with the Japanese who treated the POWs fairly. Rather, it was with those officers and guards who enforced a brutal and sadistic rule over the camps. It was in the camps where the moral argument was laid bare and stereotypes of hate held sway. To the POWs, the Japanese were lesser, utterly contemptible humans, caricatured as short, round-faced, jug-eared and buck-toothed, 'myopic behind horn-rimmed glasses'. To the Japanese, who believed death on the battlefield was the ultimate honour, Allied soldiers who had surrendered were men without honour. And Europeans in general were monsters and devils who had to be driven out of Asia. These certainties became the justification for the harsh treatment of POWs by their Japanese captors. This was a war without mercy.

The prisoners were the victims, but in inflicting the punishment, the perpetrators, who before the war would have been regarded as ordinary people, had lost their moral bearings. Whether on the Burma Railway or at Auschwitz, it was the same. Like the Nazi SS guards, the Japanese and Korean guards felt the need to conform to group values. These men were not rogue elements; rather, their actions were sanctioned by the state. By conforming, they believed they were doing the right thing – obeying orders they took to be legitimately given. This was the culture of brutality that Scott witnessed, and even extended to punishment meted out to the guards themselves by their superiors if they had committed some infraction or other.

This was a culture that was always at risk of overstepping the mark, and when it did the Australians protested. After one POW had to be admitted to hospital with a fractured jaw, inflicted by a rifle butt, Brigadier Varley investigated and, it would seem, put objections to the Japanese. Even as he did, Scott noted in his nightly letter to Marge, there had been several bashings that day. One POW had been hit on the head and laid out, and several of the boys done over. 'Green said the other night that all bashings had been cut out by order of Nagatomo,' Scott added. 'It looks like it, surely!'

Scott was unprepared when it was his turn for a 'present from Nippon'. He had been protesting to the guard nicknamed 'Wire Whiskers' that 2.2 metres per man with a 60-metre carry was excessive.

> He swung one from the knees and I got it. Never saw it coming. I called him a dirty rotten yellow bastard and went off. He was around all day trying to square off, but I wouldn't wear him. He asked me not to report him to the Jap lieutenant.

A nightmare accompanied the second anniversary of captivity. This time, Scott dreamt he was home. 'The planes came over,' he told Marge. 'I sheltered in the big gutter outside our place. Saw the bombs fall and three fell on Mitchell's draper's shop. I remember wondering if Mollie was safe. Main Street got a proper doing over, bombs everywhere.'

Anniversaries can stir memories, and all around the camp apathy and resignation were growing. And men still had to live with those memories of the fighting and surrender. As POWs, they had lived through or witnessed trauma on an almost daily basis, and nightmares were a natural consequence. Scott's were increasing in frequency. These were nights when in his dreams his mind drifted back to the last days of Singapore, conjuring up graphic images of 'bayonet charges and bombings galore'. At the time, Scott was part of the Special Reserve Battalion, which was involved in bayonet counterattacks.

One nightmare in particular woke him in a cold sweat, as he relived what happened. 'A bad night last night, fighting Japs again,' he wrote to Marge. 'I was in a bayonet charge and got stuck myself.' For some, the nightmares would subside, for others they would persist a great deal longer.

By March 1944, Scott was surprised at the number of men who were suddenly breaking down under the strain. 'I got a shock,' he admitted. 'Some fellows who a few days ago were in fair nick are now like skeletons. A dose of fever and diarrhoea soon pulls it off.'

This was the sorry point that the men had reached after two years as POWs. Scott saw the staring eyes, the beak-like noses, retracted lips, green-grey skin, and the shoulderblades like knife edges that almost cut through the skin. Then there were the knee joints twice as thick as thighs, biceps thinner than wrists, ribs almost devoid of covering, and ankles and stomachs that were bloated horribly.

The very sick wished to die, and were doing so. Men who six to nine months earlier would have recovered from diarrhoea and other endemic illnesses were listless, making no attempt to fight back. Gone was the cheerfulness that typified the digger.

Gone was the confidence that they would make it home. Scott felt for these men: he had tried to set an example of fortitude and hope, but he knew they could take only so much. 'Their spirit has been well and truly broken,' he said. 'One cannot blame them, as this experience will leave its mark on all of us.'

Everyone, to some degree, was sick. For doctors Bertie Coates, 'Pills' Anderson and Rowley Richards, it was a matter of choosing which of the frail men might survive another day of hard labour. Scott recognised that some of the men were stronger than others who had a different outlook on life. He saw himself as one of the former, and had great confidence that he would be 'coming home to you someday and you will be able to close the gate, which every night I see you holding open for me'. This remained Scott's Holy Grail: nothing had challenged the strength of the image in all the time he had been away, and especially not during the past two years.

Construction work on the railway may have finished, but dangers remained ever-present – not least from the guard known as 'the Boy Bastard'. He'd just bashed someone unmercifully and brought him back from the jungle cut and bleeding. The incident had been reported, but, as usual, there was no redress.

There was 'more bastardry' when two men were forced to stand up for twenty-four hours, others for even longer. Another two men had been punished for not selling a watch to a Japanese guard at the price he wanted to pay. 'Before lunch one collapsed,' Scott noted. 'The guard rushed out, kicked him several times, punched him and got him up again.' Two minutes later he went down again, only to be dragged up by the hair. He reeled against the hut, managed to get steady and was still standing up at lunchtime. 'The barbarous brutes,' Scott fulminated.

Viktor Frankl echoed this. He described beatings by Nazi SS guards occurring at the slightest provocation, or simply at the whim of the guard. At these times it was less the physical pain that hurt the most, but 'the mental agony caused by the injustice, the unreasonableness of it all'.

By mid-February 1944, accounts of the merciless conditions Australian POWs suffered on the Thai side of the railway had reached those on the Burma side after the two lines met. The stories were the same. But these were known only to the men who had built the line; the outside world as yet knew nothing about the horrors of the railway. Scott prayed that it one day would.

> We would not mind doing an extra six months if we
> had the assurance that these people would be made to
> pay to the last atom for the deaths of thousands of good
> men who have been foully murdered, and you can call
> it nothing else. I suppose they will shoot a few and two
> months later everything will be forgotten.

Among the men the rumblings grew louder about what was to come next. As a group, the POW officers sensed the malaise and thought it time for a morale boost by way of a pep talk given by Colonel Anderson. The men were urged to adopt a 'strength through joy' attitude and a 'morale through discipline' approach to their daily lives. Scott was dubious that the talk had hit the mark – and particularly the point when the men were reminded that they were still being paid by the Australian government. 'All the old tripe,' he reflected. 'It is too late to talk discipline now. The example required by the men had not been set by the officers since we became POWs.'

Just what the future held was still unclear. A list of men to go to Kanchanaburi was drawn up, but Scott was not on it. Two camps of 500 were to stay on the rail line for the wet season to carry out maintenance. 'I venture to say that if they leave 500 of us here, maybe 250 will march out at the finish,' he wrote. 'I look forward with a certain amount of fear to the future. I shudder as I visualise this year and the horrors to come.' Tough as the previous year had been, Scott feared that, despite his determination to make it home, he may not be so fortunate this year.

Events and circumstances were weighing more heavily on him than ever before, but a letter from his mother, which he received after it was finally released by the Japanese censors, raised his spirits. The letter was dated 25 June 1942 – nearly two years earlier. Nonetheless, Scott 'was terribly excited, but a wee bit disappointed as I wanted one from you', he wrote to Marge.

Even so, he drew comfort from the old news from his mother: Marge had gone back to Dandenong. Young John and his grandfather had been great pals, and little Doug – 'little Scott' – was well and strong. But the most important news was that Marge was well. Scott shared the letter with Jack Heathwood. 'I've read his and he mine. We were like a couple of schoolkids,' he noted afterwards. Letters from home were the greatest morale booster. Life took on a brighter aspect, and Scott felt he could face the future with more confidence.

Scott and Jack were not the only ones to receive letters – there were many who wore big smiles, and they all wanted to tell Scott about their news. 'I must be a magnet ... everyone gives me their letters to read or reads them to me. I have read them all,' he said. Later that day, the mail brought a second letter for Scott. He immediately recognised the handwriting: it was from Marge!

> Was going across to the Orderly Room when I met 'Gil' the bugler rushing over with a letter. He was nearly as excited as I was. August 3rd was the date, written over eighteen months ago. But what difference does that make? 'Tis impossible to describe my emotions as I saw the familiar writing and read that you and our bairns were well eighteen months ago. I can put up with anything they can turn on now. At last the long silence is broken.

He was elated, and could face the prospect of the next stage. Whatever was to come could not be as harrowing as the railway. He wanted to let Marge know that he expected to be moving to Japan in early March, and he hoped the mail service would be more reliable there. Murray Cheyne would be joining him on the trip there. 'I couldn't have a better mate,' he told her. 'Murray is a great lad. You'll fall in love with him when you meet him.'

As they prepared to leave Burma, the guards told the Australians to write a letter describing a 'horror' war incident and 'telling of the wonderfully kind treatment' and the 'plenitude of medical supplies' they had been given. This was an opportunity for a little sport with the guards. One of the letters caught the interest of the interpreter, who wanted the address of one 'Tom Jones' so that they could write to his widow and tell her how he died. Scott could hardly control his mirth.

The story came from the fertile imagination of a Warrant Officer in the Pioneers. It concerned Tom Jones and his destroying the German machine gun nest, being killed in the process by our artillery. Written in true Nippon propaganda style, it was a gem, and we left Tom's widow playing with a Distinguished Conduct Medal. The Japs lapped it up. The address of his widow, by the way, is Woop Woop, Snake Gully.

With his birthday on 4 March and departure imminent, Scott became reflective: three birthdays as a POW. He was 'getting ancient' at thirty-three, and he imagined he could hear Marge wishing him many happy returns. 'I don't feel very much older but I'm sneaking on,' he admitted. 'I've lost three good years over here.'

He had been certain he would be writing to Marge as a free man by now. However, he fancied himself as being gifted with a POW's nature, as he could 'sail on quite unperturbed'. He thought that perhaps he was fortunate. 'I certainly am from the health point of view, as I have had a wonderful run for over two years,' he told her. This was relative, but he had at least survived despite malaria, fever and, just recently, leg ulcers, which he had scrubbed out and filled with salt. The treatment had given him hell.

As men left the camp in stages, there were many who wanted to say farewell to Scott. 'Quite a herd of chaps were round to say goodbye, and I have a lot of addresses to look up in South Australia and New South Wales.' But, he noted on 1 March 1944, there was a chance he might be taking the long route home:

I may be on my way to Nippon shortly. 248 Dutch move
from the 108 to Kanchanaburi today, followed by their
400 sick. We follow soon afterwards, I believe. 2650 are
going into camp at Kanchanaburi, good food, clothes,
little work. Then they select 2500 and away they go to
Nippon. That is the latest camp rumour.

A move elsewhere, whatever the risks, appealed to him. Japan
seemed a better option, and he would take his chances of being
torpedoed – 'Sooner by far the trip to Japan with the tin fish
hazards,' as he put it. Scott well knew the dangers American
submarines posed. Then, on 6 March 1944, it was his turn to
leave. But the day before, there had been one more crucial task
for him to do: sew his letters into his pack.

The letters were precious: they were his link to Marge
over a long and momentous period of his life. But more than
that, they represented his love for her. The words he wrote
in her name had become the essence of his life, and he was
determined that, by whatever means, they must survive so that
she could finally read them. And he wanted to be there with
her when she held the fragile paper in her hands and came to
understand the extent of his commitment. She had kept him
alive, and he wanted her to know this.

Scott was also taking with him something else that was
special – a present of a pair of Burmese jade earrings that
he had bought in the camp. Despite food shortages, he had
saved his money to buy this gift for Marge. Jade symbolised
gentleness and nourishment and, it was said, brought luck. He
added the earrings to his small stash of keepsakes.

28

The Pact

Anticipating an easier life, Scott could afford a sense of relief as he left Burma for the Thai POW camp at Tha Markam, a journey of 300 kilometres. If he had a concern as he set out, sitting amid hundreds of men on flat-top carriages rolling along the line they had built, it was to arrive safely. His mate Keith Burrill was also on the train, along with Wal Williams, who remembered it being 'a pretty hairy trip'. This was because POWs had sabotaged the line, which clung to mountainsides and rattled over bridges with drops of 20 metres or more to rivers and gorges below. Frank McGovern recalled looking down through the timber and seeing the rails moving as they rounded the curves.

Tha Markam camp, near a bridge over the River Kwai, was the established but temporary home of 7000 Australian POWs. Crammed into long attap huts, the prisoners vied for space on their sleeping platforms. Staring out at Scott when he arrived were men with sunken eyes and skeletal bodies covered in festering sores. Many were suffering from malaria, dysentery and beriberi. Dressed in tattered clothing, some only in loincloth G-strings, the POWs were mostly barefoot and many had ulcerated legs. In the cemetery lay 284 Australians. It seemed the toll the construction of the line had taken on this side of the border was as dreadful as in Burma.

Scott was not there long before the Japanese confirmed that they would be taking the 'fittest' POWs to Japan, where there was a grave shortage of workers for the coalmines and factories the nation needed to fuel its war effort. Transporting 10,000 POWs there from the railway was an obvious answer.

There was little doubt that, compared with other emaciated, sick and injured men, Scott had held up relatively well. They may have had his body but not his mind – and that was the reason, as he saw it, that he had survived this long as a POW. His determination to make it home overrode everything. And if that involved a journey to Japan, then so be it. If Scott could handle the railway experience, he could handle anything.

First he had to walk slowly past a young dentist, who had been dubbed a medical officer to give a degree of credibility to the exercise of passing men fit to go to Japan. He gave Scott the thumbs-up; his designation was 'kumi 36 Nippon draft'. Each selected man received a shirt, shorts and hat, and a pair of split-toed rubber shoes – the first new clothes, albeit ill-fitting, they'd had in two years. Thus equipped, they were headed for the labour camps in Japan, with the prospect of freezing winter temperatures, in stark contrast to the steamy tropical heat of Burma.

Before leaving, Scott sat down with his old friend Doug McFadyen, who, although recovering well from his ulcerated leg, had not been chosen for Japan. He noticed that Baldy was 'very thin but in excellent spirits – leg healed and giving vent in good McFadyen style'. These two held each other in high regard, and had built a trust between them.

This trust was crucial to a decision that Scott knew he had to make: there was overwhelming danger involved in the voyage that now awaited him, as American submarines controlled the South China Sea. He faced a devil's choice: if he took the letters with him they could be lost forever; on the other hand, to give up the letters to a mate also carried a risk. He calculated that giving them to Baldy meant a greater likelihood they would reach Australia. Above all, Marge must know how he had never stopped loving her every day of the hell he had lived through, and how this had sustained him. With a mix of trepidation and relief, Scott extracted the letters from his pack and solemnly handed them to Baldy. They made a pact to reunite after their return to Australia. Like Lofty, Baldy was almost family.

After just a week at Tha Markam, Scott and his mate Keith Burrill joined hundreds of POWs packed into steel cattle cars – thankfully the straw and manure had been cleared away – and headed for Phnom Penh, Cambodia. It was yet another trip jammed in, with no room to stretch out, in stifling heat. The next stage of the journey was in direct contrast, involving a thirty-six-hour steamboat voyage down the Mekong River. On deck, Dr Richards enjoyed 'a fleeting moment of peace'. The guards, too, were relaxed to the point where they did not object to the men singing all the way to Saigon, a distribution point for Japanese supplies.

Dirty and dishevelled, they were marched to a dockside POW camp that had previously been French army barracks. French bystanders waved as they went, keeping their distance from the Japanese guards. Buoyed by the show of support, one of the POWs broke into the French national anthem, 'La Marseillaise', and despite objections from the guards, kept singing. It was not long before the men were singing 'Waltzing

Matilda' – an opportunity for a full-throated Scott to belt out a favourite song. They reached the camp in their best spirits for some time.

Scott was relieved to find the conditions fair and the food much improved, for which the men were pathetically grateful. Bags of rice were stacked high in the storehouse and there were fresh vegetables and a constant supply of eggs. After the deprivations of the Burma Railway, Frank McGovern thought they were eating like lords. They were soon struck by the presence of French women, some riding pushbikes. McGovern remembered that it was the first time in at least a couple of years that they had seen white women. 'Our eyes were sticking out a bit,' he admitted.

Scott was put in charge of the Orderly Room, and Keith was charged with taking out work parties. Air raids had led to tens of thousands of Vietnamese fleeing Saigon to the country, causing a shortage of local workers. Scott and Keith were soon among POWs filling the gap as they laboured on the wharves. Working under more relaxed conditions than those they had been used to, they unloaded goods from barges to the docks, and then loaded them into the holds of ships. The work, in contrast to the railway, was a picnic. And there were benefits: the odd crate could be tampered with, giving the men a small stash for trading with local Vietnamese.

The time in Saigon turned out to be a pleasant interlude, even offering opportunities to explore the town, a pastime for which Scott always had a penchant; he and Keith befriended a few French residents as they occasionally walked the streets. The food was good, plentiful and cheap. It was, Scott thought, so good that it amounted to a three months' holiday. Most men were able to regain some weight. Frequent air raids ensured Scott could not forget how close the war was, though, with Allied bombers laying 'a few close to the camp'. His mood was further boosted on 1 May when a delivery of goods arrived from a POW relief committee. He and Keith claimed a chess set each, seeing it as a memento of their war experience they would take home.

But something else excited Scott: the POWs were permitted to submit messages that would be transmitted by radio to Australia. He grabbed the opportunity to send a message to Marge, telling her that he was 'in excellent health' and 'anxious for news of you'. He ended with his customary sign-off: 'Keep smiling.'

In late June 1944, with US submarines blockading Saigon, the POWs were told: 'All men go to Singapore.' As they prepared to leave, they broke out into French songs to farewell a city they had come to enjoy. But the mood changed abruptly when they saw the enclosed cattle trucks that were to be their transport. Scott thought he was becoming a bit too familiar with carriages purpose-built for animals. After loading bags of rice, they clambered atop the sacks, thirty men plus guards to each truck, for a journey in stifling heat.

The trip took them back up the Mekong River, through Cambodia and then down through Malaya. As the train wound its way through the Malayan countryside, Scott witnessed the devastation the war had wrought, and places where Australians had died. The few Malays he saw were starving and begging at each station. 'Many of us, although terribly short on rations, could not resist the poor pathetic kids with rusty tins held out for food,' Keith Burrill recalled.

On 4 July they crossed the Causeway to Singapore. Leaving the train, they marched through the lifeless streets en route to their new tin-hut living quarters on a tiny island just off Singapore. With Korean guards viciously enforcing order, Scott and Keith laboured daily with 1000 other men for the next five weeks on Singapore Harbour, digging a large dry dock by pick and shovel, one big enough for battleships.

The island in Singapore Harbour where they were housed had no fresh water, and with meagre food rations their newly gained weight began to fall off and the tropical diseases that had been their scourge in Burma started to take hold again. They found some light relief in the form of the Korean commander in charge of their island camp: square in build, he was dubbed 'the Jeep'. The island henceforth became known as 'Jeep Island'.

During this time in Singapore, Scott wrote to his friend Major Jack Parry, who had been his commanding officer throughout the Malayan campaign and was now a POW not far away in Changi. Although personal contact was not possible, Scott wanted to bring him up to date with the experience of working on the railway and what had happened to so many men they had both served with and known well. Writing the letter, which contained a mixture of friendship and detail that was in keeping with his role as a warrant officer, caused Scott to reflect yet again on the mates he'd lost on the railway – 'all good men, pushed beyond human endurance'.

Now awaiting transportation to Japan, Scott told Parry that he hoped to see him soon. 'If we manage to swim ashore after our date with the tin fish we may be having a couple in the Port Phillip 'ere long,' he added. Scott envisaged it would make for a good yarn with Jack after the war, as they sat at the bar in Melbourne's Port Phillip Hotel.

29

Cooee

If Scott had branded as 'hellships' the Japanese tubs that transported POWs from Singapore to Burma, then his image of Dante's *Inferno* needed amendment. His memory of that hellish voyage paled in comparison with the experience on the *Rakuyo Maru*, the Japanese freighter that was to transport him to Japan.

Scott's comrade Wal Williams remembered being marched down to the docks, where a sign on the companionway stared back at him: 'Room for 187 steerage passengers'. He considered the sign and the 1317 Australian 'passengers' to be accommodated, and his heart sank. More POWs were to be transported in the *Kachidoki Maru*, making a total of about 2200 men.

The holds of the two freighters were dark, forbidding and airless. The men baulked at having to descend into they knew not what. A stand-off ensued, with men bracing themselves against the bulkheads as the guards cried, 'Go below or be driven!' With tempers rising, blood flowed as sharpened bamboo sticks were thrust at the POWs. As their defiance

When the *Rakuyo Maru* set sail from Singapore to Japan with Scott Heywood aboard, it was a doomed ship, given the control American submarines had of the South China Sea. *(NYK Maritime Museum)*

brought the confrontation to a flashpoint, the guards flourished rifles, with bayonets fixed. Brigadier Arthur Varley and his British equivalent wrangled with the guards, but to no avail. To avoid bloodshed, the men complied and were 'encouraged' down the ladder with threats of violence.

Those for whom there was no room in the hold were allowed to sleep on deck; Scott, Wal and another of his mates, Jack Flynn, were among them. The cramped holds were horizontally subdivided with a false floor, giving the men a space about 1.2 metres high, forcing them to bend over as they made their way in. To sleep, each man was crammed up against the next.

They waited thirty-six hours in steamy Singapore Harbour. With no air movement in the stifling heat below deck, this time was the worst. The toilet facility consisted of a wooden structure slung over the side of the ship, which men had to straddle. The only washing facility was a saltwater hose, and the Japanese allowed just so many on deck for a hose down.

Finally, the two transports formed up as part of a convoy of seven ships officially known as 'Hi-72', which were escorted by four coastal defence vessels. They left Singapore on 6 September 1944, carrying food, petroleum and raw materials to Japan from the captured European colonies of Burma, Malaya, the Dutch East Indies and French Indochina. By the time another three ships from Manila joined them five days later, the convoy included nine transports and five escorts sailing north across the South China Sea, taking a zigzag course in the hope of avoiding submarine attack. Little did the Japanese know that the Americans had broken the code the Japanese were using. What the Americans did not know was that POWs were on board. As they were cargo ships and had no red cross on their hulls to signify they were carrying POWs, the *Rakuyo Maru* and *Kachidoki Maru* were fair game.

On the transports, the air was hot and foul, sweat poured off the men and many collapsed. Sleep was almost impossible. So close were they to each other in the semi-darkness that when someone moved it had a domino effect. The food, as usual, was utterly inadequate, consisting of rice, watery soup and occasionally tea.

Having been through the Singapore humiliation and the tragedy of the Burma Railway, Arthur Varley knew that these men had little in reserve and begged the Japanese guards to allow them some time on deck. They needed not just fresh air but also the chance to use the latrines slung over the side. Finally, around 200 men at a time were permitted on deck, with others waiting in long lines for the privilege. There was one memorable occasion when torrential rain fell and men danced naked in sheer joy. With mouths agape, they relished the pure water stinging their faces and bodies and greedily drank it in.

A heavy veil of tension hung over the POWs and the Japanese guards alike. Scott's throwaway line of being prepared to take his chances with the 'tin fish' took on a new significance as they entered the most dangerous leg of the voyage, Luzon Strait, where US submarines lay in wait. Men who could not swim were particularly anxious, but all were grateful that some sailors from the HMAS *Perth*, including Chief Petty Officer Vic Duncan and Able Seaman Frank McGovern, were on board. In an emergency, the sailors would know the procedures for abandoning a sinking ship. When the men had boarded in Singapore, they were each given a block of rubber with an attached handle, which the Japanese assured them would act as a life preserver. No one believed the solid block would even float.

Around 2 am on 12 September 1944, the convoy crossed the path of three American submarines waiting in a wolf pack, the USS *Growler*, *Pampanito* and *Sealion II*. The escort vessel *Hirado* was torpedoed by *Growler* and sank quickly. Sleeping on deck, Wal Williams saw the *Hirado* break in two, and 'down she went in thirty seconds'. Despite the panic all felt, the convoy had no option but to sail on. In the darkness, everyone knew another attack was certain. As the sun rose, the *Sealion* torpedoed the escort *Nankai*, a mere 400 metres for'ard of the *Rakuyo Maru*.

Immediately after, at 5.31 am, a torpedo hit the *Rakuyo Maru*, penetrating the No. 1 hold, which was filled with rubber. Seconds later there was a dull thud as a second torpedo crashed into the engine room. From his vantage point on the deck, Wal Williams watched the torpedoes hit. 'You could see them coming,' he later recalled. 'One hit in the engine room and that stopped the ship. The second hit right in the bows of the ship.'

The disabled ship shuddered, and the bow dug in. On deck, Scott and his mate Jack Flynn had been trying to sleep among the winches but the force of the explosion tossed them up into the air 'in a great squirt of water', and they landed heavily back on the deck. Wal was washed off the rafts and slid along the deck. 'It was just like being in the surf,' he said.

The torpedoes tore a massive hole in the side of the *Rakuyo Maru* – big enough to drive a double-decker bus through – and killed several engine-room crew. Debris lay everywhere, and although no prisoners were killed in the blast, a Japanese gunner lay dead over the guardrail. In the hold, panic spread as hundreds of men began to desperately clamber through the narrow gangway.

The crew hastily tried to launch the lifeboats. It was now every man for himself, and as POWs edged threateningly closer, the crew used staves to beat them off. With the drainage pumps inoperative, the *Rakuyo Maru* took on water and settled three or four metres lower in the water. The cargo of rubber gave her some buoyancy but she was drifting out of control. Shortly before 7 am, the Japanese lowered ten lifeboats, together with a smaller rowboat and a punt, and abandoned ship. In their haste to get away, crew members jumped overboard, some breaking their necks on hitting the water as their life preservers jolted upwards into their chins. A Japanese officer on the bridge, complete with Wellington boots and Samurai sword, was among those who were seen jumping; he didn't surface. Others in the water died when hit by hatch covers and other debris.

As it became clear they were being left to their own devices to survive, years of pent-up anger among the POWs erupted. They were not going to miss this chance to exact some revenge on the Japanese. Some were hacked with swords, others bashed with iron bars and thrown overboard; yet more who were in the water were later pinioned and drowned.

In the mayhem, the *Growler* came back for another attack, and torpedoed two more escorts. As the *Rakuyo Maru* settled slowly in the sea, Scott, Keith Burrill, Wal Williams and Vic Duncan, along with some HMAS *Perth* POWs, jettisoned life rafts from the bridge. 'Anything that was floatable we got rid of it, tossed it over,' Wal remembered. Keith called out, 'Keep one for ourselves, Scotty.' But in the noise and panic, Scott didn't hear the call clearly. 'He misunderstood me, and by the time we had finished throwing them over, we found ourselves with no rafts.'

Frank McGovern searched the bridge, finding some charts; a quick search for food netted him a can of condensed milk. As the threat of the ship sinking became urgent, the men began jumping into the water, desperately searching for whatever they could hang onto. Wal and his navy mate Max Campbell jumped into the oil-slicked water and clutched a raft. Not far away, the oil on the surface was on fire. Fearing they were going to drift into the flames, he and Max began to swim back to the ship.

When they were about halfway back, the Japanese depth-charged the submarines. 'Quick, get on your back,' Max yelled at Wal. 'You should take it through your back. If you tread water and it hits you in your tummy, then it can crush your intestines.' They made it back to the ship and climbed up a rope ladder. On deck they noticed that the crew had left a 'comfort woman' behind. She was crying hysterically, but Wal saw the humour in the situation:

> I'll always remember this bloke out of my unit, he was a lot older than me and he was bald-headed, and he was in the nuddy. He was saying to this Japanese girl who was sitting on this step, 'Everything will be right,' and I said, 'Have a look at yourself!' All he had on was an AIF hat, so he whipped his hat off and put it over his privates.
> So funny, she didn't seem bothered and would have seen more of that than hot dinners. He was so embarrassed!

Fortuitously, there were still a couple of lifeboats that the Japanese had been unable to launch. The men set about trying to free and then lower them over the side, Scott and Vic Duncan among them. As Frank McGovern recalled:

> Vic Duncan and a few more of them, army fellows too, were trying to manage this lifeboat that had been jammed in the davits by the Nips in their panic to get it away. It took us a couple of hours to get the thing free. We finally got the lifeboat out clear of the ship to lower.

An axe was used to chop through the halyards, but in the process the lifeboat was tipped on its side, losing all the supplies that had been gathered. When the boat hit the water its planks were sprung, but it still floated. Men jumped overboard and clambered aboard, the first finding some cloth inside the lifeboat to pack the leaks. They took turns to bail out the water.

By now the second lifeboat had also been launched and was soon filled with survivors. Among them was the comfort woman who had been sitting crying on deck, fearing she would be left behind. Frank McGovern recalled that they had lowered her into the boat. 'We slid down the rope, but you couldn't get into the boat because it was packed, there must have been about 100 on there,' he said. 'Two inches of freeboard, so we hung onto the side of the boat.'

Scott had a money belt tied around his waist, with currency that could be used to buy food and medicine when he and Keith reached Japan. But Dr Rowley Richards had warned the men that when they went overboard, they should discard all excess clothing and footwear. 'Hit the water as lightly clad as possible,' he told them. As soon as he jumped into the water, Scott realised that the weight of the coins was dragging him down. He had no option but to unbuckle the money belt and watch it sink.

As the ship sank lower, Harold Ramsey remembered a British POW saying to him, 'We've got no hope, Aussie. Let's see if we can find some booze and go down with the ship.' Harold didn't agree. 'I'd be the world's greatest optimist and I said, "Not me, I'll get out of this." The last I saw of him he was on the bridge of the ship, and he would have gone down with it.'

On the water, the Australians saw Japanese in a lifeboat not far away. Wal remembered that they signalled to them, trying to get them to come over to take the prostitute. 'We had a devil's own job trying to get the Japs to take her,' he said. 'They didn't want her. Anyway eventually a boat rowed over and we got rid of this woman, and while they came over, they stood over us with a rifle. We had two barrels of water and they took one.'

At dusk, two unarmed Japanese frigates from the original convoy approached, searching for their own survivors. The Australians thought they were about to be rescued, but anyone who tried to climb the scramble nets thrown over the side was pushed back into the water. Within the next thirty minutes the Japanese had picked up everyone they were going to rescue – only Japanese survivors. As the escorts were leaving the scene, they ploughed straight through the middle of POWs who were still floating, the screws of the ships chopping many to pieces.

About 1200 Australian and British POWs were left despairing in the water. Through a loudhailer, a Japanese officer said, 'Goodbye, goodbye.' And waved. The contempt accompanying this farewell was galling. 'We thought, you lousy lot of bastards,' Frank recalled.

But at least there were now ten empty lifeboats, and the Australians in the water made for them. All were recovered, and up to forty men were able to climb into each. There were now twelve lifeboats, but still they were not enough to rescue all the men in the water, which had become choppy from the tail end of a typhoon.

At 6.30 that evening, the *Rakuyo Maru* disappeared beneath the waves. As she sank, 2/10th Field Regiment gunner Kitch Loughnan was overwhelmed by the feeling of vastness: he was a mere dot in the South China Sea. With the survivors becoming more and more spread out, he cooeed, hoping to make contact with anyone who might hear him. 'A lifeboat, with some of our chaps on it, picked us up,' he said later. 'I could have hugged them. We rowed around picking up other chaps, until our boat was filled.'

In time, many of the rafts drifted together and, with much cooeeing, several boats made contact and lashed themselves together to form a convoy. Seldom had a shrill cry from the Australian bush carried such urgency.

30

Slow Boat to China

For the first time in two and a half years the men found themselves free and unguarded – and, for the moment, no longer POWs. They desperately hoped they could survive the open seas in their lifeboats. So too did the POWs from the *Kachidoki Maru*, which had steamed north with five accompanying ships when the mayhem of the submarine attacks on the convoy had begun.

Just before midnight, as they were about to change course toward Hainan, the USS *Pampanito* had caught up with the ship, firing several torpedoes. Two thudded into the *Kachidoki Maru*, one hitting the No. 7 hold and splitting the vessel's seams along the water line. The engine room instantly flooded, the engine stopped, and minutes later the order to abandon ship was given. Shortly after, the *Kachidoki Maru* took a heavy list and slipped below the surface. Although just twelve crew were lost, 476 passengers and POWs were killed. Five ships had gone down in a day of carnage on a scale seldom witnessed at sea.

When dawn broke on 13 September, Australian and British survivors from the two ships were spread out as far as the eye could see. Those from the *Rakuyo Maru* clung desperately to anything that would float, from lifeboats barely above water level, and with no room aboard for any more men, to makeshift rafts. They had been abandoned. They did not know if the Japanese would return to rescue or kill them.

On the one hand, they felt liberated, but now they faced another daunting challenge: how would they reach land? The Chinese coast was some 600 kilometres away. 'We knew we were somewhere between the Philippines and the China coast,' Wal Williams remembered. 'We didn't know how many miles away, so we reasoned that it was a big hunk of land [and] allowing for currents and everything else we were heading due west, so we might hit the land somewhere.'

Some thought their best hope was to be rescued by an American submarine. Clinging to a raft, Kitch Loughnan recalled one of his mates saying, 'Don't worry, the Yanks will pick us up.' If not, they thought they might reach China after another ten or so days at sea.

Early on the evening of that second day, Rowley Richards' group of three lifeboats drifted into Arthur Varley's convoy of eight lifeboats tied together, which carried about 150 men. Varley asked what course they were on. When told due west, he responded that they were going north-west. With the POWs from the HMAS *Perth* in charge, they turned down Varley's offer to join them and continued on their own course, thinking they could navigate their way to freedom on, as Frank McGovern put it, a 'slow boat to China'. One of the Varley group of lifeboats decided to join them. They bade farewell and headed in separate directions.

They were all at the mercy of chance. For the survivors in both groups, the less appealing outcome was to be picked up by a Japanese ship. Although that was preferable to dying at sea, after a brief taste of freedom it would mean a return to POW status.

Scott knew the risks. When he'd plunged into the sea, most of his possessions had been lost: the Saigon chess set, the jade earrings he had bought for Marge, and his money. He was gutted when he realised how little he now owned. He had also lost the photo of Marge standing at the gate – the photo that he had so treasured on the railway. Somehow, he had managed to hold onto his spoon, something basic but so fundamental to a POW's survival. Importantly, too, he still had the signet ring Marge had sent him. It had brought him through thick and thin. And he was alive.

Scott and Keith decided to stay with the Richards group, thinking that heading for China offered the best chance of finally ending their ordeal of the past two and a half years. But this was an ordeal in its own right: the sun was merciless and the men's skin was blistering. Suffering from exhaustion and dehydration, they gratefully sucked the dew that formed on their arms. They found an old tin of cigarettes in the bottom of the lifeboat and shared them around. To cool off, some eased themselves over the side during the middle of the day, keeping watch for sharks. In desperation, some gave in to drinking sea water; those who did died. As they became delirious, they just slipped away from their rafts, and from life.

At first light the next morning the Richards group heard gunfire, the sound travelling clearly across the water from the horizon. The bursts came from the same direction the Varley boats had headed. Frank McGovern knew the sound of naval fire and was certain of what he heard:

It was heavier than machine-gun, naval pom-pom
gun, I heard naval two-inch shells, pom-poms going
off. We didn't sight anything, we just heard it, because
sound travels over the water as you know, and we
never sighted those boatloads either from that day.
We four boatloads [were] headed towards China, as
we thought.

It seemed clear to those in the Richards convoy that Varley's
men had been killed by the gunfire they had heard.

Things took a worrying turn. In the distance, they saw a
Japanese frigate and two corvettes heading straight towards
them. Convinced they were about to suffer the same fate as
the Varley group, they calmly said their goodbyes and awaited
their fate. One of the corvettes peeled off and, with guns fully
manned, slowed as it came alongside the lifeboats. Seriously
alarmed, Vic Duncan said to the men, 'If you believe in God,
say your prayers now.' And they did.

So they were taken aback when a Japanese voice rang out:
'Are you American?'

'No', replied the castaways.

'Are you British?'

'No, we're Australian,' they shouted.

To their amazement, a scrambling net tumbled down the
side of the ship. The 157 Australian and British POWs from the
lifeboat convoy climbed aboard. If they weren't suffering from
exposure and sunburn, then it was dehydration and dysentery.
But they were elated to be alive.

Scott and Keith wondered why they had been picked up.
Wal Williams had a theory: 'We, the survivors, maintained
the Varley group had been done over by the Japs, and we were

picked up more or less so they could save face by saying they had picked up survivors from the convoy.' Others thought the Japanese had returned not out of any humanitarian concern, but because they needed to fulfil their commitment to deliver a work gang to Japan and not arrive empty-handed.

The ship steamed towards Yulin, on the island of Hainan. From here the men were transferred to an oil tanker, where they met British survivors from the *Kachidoki Maru*. They were in a bad way, many with burns and broken limbs. All knew that an oil tanker had little chance of making it to Japan without being torpedoed. Observing their mood, the Japanese threatened to turn machine guns on them if they didn't go below. It was only when the officer in charge of the voyage came aboard that the confrontation was defused: he too realised the tanker would have little or no chance of getting through, and arranged for the POWs to be transferred to a whaler for the voyage.

Three days after the *Rakuyo Maru* sank, a lookout on the USS *Pampanito* saw rafts carrying men frantically waving. Assuming them to be Japanese survivors from the damage the submarines had wrought on the convoy, the Americans were armed and ready to shoot, but were stunned when an unmistakably Australian voice yelled: 'First you bloody Yanks sink us, now you're bloody well going to shoot us!' When 'Curly' Martin – a different 'Curly' from Scott's close friend, the cook in Burma – took off his cap to reveal his blond curls, there was an immediate change in attitude.

The *Pampanito* moved slowly, searching for more survivors. Some ninety-two Australians and sixty British were rescued, many still clinging desperately to the edge of makeshift rafts, their condition deteriorating by the hour, and most covered with oil.

The *Pampanito* broke radio silence and called the *Sealion*, which lay about 30 nautical miles to the north-east, asking for help. The *Sealion* steamed down at flank speed and began rescuing more survivors. As night fell, the *Pampanito* had rescued seventy-three more men, and the *Sealion* another fifty-four. Later, the submarines *Barb* and *Queenfish* rescued a further thirty-two.

The commander of the *Pampanito*, Lieutenant Commander Paul Summers, commented that it was a 'pitiful sight none of us will ever forget'. The rescued POWs were profoundly grateful for the care the American crew bestowed on them, despite the fact that it had been American torpedoes that had sunk the *Rakuyo Maru*.

These men were the lucky ones. Their war was over. They would now return to Australia and Britain. Importantly, they would soon be able to tell their stories of the Burma Railway to a shocked nation.

31

Wretches

The signet ring Marge had sent Scott in Malaya had done its work. He was not free, but he had survived. Inside the dark and cavernous hold of the *Kibitsu Maru* as it left Yulin harbour at Hainan, Scott knew just how near he had come to freedom, and yet how far away it remained. The American submarines that had played havoc with the *Rakuyo Maru* and other ships in the Japanese convoy had now rescued many of his comrades. For them, there had been a nip of brandy, a wash, clean clothes and something to eat. And then sleep – and the knowledge that they would be heading home. They were really free.

But Scott was not among them. He was one of only 157 POWs from the *Rakuyo Maru* and another 520 from the *Kachidoki Maru* who sat tightly packed in the gloom of the whaling ship's vast hold, converted during wartime for the use of landing craft. Although the hold extended the full length of the ship, each of the survivors had less than 1 metre by 3 metres to lie down on grass mats.

There was just one ladder to climb out of the hold onto the deck. Scott was thankful for the small mercy that there was not a false ceiling like the one on the hellships, which had created such stifling heat. Daylight filtered through the single hatch, and the few sparse interior lights caught the relief on the sunburnt faces of the men, who were thankful to be in this cooler space. Keith Burrill had come down with malaria once more. He considered himself fortunate, though, as all around lay men with fractured limbs and skin and eyes burned and blackened with oil from the explosions.

Amid the stench of latrine buckets, everyone was jittery. There would be no escape from another submarine attack, they knew. As the *Kibitsu Maru* made for Japan, a typhoon struck, the 44-gallon drums that lined the walls banging violently against the ship's hull as it lurched and rolled through the South China Sea. Four days into the voyage, B-24 Liberator bombers attacked the convoy, damaging most ships – but not, serendipitously, the *Kibitsu Maru*, which joined a new convoy and headed for the port of Moji on the island of Kyushu.

The waters were alive with US Navy submarines. Scott and Keith witnessed a Japanese corvette explode just 100 metres from them. Together, they prayed. Their ship finally berthed at Moji as dusk settled over the port on 28 September 1944. Eight men had died on the voyage and were buried at sea.

The Australians were a sorry lot as they disembarked at Kyushu's main port. Most were cursed with malaria or dysentery, Keith among them. They left the station barefoot and with only blankets wrapped around their shoulders. Although many were almost too weak to stand, they were deloused in hot-water tanks, guards shoving them under, into the disinfected water, with long bamboo poles. They felt like sheep being dipped. The humiliation did not stop there. They were marched to just-vacated horse stalls, where they sat for hours in the enveloping cold of autumn, many clad only in their tattered G-strings. But some nationalistic pride had taken hold and most had somehow kept their slouch hats.

The POWs were split into two groups, with the larger one, led by Dr Rowley Richards, bound for Sakata, in north-west Japan. The remaining fifty men were to be sent to work at the port city of Yokohama, south of Tokyo. As they shuffled through the streets to the railway station, those with dysentery lost control of their bowels. Onlookers surrounded them, some jeering, laughing and spitting, while others seemed stunned by the sight of such miserable souls. This was almost too much to bear. The Australians had no option but to keep their heads high and defiantly look straight ahead, shutting out the embarrassment of this walk of shame. It was one of the lowest points of their POW experience.

Scott, Keith and Frank McGovern were among the group who undertook the thirty-six-hour train trip to Yokohama. On arrival, they found the mood angry. The city was being bombed, and the POWs were allies of the Americans. The three were among those sent to camp 11D, located in the densely populated industrial area of Yokohama and Kawasaki, 30 kilometres from Tokyo. They were each given a thin, hessian-like tunic, a pair of canvas shoes, a cap and a number.

Along with another 189 Dutch, British, American and Australian POWs, they were housed in a two-storey barracks that was infested by lice and other pests. They slept on straw mats and were given just a few thin blankets which provided little warmth, forcing them to sleep in their work clothes and huddle together in bed. If beds were left unmade, or blankets not square, men were bashed. Once their shoes wore out, rags wrapped around feet became standard. Surrounding the camp was a 7-metre-high stockade wall, creating a confined space, in complete contrast to the openness of the prison camps in Burma. The jungle, rather than walls, had ensured they did not escape.

The camp had an irregular water supply, poor bathing facilities and pit latrines. The men were responsible for their own cooking, and as labourers were entitled to a meagre diet of barley, rice, sorghum and noodles. Fish, meat and soup initially supplemented the diet for extra protein. As so many men were unable to digest their food, beriberi persisted. Within days Keith Burrill succumbed. 'Yes, I have beriberi in the legs. Food very light and lacks vitamins,' he wrote in his diary.

Across Japan, POWs worked in factories, foundries, mines and dockyards. In mid-October 1944, Scott and Keith started work at the Toshiba Electric Company at Yokohama. With Scott in charge of a group comprising twenty-five men, he and Keith were soon manufacturing components for industrial motors and radio transmitters. Their tasks included operating lathes, oxyacetylene welding equipment and other metal fabricating machines. They all bitterly resented the thought that they were working for the Japanese war machine. The signs around the factory urging them to 'Work cheerfully' engendered as much enthusiasm as the 'Work will make you free' sign that was emblazoned on the gates at the entrance to the Auschwitz concentration camp.

The POWs were paid in accordance with Japanese Army regulations. As warrant officers, Scott and Keith were paid 25 *sen* (or cents) a day. When POWs wanted to spend money, they received cash from the POW officer and shopped outside the camp, accompanied by a Japanese guard. It was unfathomable that they were not permitted to buy food.

As the Japanese winter set in, Keith contracted pneumonia, a complication of a relapse of malaria, compounded by the daily fifty-minute walk, often in rain, to the factory. Quasi-military guards in nondescript uniforms marched the men to and from work, keeping watch as they worked and bashing them for minor transgressions. These so-called 'Foo Men' were army rejects and carried metre-long hexagonal staves, with which they enthusiastically meted out punishment. If they weren't using the staves or their fists, they were using judo throws to punish the men. Scott and Keith watched aghast one day as a Foo Man beat a Dutch POW unconscious. He was refused hospital treatment and died the next day.

Of the punishment, Frank McGovern recalled:

> They were a bad lot of wretches. Some of the blokes who had committed a misdemeanour, some slight thing, they'd be standing outside to attention for up to six hours at a time, outside the guardhouse just away from the braziers so that they wouldn't get any warmth. The change of guard would give them a bit of a bash as they went through. They'd be like blocks of ice when they'd come in.

US Air Force bombing raids over the Tokyo area began in earnest in early November 1944. The screech of sirens at night became incessant, heralding the approach of B-29 Superfortress bombers. There a further cause for concern: in an earthquake-prone country, tremors were frequent. The work was different, the climate the polar opposite from Burma, but the same sense of brutality, and the threat to survival, hung heavy.

32

A Welcome Diversion

Each time Marge caught sight of a telegram boy pedalling his bike along her street, she froze, praying he wouldn't stop at her house. Only when he was well down the street would her feeling of dread subside. These were the days when telegrams were a common form of communication, and she'd had her fair share. She could breathe easy until the next time.

Now living in Hamilton following her father's transfer from Mildura, Marge had not had any word from Scott for almost a year. At that time, his card had been the proof she needed to be sure he was alive, even if he had to bear the indignity of being a POW and tolerate hardships she could only imagine. He was alive – and with his mates. But she knew the card's sign-off – 'Keep smiling' – was pure Scott.

Starved of further news, Marge had continued to write – to the army, to the Red Cross, even through Papal channels – pleading for information. Was he well? How could she get a letter or parcel to him? The letters she did write were often returned. Letters became an act of faith as she wrote and wrote into a void, but as long as a sliver of hope existed, she kept writing. Of course, this was just what Scott was doing. He wrote and wrote, knowing the letters could not be posted, but he wrote just the same.

Reading newspaper headlines and news of the war was torment for Marge and other wives and families back in Australia. When she read that a convoy of Japanese ships thought to be carrying POWs had been torpedoed by American submarines in the South China Sea on 12 September 1944, it was yet another news item that could have involved Scott – or not. Previous headlines of POWs lost at sea had gripped Marge with fear. It was a common enough occurrence. And then the fear would pass when there were no follow-up telegrams.

Five weeks after the torpedoing, news began to filter through. The first official announcement came in the form of a press release from the War Office in London:

86 AUSTRALIANS SAVED FROM TORPEDOED JAP SHIP LONDON, Monday, AAP
The War Office announced today that 58 British and 86 Australian prisoners of war from Malaya and Siam have been recovered from a Japanese transport which was torpedoed in the Pacific last month.

In Melbourne, *The Argus* reported on 17 October 1944 that the men had been picked up by the wolf pack of American submarines responsible for torpedoing the *Rakuyo Maru* – which just happened to be in the area. These men were now on their way home. The article finished with ominous words. 'It was feared that a number of prisoners of war lost their lives when the transport was torpedoed.'

The relatives of the eighty-six Australian survivors saved by the Americans had indeed been notified – an enormous relief for them. But Marge was still in the dark, not knowing if Scott had been on the torpedoed ship or remained in Burma. The rescued POWs were kept in virtual isolation in Australia for some weeks. And while convalescing, they were intensively questioned about their experience in captivity on the Burma Railway. Not only did they provide the first descriptions of the callous mistreatment of POWs, they also compiled lists of their comrades on board the ill-fated transports. They were not permitted to contact their families until they had been adequately debriefed.

The government was in a quandary: how much detail of the atrocities should be made public? Saying too much could be very disturbing for the relatives of those POWs still in captivity – it would be painful to know details of the brutality, disease and privation they were experiencing. Yet for the relatives of those thought to have died on the *Rakuyo Maru*, those rescued may well have vital information they were craving.

If Scott had been on the *Rakuyo Maru*, Marge realised, then the chances of his having been rescued were diminishing. As she tried to understand what had happened, a letter arrived from Melbourne. It was from military headquarters. With her heart in her mouth, she opened it:

RE VX39162, HEYWOOD, W.S.
30 October 1944
    I regret having to inform you on behalf of the Minister for the Army that, from information supplied by survivors of a torpedoed Japanese transport, it is feared that your husband, the above-named soldier, lost his life, and that his records will now be endorsed 'Previously reported

Prisoner of War now reported Missing believed Deceased
on or after 12/9/44'.

Shock, incomprehension and grief hit her. For Scott to have
survived the years on the railway, only then to die at sea
from an Allied torpedo, was her worst nightmare. As she
struggled with what it meant, a week later, on 8 November
1944, she opened a copy of *The Sun*. And there it was in
black and white:

> Men Drowned on Jap Prison Ship. The following list of
> Army casualties establishes the fate of scores of Victorian
> soldiers previously posted as missing or prisoners.
> Previously Reported Prisoner of War, Now Reported
> Killed in Action – W/02 W.S. Heywood, Dandenong.

Acting Prime Minister Frank Forde addressed the House
of Representatives nine days later about the sinking of the
Rakuyo Maru, describing heart-rending and dramatic stories
of the POWs adrift in the South China Sea. Evidence given
by the rescued men made it clear beyond all doubt that the
Japanese intended to leave all prisoners of war to drown.

Information about the POW camps now began to emerge.
On 18 November, *The Argus* ran with the headline 'Grim
Story Told by Survivors Shocks Parliament'.

> An early estimate places a death toll of Australian
> prisoners of war in Japanese prison camps in Burma and
> Siam at about 2,000 out of 10,000. Mr Forde said main
> causes of death ... were malnutrition, dysentery, malaria
> and exhaustion, and in some places, cholera.

During the debriefing process, several of the rescued POWs had spoken of seeing lifeboats turned adrift in the water, presumably abandoned by the Japanese when they were picked up by their own ships on the first day. One survivor stated that he saw in the distance six or seven lifeboats loaded with survivors.

The angry reaction to the sinking in Allied nations provoked a Japanese government response. At a press conference in Japan with foreign correspondents on 6 December 1944, a Japanese spokesman for the Board of Information, Mr Iguchi, contradicted statements by the Australians and British that the Japanese had not rescued any POWs in the aftermath of the sinking of the *Rakuyo Maru*. According to Iguchi, 136 POWs had indeed been rescued and were in Tokyo and Fukuoka. The men were reported to be 'in sound health and are deeply appreciative'.

In Canberra, a memo from the Secretary of Defence to the Acting Prime Minister on 9 December 1944 suggested that Forde make a statement concerning the 136 POWs purportedly rescued and held prisoner in Japan. However, there was concern that this information would raise hopes in vain. The Acting Prime Minister responded that he thought it unlikely there were other Australian survivors; rather, they were 'probably' lost at sea.

After some weeks, the rescued men from the *Rakuyo Maru* were released on three months' leave to rejoin their families and, for the first time in years, enjoy Christmas at home.

For Scott, his fourth Christmas away from home brought brief but welcome respite. He and Keith were delighted to receive their first Red Cross parcel since arriving in Japan and to be able to decorate the huts to celebrate the day. There were sweet beans, bread and fish, and songs and music on Christmas Day. They joined their forty-eight fellow Australians in singing 'Advance Australia Fair' and 'God Save the King'. Both men had an emotional, heart-rending day; Keith said it was 'one of the greatest thrills' he had experienced during the years in captivity. They finished the day with 'Auld Lang Syne'. 'Our best Xmas as POWs,' Keith noted.

It was a momentary but priceless diversion.

33

Rollercoaster

As long as the word 'missing' was part of the official wording used by the Department of Defence, Marge could hope that 'presumed dead' may not be true. In a letter to Auntie Gert on 31 January 1945, she entertained scenarios that included Scott washing up on an island or being rescued at sea. There was no conclusive proof of his death, so she could have hope.

News of the Japanese brutality began to appear in the papers as survivors personally shared what they knew. There were public appearances, with more and more details reported and read, of course, by Marge and other wives and families of missing men. Not only had she been told Scott was presumed dead, now she had to absorb details of the horrific conditions he had endured at the hands of his Japanese captors in Burma.

Marge read that among the survivors was Warrant Officer John Flynn, a member of the AASC's 105 General Transport Company, who had been one of those the Americans had rescued. He was recuperating in hospital in Brisbane, and she wrote to him, wondering if he could shed any light on what had happened to Scott. Flynn responded, saying that the last time he saw Scott was after the ship was hit.

> He was doing a grand job organising and keeping the men calm and in order. I knew Scotty for a long time while we were prisoners. As a matter of fact, we were in the same camps quite a lot. We had a lot of parades and he was the Camp Sergeant Major, a job that took a lot of doing, but he handled it perfectly. My admiration for Scotty as a man was very high, but what I admired him for most was his ability and courage as a soldier – he is one of the best and he has what it takes. This is a very hard job for me, Mrs Heywood, I wish I could tell you he is safe and well. All I can do is to join with you in sincerely hoping he was one of the 136, which I think could be possible, and that we see him again soon.

Marge was not alone in living this nightmare. Relatives, desperate for information, besieged the survivors at public meetings. In Sydney, the *Daily Telegraph* reported that women seeking information about relatives mobbed repatriated POWs at the Sydney Town Hall. As the men walked onto the stage, the audience stood and burst into a rendition of 'For They Are Jolly Good Fellows'. Desperate for any news, mayhem erupted as women climbed over press tables to reach the stage, waving photographs, letters and names on scraps of paper. One *Rakuyo Maru* survivor was able to recognise a few photos of men whom he knew to be alive and well. 'Hundreds of women just told me names,' he told the paper. 'I couldn't help them, because we only knew them by nicknames.'

*

The next day, 26 January 1945, the Japanese radio broadcast 'Humanity Call' engendered desperately needed hope by confirming that Australian survivors from the *Rakuyo Maru* had been picked up by a Japanese ship. This official notification, amplifying the Japanese government's insistence that POWs had indeed been rescued, revealed that eighty Australian prisoners previously classified as missing and presumed dead were prisoners of the Japanese once more.

Three days later, the telegram boy stopped at Marge's house and her world was turned upside down again:

IT IS WITH PLEASURE THAT I HAVE TO ADVISE YOU THAT
TOKIO [SIC] RADIO BROADCAST 26 JANUARY REPORTS
FOLLOWING SURVIVOR FROM JAPANESE TRANSPORT
SUNK 12 SEPTEMBER 44 IN TOKIO PW CAMP PENDING
CONFIRMATION THROUGH IRC GENEVA VX 39162 HEYWOOD
WS WILL BE RECORDED AS PREVIOUSLY REPORTED MISSING
BELIEVED DECEASED ON OR AFTER 12 SEPTEMBER 44 NOW
REPORTED MISSING BELIEVED PRISONER OF WAR INTERNED
TOKIO CAMP. MINISTER FOR THE ARMY.

For Marge, this was a rollercoaster. After all this time and mistaken messages, this was real. Scott was alive! A POW in Tokyo he may have been, but he was alive! Once again, she could afford to hope, to believe that he would be coming home. After all, the Allies were winning and the war with Japan seemed to be nearing an end. If she needed any further verification, it came in the form of a letter from the Records Office on 3 February 1945:

Dear Madam,

It is advised that in a message broadcast by Japanese Radio from Saigon on 13/1/45, a member of the AIF is alleged to have stated that I am with Scotty and we are both fit and strong.

The name mentioned in the message would appear to refer to the above-named soldier, and the information is conveyed to you with that warning, that in view of the nature of its receipt and that it emanates from an enemy source it should be accepted with reserve.

Another telegram came from Vera White, advising Marge that a message had been sent to her via the Red Cross in Geneva from Scott: 'Health fine hope well Happy New Year Love Scott.' This was all the verification she needed.

The collective relief surfaced in the *Dandenong Journal*, which reported that Scott and Private Harold Ramsey, who was also a POW on the *Rakuyo Maru*, had survived the sinking of the transport: 'Dandenong friends of W.O. Scotty Heywood, who was reported presumed dead after the sinking of the same transport, will be delighted to know that he is still alive and is now a prisoner in Tokyo.'

To Marge's joy, a letter from the Red Cross arrived with an authority to send Scott a cable. Having had nothing directly from Scott for so long, and no luck in sending him mail, this was more personal, even in the abridged prose of a telegram. Just maybe, Scott could send a reply.

Soon after, Marge was deluged with messages from people from as far afield as Maylands in Western Australia, Queenstown in Tasmania, Rockhampton in Queensland and Daylesford in Victoria. They had all been listening to short-wave radio and had heard a message from Scott broadcast by a Japanese radio station:

> Hope yourself, bairns and families are well. Love to you
> all. I am in excellent health. Anxious for news of you.
> Alan [Campbell] and Doug [Baldy McFadyen] are well.
> I am with Frank Phillips, Murray [Cheyne] and Wimpy,
> who are all well. Regards to all friends at home. Keep
> smiling. Scott

Marge would have been heartened by the appearance of two of Scott's favourite turns of phrase: 'bairns' and 'keep smiling'. She therefore had no doubt that the message was genuine.

Those sending the message on to Marge evidently had cause to be listening to Japanese radio, and the poignancy of their accompanying messages touched her. All were strangers, yet one happened to know Scott's parents in Stawell. Another woman's husband had recently been liberated from a POW camp in Germany. Yet another had a son who was still a POW, and listened every night in the hope of hearing news from him. Another rightly suggested the message could have been recorded as long ago as May or June 1944; this would accord with Scott taking the opportunity to send a message when in Saigon. All those tuning in and hoping to catch a Japanese information broadcast were part of a disparate community who held in common the worry about family members with whom contact had been lost in the war. They understood Marge's fears.

*

Meanwhile, unknown to Marge, the war was entering a dangerous phase as the Americans closed in on Japan.

The push for victory was unstoppable, which meant ramping up the bombing of the Japanese mainland. Fear gripped the men in the POW camps. They'd endured the coldest winter in Japan in seventy years. By late February the snow was too deep to walk through. Inadequately clad and desperately hungry, they huddled around fires in their huts trying to draw a little warmth. Pneumonia and beriberi took hold. And all the while they heard the worrying sound of the B-29s.

Then, on 9–10 March, came the 'Night of the Black Snow'. Some 334 B-29 bombers struck, dropping 2000 tons of incendiary bombs on Tokyo and its surrounding district. During the course of the next forty-eight hours they delivered sheer, unimaginable terror. Flying at a mere 500 feet, the Superfortresses created a giant bonfire, while 30-knot winds spread the flames throughout the area of Tokyo, Kawasaki and Yokohama.

Under orders from the camp commandant, the POWs fled. Outside, the scene reminded the Australians of great bushfires, with a wall of flame rolling and roaring up the street, consuming everything in its path. The road was packed with terrified women and children. An angry crowd confronted the POWs, forcing the commandant to draw his sword. As he waved it around, flames reflected off the polished blade. With guards fixing their bayonets, a path was cleared.

The POWs stayed in an open field that night, returning the next day to find an area of 6 square kilometres destroyed. In all, more than 41 square kilometres in and around Tokyo were razed by the bombs and fire; amid scenes of pandemonium and horror, between 80,000 and 130,000 Japanese civilians were killed, their bodies melted by the intense heat. It was the worst single firestorm in recorded history.

In early April, as more bombing raids were conducted, Scott was hospitalised to have his appendix removed. He returned to the camp to light duties just in time to be caught up in yet another raid on 13 April, when incendiary bombs finally destroyed the camp. Scott and Keith took refuge in the mess of a nearby factory. Everything was disorganised. 'Things look pretty black for all here at present,' Keith observed. They moved to another camp, 14B, inside the Kawasaki factory area, and Scott resumed work. As he did so, Keith Burrill was hospitalised with beriberi, which left him unable to walk.

With Japan reeling from the effects of a US naval blockade and the air offensive, which had destroyed more than 2.5 million homes and left millions of people homeless, food became even scarcer; people were told to collect acorns. Making things even worse for the POWs, the Japanese guards purloined the Red Cross food supplies intended for the prisoners. Scott and Keith were incensed. As Keith put it:

> Japs tell us we have no further claim on Red Cross
> because Yanks have sunk Jap Red Cross boat. We know
> their Red Cross boats only too well. Japs here are still
> eating Red Cross parcels & smoking American Red Cross
> cigs & I will bet Nip airmen keep going on our Red Cross
> food.

They thought the scarcity of food the worst they had experienced as POWs. There were tiny loaves of mouldy black bread, thin soup of boiled turnip tops and greens grown on latrine waste, with no salt to hide the taste. With the approach of summer, fleas and mosquitoes came in plague proportions. Each season brought its own hazards.

Germany's surrender on 8 May brought the war in Europe to an end. The full focus of the Allied offensive turned to defeating Japan. From May to June 1945, nine POW camps in the Tokyo–Kawasaki–Yokohama area were closed, and the prisoners transferred to camps in northern Japan because of the threat from ongoing air raids. One group, including Scott, remained in order to keep the factories running. A report compiled later by Allied HQ revealed that by July the Japanese knew it was dangerous to leave the prisoners in a primary air target area such as the Yokohama waterfront – and so too did the POWs. The country was being pounded into submission.

From the start of July, the Americans dropped leaflets, which the POWs saw as an ominous warning of forthcoming raids. They complained about the camp being located alongside a factory, a plum target, and they argued for the camp to be moved. The camp commander agreed and recommended to the military authorities that it should be shifted. An inspection by senior military figures followed, but the camp remained where it was.

After another spell in hospital with sickness, Scott was anxious to get back to the men. He saw that as his duty. He returned to the barracks amid grave concerns about the safety of the factory area – there were up to three raids each night now. Finally, the Japanese decided to send twenty-three of the men to another camp at the port city of Niigata, some 250 kilometres north-west of Yokohama. Scott was selected but, along with Keith Mills from Perth, was too weak to travel. As Private Harold Ramsey recalled, 'My mate and I were sent in their places.' Harold was happy to go, as the raids were getting heavier, the guards more brutal and the bashings more frequent.

Although Scott couldn't join them, the men were keen for him to have what they regarded as the most comfortable bed in the barracks. In his cheerful and optimistic manner, he refused. A game of cards followed, rigged so that Scott would win. As mid-July approached, he was in the best bed in the barracks.

34

Black Friday

Everyone was on edge. The prelude to the raid on 13 July at camp 14B was the sound of fifty B-29 bombers coming closer. Panic spread among the POWs left in Yokohama. They demanded to be let into the air-raid shelters that they had laboured to build just outside the barracks. But these were for Japanese only. According to an official report, the Japanese were crammed into the sandbagged shelter. Guards stood by the entrance to prevent the POWs from entering. They had no option but to return to their barracks and wait.

The camp had not been marked to indicate the presence of POWs when the B-29s flew over Yokohama in that night's raid. It seemed to go on forever. To the pilots and crew, it was just another industrial area to be targeted with 100 bombs in a raid that lit up the night sky and laid waste to many factories. Around midnight, a 1000-pound bomb was dropped and scored a direct hit on the barracks at the Toshiba factory.

Harold Ramsey was devastated. 'They dropped the bomb right where we slept, our mates were blown to bits.' Frank

McGovern remembered a heap of bricks crashing down as he sat talking to his mate Keith Mills.

> Keith was standing up. I rolled over and then the next
> minute I was up in the air, like slow motion. Fortunately,
> I came down feet first into a crater, water up to my chin.
> When my head came up I hit something and I could see
> flames. I put my hands up and held on to something and it
> was the timber roofing – the place had been blown apart,
> and all the timber had come down across the crater where I
> was. I held [it] up with my hands, I saw the shadowy figures
> silhouetted against the flames and it looked like Dante's
> *Inferno*. I felt this terrific pain in my back. It turned out it
> was a compression fracture of the vertebrae in the lumbar.
> One of the Yanks came along and he dragged me out.

Only rubble from the building was left. Amid the yells and screams from injured men that followed, Frank was laid on the ground, temporarily paralysed from the waist down, with more wounded placed alongside him.

> I turned my head to this bloke and spoke to him and he
> didn't answer – he was dead. So I spoke to the bloke next
> to me on the other side – no answer. So I'm just lying there
> in among all these dead. I think I said a few prayers. I was
> there until dawn broke and the rain put the fires out.

Scott was in bed when the bomb struck. He was killed instantly, the explosion blowing him onto the roof. His death certificate stated that he had suffered a fracture at the base of his cranium and submaxillary bone, a complex fracture of the right foot and a fracture of the left foot. He was just thirty-four. Another twenty-nine POWs died that night. An official Japanese report concluded that the death of the thirty men was the fault 'of the Japanese camp personnel for permitting the camp to remain in the factory area'.

Serendipitously, Keith Burrill was still in hospital, which had escaped the bombing. But he was grief-stricken: he had lost a close mate. He'd known there was no way the camp would avoid the bombing. It had been built among many prime targets – factories, shipyards and oil refineries. '[It was] Black Friday for our camp,' Keith said. He and Scott had been through the hellships, the Burma Railway and the sinking of the *Rakuyo Maru*, and had survived them all. Until now.

Frank McGovern lost three of his mates from the HMAS *Perth* in the raid. In all, seven Australians died that night, along with twenty-one Dutch POWs. Another sixteen men were injured, two of whom died later. These thirty men had lost their lives to 'friendly fire', hapless victims in a war that was about to end. There was to be just one more raid on the area. On 25 July, camp No. 2, located at Kawasaki city, close to Yokohama, was bombed, killing twenty-two POWs, four of whom were Australians.

According to an official Japanese estimate, Allied bombing had by then destroyed half of Japan's productive machinery, much of it in the Yokohama–Kawasaki industrial area, which was home to the steelworks and heavy industry necessary for the war effort. The atomic bomb that obliterated Hiroshima was unleashed on 6 August. Three days later, a second atomic bomb destroyed Nagasaki.

Scott had survived for so long, but all his strategies, conscious and instinctive, were not enough to withstand a bomb from a B-29 a mere twenty-four days before these exponentially bigger bombs ended the war. Japan would surrender on 15 August 1945.

*

In Hamilton, Marge greeted the news of the end of the war with huge relief. She had been assured that Scott was alive, and it would only be a matter of time until he came home. She scoured the newspapers for any hint of his return. *The Argus* splashed over the front page on 1 September a story by war correspondent George Johnston, who was one of the first on the scene in the Yokohama–Kawasaki area. After meeting some Australians, he wrote of the 'misery and degradation' the POWs had suffered in the camps. 'They told of their existence in rat and disease-ridden hovels,' he wrote, 'of meagre food allowances, and of painful tortures and brutal floggings.'

Johnston, who would later author the acclaimed World War I novel *My Brother Jack*, was writing about the bombing raid that had occurred on 25 July. The POW camp was now a mass of splintered timber, strewn around the colossal bomb crater where many of the bodies were still buried. Those who spoke to him were bitter and angry because of the Japanese insistence on retaining camp locations in 'the heart of Japan's richest bombing targets'. He painted a grim and desolate picture of the ruined Yokohama–Kawasaki industrial area, and the environment in which the Australians had battled to survive.

At the fringe of this scarred, black ugliness he saw a battered, grey, tumbledown shack of wood on which the letters 'POW' appeared in black on yellow, alongside crudely painted British and American flags and the word 'Australians'.

Johnston and the four other correspondents with him began to move towards the hut, making slow progress before vast water-filled craters made it impossible to drive any further. He continued on foot.

> I ran toward the shack, and as I came round a twisted
> heap of blackened girders I could see a large group of men
> in khaki. They jumped to their feet when they saw me,
> and, noticing my slouch hat, suddenly started shouting
> frantically and running toward me. They shook my hand
> until I thought my arm would drop off; they shouted and
> laughed and cheered like madmen. Never in my life have I
> seen such an exhibition of unrestrained joy.

There were just nine Australians out of nearly 200 POWs; the remainder were British, American and Dutch.

> Then everybody started talking at once. It was a
> wonderful moment, almost as wonderful for me as it
> was for them, and we entirely ignored the heavily armed
> Japanese guards sitting among the bomb wreckage and
> watching apathetically.

Regulations prohibited Johnston from mentioning the names of these POWs until their relatives had been notified, but such graphic accounts brought home to Australians the horrors the men had suffered. Marge could not have avoided reading them. Her family and her close circle encouraged one another to be positive and not to jump to conclusions. That was also the message from *The P.O.W.* – the monthly newsletter of the Australian Prisoners of War Relatives' Association. An editorial urged relatives 'to keep a stiff upper lip' because the day of liberation was nearing.

Marge knew the POWs were being shipped home, so some delay was to be expected. While she could wait, she expected it would happen soon. On 15 September, a Saturday morning, she read that more 8th Division ex-POWs were due in Melbourne in a few days. Frank Forde, the Minister for the Army, gave an assurance that everything possible was being done to speed up the release of names and the return of the POWs from Japan.

Marge hardly slept that night. She would go to Melbourne in the morning and be there to meet Scott when he came home. It would only be a few days until he was here. She had carefully selected what she would wear. In the morning she would walk down the front path and along the street to catch the bus to Ballarat and then the train to Melbourne. She was ready.

35

The Shoebox

At she reached the front gate, Marge turned to wave to her parents and her two sons standing on the verandah. But then a sense of foreboding gripped her. She recognised the peaked cap of the Hamilton telegram boy as he rode towards her. He stopped and handed her a telegram. Inside were the words Marge had long feared:

IT IS WITH DEEP REGRET THAT I HAVE TO INFORM YOU THAT VX-39162 HEYWOOD W S WAS KILLED IN ACTION TOKIO CAMP ON 13TH JULY [1945] RESULT OF AN AIR RAID AND DESIRE TO CONVEY TO YOU THE PROFOUND SYMPATHY OF THE MINISTER FOR THE ARMY.

The telegram had left Melbourne at 11.50 pm the previous day, 15 September 1945. That night, as Marge would later explain to John and Doug, she'd had a dream in which St Peter had handed her a letter. Now Marge understood what it was, and the full horror of the dream hit.

She knew that this time there was no mistake – this time

it was real. She had been through an upheaval of emotions, not least in the past month after Japan's surrender. So many women like her had struggled to find out what had happened to a POW husband, son or brother. To know that Scott had come so close to surviving the war only added to her heartbreak.

Marge had endured so much trauma about whether he was alive or dead. Finally there had been relief in the apparent certainty that he was alive and would be returning home. She had been excited that Scott would soon be making the train trip back to Hamilton. With her! They would walk through the gate and close it behind them. The nightmare would be over. But not now.

Marge was just twenty-six years old, and had two small boys to raise. Her world had been ripped apart. How could this be? She was plunged into unimaginable torment in what was doubtless the worst week of her life. Nothing could ever surpass the gut-churning awfulness of that week in September. It was too much to bear.

What made the pain worse were the stories and photos on the front pages of Melbourne's daily newspapers as 8th Division POWs arrived by hospital train at Spencer Street Station in the days that followed. Thousands of people lined the city's streets and cheered their return. Scenes of unadulterated joy were splashed across the front page of *The Argus*, which also described the scene:

> Melbourne gave 119 lean, wan-faced men an unforgettable welcome yesterday afternoon. They were the first group of Australian POWs recovered from the Japanese hands to reach Victoria. Included in the group were 63 Victorians, for whom the welcome was specially memorable.

Cheering thousands in the city lined the route, flags were waved excitedly, home-made confetti was flung in profusion by laughing girls over the decorated cars which carried the soldiers, and wave after wave of cheers accompanied the rapidly moving procession.

And staring out at Marge were the images of returned POWs greeted by wives and children, being reunited once more. One caption read: 'When WO F.A. Foley, of Glen Iris, saw his wife and his mother at Spencer street station he leapt from the car he was in and embraced them both at the barrier.' Another read: 'Making friends with his two small children was a task for Cpl F.L. Couacaud, of Longwarry, when his wife brought them to Heidelberg Military Hospital yesterday.'

This very experience was what Marge had longed for – what she had imagined would happen when she travelled to Melbourne. These men had been given the chance to resume a normal, happy family life. But instead of that, a wave of grief washed over the Heywood and Hawkins families.

First they had to deal with the grim task of posting death notices. In *The Age*, under 'Deaths on Active Service', Scott was remembered as Marge's 'dearly loved husband' and 'loved daddy of John and Douglas'. His parents, Fred and Margaret, placed a similar notice in *The Argus*, which concluded with the phrase 'Duty nobly done'. Yet another in *The Age* poignantly noted that Scott was the esteemed friend of the late Warrant Officer Class 1 Henry Heath Waters. Lofty had died of dysentery on 9 November 1943, while working on the Thai end of the railway. Scott had never known; such were the vicissitudes of war. Scott and Lofty would both have enjoyed the words printed in the notice: 'Together again'.

The communities that knew Scott mourned his passing. Recording his death, the *Stawell Times* commented that he had been one of the town's favourite sons, someone who was 'a particularly fine type of young man'. Scott had had a successful military career and had quickly risen in the service. He was, the paper concluded, 'recognised as a particularly fine officer, respected by officers and men alike'.

Scott's father, Fred Heywood, who had been in indifferent health for some time, was plunged into a deep grief. In early November 1945 he suffered a stroke; a fortnight later he died, aged sixty-eight. The flags in Stawell flew at half-mast, and his obituary observed that Scott's death 'brought on the illness from which Mr Heywood never recovered'. Shortly after, the family cordial business was sold.

*

In Japan, in the wake of the blast, Vic Duncan, who had been uninjured, had the grim task of identifying Scott's body. He did so with a heavy heart, after which Scott was cremated, along with the other twenty-nine fatalities. Vic, too, had seen so much death; it was all the harder to take when it was a mate, and Scott had become a close mate, someone he respected, someone whose values had made a lasting impact on him. Vic was determined to ensure that, in death, Scott did not become just another statistic. His family needed to know how highly he was regarded by his comrades.

Vic returned to Australia with a memento of Scott's: the dessert spoon which he had used over the years of captivity, a utensil so simple and tangible, yet so very personal. He wanted to deliver it to Marge in person. In a letter to her just a few days after the news of Scott's death broke in Australia, Vic wrote:

I knew Scotty in Burma, Thailand, Indochina, Singapore,
the sinking of the *Rakuyo* and finally Japan. His spirit
was incorrigible in those hard times and I have nothing
but admiration for him. I speak not as a stranger but as
one who knew him fairly closely. Scotty's signet ring and
R.S.M. badge I personally attended to. The Japs assured
me they would be placed in the box of ashes. I saw these
boxes, they were imprinted with the name, number, etc., of
each man and will, I am sure, eventually reach Australia.

In taking such care regarding Scott's remains and valued
possessions, Vic ensured that in death he was reunited,
symbolically at least, with his beloved Marge.

In her grief, Marge wrote to Dave Quick, a RAAF corporal,
in early January 1946. She had seen his name in the papers,
along with information that he lived in inner Melbourne, and
she asked what he knew of the day Scott died. Dave replied
quickly, telling her how much he'd enjoyed Scott's cheerfulness
and optimism. 'Scotty was one of the fairest and the best and
respected by all his men,' he wrote. Dave had been with Scott
when the bomb exploded.

[W]e only received one direct hit and that was from
the last stick of bombs dropped. It was a long hut,
with the Jap quarters occupying one end, the far end
being occupied by 19 Australians and some Dutchmen,
and it was this end which received the full force of the
explosion … I had a miraculous escape, I was knocked
unconscious and found myself in a canal, on coming to,
with the roof of the building on top of me. I was lucky
enough to find a small opening through which to drag

myself out … Men from our rescue party said those who were killed would not have suffered pain, as in all cases death had been instantaneous, and I know from my own experience this must have been so, as I did not even hear the explosion.

Major Jack Parry also wrote to Marge, describing Scott as a loyal friend and someone who had the qualities that made a fine soldier. As well, Scott was cheerful and quick to help others. Parry had heard good reports of Scott, both from his senior officers and from his men. In talking to survivors of the *Rakuyo Maru*, Parry had listened to stories of Scott's particular bravery in helping to save men during the sinking. 'It is no more than I would expect of him,' he told Marge.

A letter in February 1946 from Scott's close mate Murray Cheyne would have warmed Marge's heart. He told her that a night never passed without Scott taking out his photos of home and the family; sometimes they would look at them together. Murray had seen the photos so often that, even though he had never met her, he felt that he knew Marge extremely well. 'I will even go as far as to say that if I passed you in the street, I would recognise you,' he wrote.

Even though I only met Scotty in 1942 I think I can claim the honour of saying that I was one of his best and closest friends – we worked side-by-side on the Burma Railway and had a chance to study each other during that period. I can say quite truthfully, and without any fear of contradiction, that Scotty did more for the men on the working parties than any other officer, NCO or private, nothing was ever too much for him.

Murray recalled the day they had received their first mail in Saigon, in June 1944. They were both ecstatic. 'Scotty would read mine, and I his,' he told her. 'It seemed only natural for us to do so.'

In 2020, Wal Williams, who endured the construction of the railway, the sinking of the *Rakuyo Maru* and time as a POW in Japan, recalled his association with Scotty during those years and how much he admired him.

> He was a well-respected bloke. You're very fortunate to get first-hand the story of the Burma railroad in the way that Scotty was able to write about it. When people ask me about it, I think of what happened in weeks or months, but he captured it daily. I don't know how he did it.

Shortly after the war ended, the British Commonwealth Mausoleum was built at Yokohama, and the ashes of eighty Australian POWs who died in Japanese camps in various parts of the home islands were placed there. On 30 November 1945, this became Scott's final resting place.

A letter to Marge from the Directorate of War Graves Services assured her that his ashes would receive reverent care and attention for all time, in a building that stood as 'a monument to the courage, unselfishness and patriotism of all the men who have given their lives in the service of the country'.

As was common, a condolence letter from Buckingham Palace and King George VI followed. Although she appreciated this, and outwardly maintained a 'stiff upper lip', Marge struggled to come to terms with her loss and the emptiness it left in her life. She now knew how Scott had died, and of the high regard in which he was held. But what

Scott Heywood's grave in Yokohama.

had happened during those years in captivity in Burma was still a mystery to her.

In early 1946, Marge received news that Baldy McFadyen was recuperating in Heidelberg Hospital and, on discharge, intended to travel to Hamilton to deliver a cache of letters that Scott had written to her in captivity – all 389 of them.

Baldy made the solemn journey later that year, and Marge warmly welcomed him into her home. Her son Doug has a distant memory of the occasion: that the two talked over a cup of tea. Then Scott's old friend walked down the front path and closed the gate behind him – the gate Marge had always envisaged Scott walking through.

Scott's story was now within Marge's grasp to read and comprehend. But the thought of coming to terms with the content of the letters was overwhelming to her. Just holding them was as much as she could manage.

Each had been the other's 'whole life'. These were words that Scott never forgot. So many times Scott had assured her of this. He wanted Marge to know she was, and always would be, all he wanted in the world.

In the quiet of her home, Marge put the letters in a shoebox and placed it at the back of a linen press. There they lay, hidden away. She could never bring herself to read them.

36

The Camphor Chest

With good reason, Viktor Frankl worried that he might die before reuniting with Tilly when the war ended. He asked his trusted friend Otto whether, in the event of his death, he would tell Tilly that he spoke of her daily, hourly even. And that he loved her more than anything in the world. For him, their brief marriage outweighed everything they had both been through.

Frankl didn't die. He was liberated from Turkheim, his final concentration camp, in Bavaria, in April 1945. Tasting newfound freedom, he was wandering through a nearby field when he came across another recently liberated man. While they were talking, Frankl noticed he was absent-mindedly rolling a small object in his hand. It was a tiny gold globe pendant, exactly like the one he had given Tilly for her birthday before the war. Frankl worked it back in his mind: an SS storehouse of confiscated jewellery was located nearby – it had to have been the same one stripped from Tilly when she'd entered Auschwitz. Frankl bought the trinket from the man.

With a mixture of anticipation and trepidation, Frankl returned home to Vienna. And began to search for Tilly. It

With the war over, and the dream of life with Scott lost forever, Marge's sons Doug (left) and John (right) became the centre of her life.

was the next morning when he heard the news from a friend: Tilly had died at Bergen-Belsen after indescribable suffering. 'I am terribly tired, terribly sad, terribly lonely … So now I'm all alone,' Frankl wrote. 'Whoever has not shared a similar fate cannot understand me.'

There was one who could: Marge. She had lost a husband and father to two young boys. This was an era of families left shattered by the war. More than 39,000 Australian servicemen and women had died either in war or in captivity. Just as in the aftermath of the Great War, families would never be the same, as the tentacles of trauma spread wide. Communities experienced collective grief. The men who returned knew what it was to be morose, to suffer nightmares and the blackness of depression as they relived the terrors of the battlefield and in the POW camps.

For widows like Marge, there was no formal mechanism for mourning her lost husband, no final goodbye. That Scott's body could not be sent home denied Marge and the wider family the rituals associated with a funeral that might have helped them reconcile themselves to his loss. As a young widow and mother, Marge found herself suddenly alone. Somehow, in her numbness, she had to construct a future for the rest of her life. And how, beset by overwhelming grief, could she achieve that?

The situation she now found herself in was so different from what Scott had imagined for them. As he'd prepared to leave Australia, Marge's financial security had been uppermost in his mind. A buoyant Scott had assured her: 'I can see us living in luxury when I come home.' Two years later, while at 105 Kilo camp, he'd written that with two years' deferred pay in his book, amounting to £110, they would 'be millionaires when I come home'.

Marge would never be wealthy – not that she had ever aspired to that. She had simply wanted a normal life with Scott. She had little choice but to get on with it. With two sons to raise, she was helped by her mother and father, and her brother, Ian. In the immediate post-war years, they all lived in the same house in Hamilton.

These years were a time of austerity in Australia. A time when society wanted people to put the war behind them. A time for economic reconstruction. For many families, money was tight, not least in the Heywood/Hawkins household. They made their own entertainment; besides play readings, musical evenings were a regular event. Marge would sing and play the cello, her mother would accompany her on piano, while her elder son, John, played the violin. Marge was an accomplished singer, even performing on the local Hamilton radio station. Music was the theme that ran through Marge's life, and the next generations.

Marge's father died in 1948, and soon after that John won a scholarship to study the violin in Melbourne. The family moved there and, in 1952, with the help of a new war service loan to boost Scott's superannuation, Marge bought a house in the industrial bayside suburb of Williamstown.

Now the main breadwinner for the family, she trained as a kindergarten teacher and taught at a local school. Later, she retrained as a law clerk, embarking on a second career. Marge's singing took her to the National Theatre Opera Company and the Australian Elizabethan Theatre Trust Opera Company. Importantly, a small sleepout at the back of her house became her art studio. Here she retreated to paint intricate bark paintings, from which she derived not only satisfaction but a level of peace.

As a sixteen-year-old, Doug Heywood stumbled upon his father's letters in the shoebox, carefully stowed at the bottom

Marge took solace in singing. In this photo she was part of the chorus in a production of Verdi's opera *La Traviata*, staged by the Australian Elizabethan Theatre Trust in 1962.

Doug Heywood OAM spent years coming to grips with the wartime
letters of a father he never knew.

of a wardrobe. He was intrigued. He knew that his father had been killed in Japan during the war, and that Anzac Day was a time to remember those who had died, but beyond that he had little knowledge of Scott. When he and John asked about their father, there was a stock answer: 'Your father was a good man – he served his country and you should be proud of him.' Relatives counselled them against asking their mother questions, warning that it would only upset her. 'Least spoken, soonest mended' was the mantra of the day. A small framed photo of Scott sat on the dresser in the family's living room for decades, along with the framed message from King George VI. These were the only overt references to Scott in the house.

Doug started the painstaking task of sorting the letters, and thus began the journey of a young man getting to know his father. Over the ensuing years he read and transcribed each fragile letter, neatly written in Scott's tight cursive script on thin, fragile paper, yellowed with age. Doing so stirred deep emotions in him. Layer by layer, Doug took on the task of bringing his father to life, but it was not an easy process.

It was not until 2011, the hundredth anniversary of Scott's birth, that Doug seriously put his mind to finishing transcribing the hundreds of letters. After completing this, he privately published them as a book for the family, *Guests of the Uncivilised* – the title Scott had proposed using for a book about his life as a POW.

'I came to understand the deep loving bond that he and my mother shared,' Doug explained. 'I admire and respect my father's inner strength through all the suffering that he endured; his honesty and integrity is beyond doubt, his sense of duty unshakable, his thoughtfulness and care for others is frequently apparent, and his love for his wife and family is unquestionable.'

Marge was comfortable enough with Doug taking such an interest in the letters, but she didn't speak about Scott at all. She couldn't. She just shut it out. Outwardly, she was successful. She led a quiet, simple life, not seeking solace from the company of other widows, but enjoying her local community and, of course, her singing.

There were times over the years when Marge felt overwhelmed. Her stoicism would crack, and she would be admitted to hospital for a rest. This gave her space to just be. She was surrounded by caring health workers. The word 'depression' was mentioned. Her sons would visit, she would cry sometimes, but no one asked and she did not say – it remained unspoken. An aura of widowhood settled on her.

After interviewing POW widows, the historian Joy Damousi found a clear consistency: their stories were 'shaped around ideas of romance, lost opportunities and perfect love'. It was like a time warp. Seen through the lens of nostalgia, this gave the women a justification for not remarrying. With no space or place or permission to grieve, feelings were repressed and denied. And they didn't go away. Despite various suitors, and the encouragement of her sons, Marge never remarried.

Widows were encouraged to just get on with life. During the years in which their husbands were in captivity, they absorbed and internalised the trauma of their spouse's war experience, playing nightmare scenarios over and over in their minds. Yet, at the end of the war, there had been no prize – the return of the men they loved was denied them. Now they had to adjust to their absence permanently, silently.

The returning POWs from the Burma Railway spoke little of their experience. It was too close, too brutal, too hard to put into words, and probably too hard for those at home to hear; much easier to remain silent and tamp down the memories. Many were suffering from the effects of up to four years in captivity, and there was little understanding of their trauma, or its treatment.

It was not until the 1990s, around the fiftieth anniversary of the war's end, that the silence was finally broken and pilgrimages were made back to Burma and Thailand. The ex-POWs were in their seventies and eighties as they trod the ground where so many memories lay. They had seen the war crimes trials play out immediately after the war, and verdicts that had led to Nagatomo and the Boy Bastard, among others, being hanged. For such men there was no sympathy. As old mates reconnected, and wartime stories were revived and worked through, there were many laughs, with the help of a glass or two. Perhaps some demons were laid to rest.

For Marge, no such catharsis was possible. Her nostalgia was bittersweet: idealised memories that she carried through the years, coupled with the loneliness of unrealised dreams. From the perspective of the 2020s, it is not too much of a stretch to suggest that Marge was experiencing a degree of vicarious traumatic stress that complicated what should have been a normal grieving process.

No one really knows how Marge dealt with the trauma of Scott's captivity and the blow of being informed that he was presumed dead, then that he was alive, before finally receiving the awful truth that he really was dead. Marge never talked about it. She locked it away, and with it she shut down the very normal emotions that accompany grief. When Scott's letters were delivered to her, she hid them away, undoubtedly fearful of the strong emotions she knew they would elicit in her. And there they stayed.

Understandably, Marge sought to avoid reminders of Scott, and to push down any random thoughts or emotions that might cause her pain. In her trips to hospital over the next fifty years, there were many diagnoses. Consistent were headaches, insomnia, anxiety and reactive depression. Furthermore, her many physical complaints over the years were described in hospital notes as a 'hypochondriacal concern with bodily functions'. Mostly, no physical basis for her symptoms could be found. Her locked-down emotions had found a means of expression.

It is astounding that, in her hospital notes over decades, it wasn't until 1992 that a medical professional linked Marge's depression 'to the disappointment of her husband's death in the last weeks of WWII'. To describe Marge's reactions to Scott's death as 'disappointment' doesn't come close. Indeed, it diminishes her suffering, as it fails to comprehend the depth of her pain.

While Scott physically experienced the trauma of captivity and constant threat of death, Marge had only the scenarios playing out in her head of what she imagined Scott was enduring. It was as though his death caused an emotional shockwave that reverberated down the years. She existed in a cone of silence, one that would last the rest of her life.

What was remarkable was that she was able to lead so seemingly successful a life with her two sons – with art and music as a focus – and a successful career as a law clerk. Marge had a lovely voice. Perhaps, for both Marge the soprano and Scott the tenor, singing became a mechanism by which they coped – even if they were half a world away from each other. And for Marge, singing would provide not only solace but a connection to Scott for the rest of her life.

Marge died on 25 January 2004 and was finally returned to and laid to rest in Stawell, the very town where, seven decades earlier, she had met and fallen in love with Scott and enjoyed the happiest times of her life. While clearing out her house, Doug came across a small yellow cardboard box, inside a camphor chest in which his mother had her precious keepsakes. On the lid were Scott's name and his army number, VX39162. Inside was the lock of light brown hair, a curl, that Scott had sent to her, shortly before leaving Australia for war, when his hair was shorn – army style.

Left: Marge
Heywood in
later life.

Below: The camphor
chest in which Marge
Heywood kept
her most precious
keepsakes.

Authors' Note

The story of Scott Heywood began for us amid the catastrophic Australian bushfires of 2019–20, and we wrote this book against the background of the coronavirus pandemic. A friend had introduced us to Doug Heywood, Scott's younger son. He showed us an extraordinary cache of nearly 600 letters his father had written to his mother over several years, but especially during his time as a POW. We were immediately captivated.

As well as describing a poignant love story, the letters offered great insight into what drove Scott and how he stayed alive for so long in the brutal conditions he experienced. Instinctively, he laid down strategies for survival when faced with the consequences of inhumane incarceration. It quickly became clear to us that these strategies are as relevant today for Australians as they deal with the impact of the recent bushfires and the disease that has come to define contemporary life.

While Peter's background is journalism, he has been writing about men and women of Australian military history for the past twenty years. This story touched him differently:

it was not just one of war and captivity, but one of hope and inspiration.

Sue, a psychologist, was immediately struck by the parallels between Scott's story of captivity in Burma and Viktor Frankl's story of internment in the Nazis' concentration camps. It seemed natural to weave Frankl's survival story through Scott's. Both stand as a tribute to the resilience of the human spirit. Scott developed his strategies through raw instinct, while Frankl had developed theories during his psychiatric training, and these were validated by his experience at Auschwitz.

At the war's end, Frankl wrote a slim volume titled *Man's Search for Meaning*, chronicling his experience. It sold – and continues to sell – millions of copies. Scott went to extraordinary lengths to save his letters and ensure that they reached Marge. We can conjecture that his motivations in this were mixed. He wanted Marge to read the letters, to understand his commitment and unwavering love for her. He also felt a driving need for retribution against the worst of the Japanese and Korean guards. And he was considering writing a book about his experiences as a POW.

As we have seen, Marge was so traumatised she could never bring herself to read Scott's letters. And, of course, Scott was never able to write his book. Doug Heywood took up the challenge, and over many years assiduously and accurately transcribed his father's letters. Our aim was to bring these powerful emotional and historical strands together to document a unique story of love.

Endnotes

1. A Spray of Orchids

Information regarding the Stawell Gift was sourced from Stawell Historical Society.

Regarding Scott's car accident, see the *Horsham Times*, 17 August 1934.

Regarding the poor standing of the police, see the *Horsham Times*, 7 July 1936 and 30 June 1936.

Information on Margery Heywood's head injury was drawn from Department of Veterans' Affairs files, held by the Heywood family.

For Viktor Frankl references, see: Viktor Frankl, *Recollections: An Autobiography*, Basic Books, 2000, pp. 84, 88.

Scott Heywood's letters were dated 18 June 1938; undated May 1939; undated July/August 1938; undated, August 1939; 20 September 1939; 15 December 1939; and 17 January 1940.

For information on the government's army plans, see the *Sydney Morning Herald*, 16 September 1939, p. 15.

2. Keeping Close

Scott Heywood's letters were dated 17 February 1940; 19 February
 1940; 7 March 1940; 14 March 1940; 26 January 1941;
 9 February 1941; 18 April 1941; 2 May 1941; 4 May 1941;
 21 May 1941; 24 July 1941; and 1 August 1941.

For background to the Australian Army Service Corps (AASC),
 see Colonel Neville Lindsay, *Equal to the Task*, Historia
 Productions, Kenmore, 1991, www.historia.net.au/equal-to-
 the-task_v1-raasc/e1-fore/index.html.

G. McKenzie-Smith, 'The Army's Grocers and Truckies:
 Understanding the Australian Army Service Corps in WWII',
 Sabretache, vol. 56, March 2015.

The Age's account of the march through Melbourne's streets was
 carried on 15 February 1941.

3. Daydreaming

George Fletcher's quote on his arrival at Singapore was drawn from
 his diary, 15 August 1941. The diary is held by his family. His
 entries on race relations were dated 26 November 1941 and
 20 November 1941. His entry on his doubts over Singapore's
 security was dated 1 October 1941.

Major General Gordon Bennett was quoted in *The Herald*
 (Melbourne), 16 August 1941.

Scott Heywood's telegram to Marge on his arrival in Singapore is
 held by the Heywood family.

Scott Heywood's letters were dated 18 August 1941; 20 August
 1941; 19–20 August 1941; 2 October 1941; 2 November
 1941; 1 September 1941; 28 August 1941; 8 October 1941;
 7 September 1941; 19 September 1941; 25 October 1941;
 21 September 1941; 24 September 1941; 7 November 1941;
 12 October 1941; 22 October 1941; 29 October 1941;

26 September 1941; 1 October 1941; 2 October 1941;
29 September 1941; 11 October 1941; 14 October 1941; and
16 November 1941.

Details on the strength of Scott's unit were drawn from the War
Diary of No. 2 Company AASC, February 1942. See AWM52,
10/2/23/5; 10/2/23/6.

Ken Dumbrell's comments were drawn from Colin E. Finkemeyer,
*It Happened to Us: The Unique Experiences of 20 Members
of the 4th Anti-Tank Regiment*, Melbourne, 1994, https://
s3-ap-southeast-2.amazonaws.com/awm-media/collection/
MSS2350/document/6187721.PDF.

4. Thunder Be Buggered

Scott Heywood's letters were dated 9 December 1941;
11 December 1941; 19 December 1941; 20 December 1941;
21 December 1941; 20 December 1941; 16 December 1941;
19 December 1941; 21 December 1941; 23–24 December
1941; 25 December 1941; 26 December 1941; 28 December
1941; 29 December 1941; 30 December 1941; 27 December
1941; 3 January 1942; 27 December 1941; 31 December
1941; 27, 28 and 31 December 1941; 29 December 1941, 1 &
10 January 1942; 5 January 1942; 4 January 1942; 5 January
1942; and 7 January 1942.

George Fletcher's diary entry was dated 18 December 1941.

Prime Minister John Curtin's speech was published in *The Herald*
(Melbourne), 27 December 1941.

The Argus's report on heavy fighting in Malaya was published on
17 December 1941.

For the description of the Japanese Army, see *2/29th Battalion
Unit Diary*, 21 December 1941, p. 79; AWM52 8/3/29.

Details of the work of Scott Heywood's unit were drawn from the
War Diary of No. 2 AASC, 8 January 1942.

5. Where Are the Planes?

Scott Heywood's letters were dated 12 January 1942; 8 &
10 January 1942; 13 January 1942; 18 January 1942; 13 &
16 January 1942; 17 January 1942; 16 & 19 January 1942;
17 & 18 January 1942; 18 January 1942; 20 January 1942;
the date on the letter wondering where the planes were was
censored; 21 January 1942; the letter asking Marge to pray for
Lofty's safety was undated, January 1942; 30 January 1942;
10 November 1942; 30 January 1942; the date of the letter
referencing Tobruk was censored; and 1 February 1942.

George Fletcher's diary accounts of meeting the AASC and the
general devastation were dated 15 January 1942. His account
of the results of fighting was dated 16 January 1942. His
account of Muar River fighting was dated 24 January 1942.

The description of the work of Scott's unit was drawn from the
War Diary of No. 2 Company AASC, entries dated 14 and
17 January 1942; reference to the narrow escape was drawn
from 17–18 January 1942; for the preparations for evacuation,
see 25 January 1942. Details of the evacuation were drawn
from entries for January 1942.

The account of Major General Bennett's wishful confidence was
published in the *Singapore Times* on 16 January 1942.

6. Battle Stations

Scott Heywood's letter was dated 2 February 1942.

Major Jack Parry's letter to Marge Heywood was dated 25 March
1946.

For the Special Reserve Battalion being formed from surplus
    Service Corps, Ordnance Corps and 2/4th Machine Gun
    Battalion reinforcements, see Lionel Wigmore, *The Japanese
    Thrust*, AWM, Canberra, 1957, p. 302.

For the formation of the rifle companies, see the War Diary
    of No. 2 Company AASC, February 1942; for the heavy
    bombing, see entry for 14 February 1942.

George Fletcher's diary account of the shelling was dated
    8 February 1942; of going back to Holland Road, see
    9 February 1942; for his account of taking shelter, see
    12 February 1942; of hearing of the birth of his daughter, see
    13 February 1942; of coming across the stricken child, see
    15 February 1942.

Brigadier Arthur Varley's diary entry on the shelling is cited in
    Wigmore, *The Japanese Thrust*, p. 308.

The account of the Japanese landing was drawn from a speech
    by Andrew Warland, 15 February 2020 at The Shrine,
    Melbourne.

The account of the bayonet charge was drawn from Wigmore,
    The Japanese Thrust, p. 349.

7. Rats in a Trap

For the account of the surrender of weapons, see the War Diary of
    No. 2 Company AASC, February 1942.

Scott Heywood's letters were dated 17 July 1942; 15 February
    1943; 23 September 1942; 17 September 1942; and 21 July
    1942.

George Fletcher's account of his escape was drawn from his
    National Archives of Australia file (NAA: B883, NX29466),
    and from his own diary entries for 10 February 1942 and
    10 April 1942.

Keith Murdoch's description of the fall of Singapore was published
in *The Herald* (Melbourne), 15 August 1942.

8. Naked Existence

For Viktor Frankl's accounts in this chapter, see Frankl,
Recollections, pp. 87, 89, 90, 93.

For Frankl's quote regarding 'our naked existence', see *Man's
Search for Meaning*, Washington Square Press, New York,
1984, p. 28.

Scott Heywood's letters were dated 19 July 1942 and 22 July
1942.

The Department of the Army letter to Marge was dated 30 March
1942; it is now held by Doug Heywood.

Marge Heywood's letter to the unnamed escapee from Singapore
was dated 31 March 1942; it is now held by Doug Heywood.

The District Records Office letter to Marge Heywood was dated
21 April 1942; it is now held by Doug Heywood.

The Red Cross letter to Marge Heywood was dated 1 May 1942; it
is now held by Doug Heywood.

For Dr Rowley Richards' account of the voyage, see his *A Doctor's
War*, HarperCollins Publishers, Sydney, 2008, p. 83.

John Garran's account of his arrival at Victoria Point was drawn
from his diary entry for 7 June 1942; his diary is privately held
by his family.

9. The Photo

Scott Heywood's letters were dated 17 July 1942; 21 July 1942;
22 July 1942; 25 June 1942; 19 July 1942; 17 March 1943;
25 July 1942; 17 July 1942; 25 July 1942; 24 July 1942;
21 July 1942; 3 August 1942; 11 August 1942; 24 July 1942;
and 9 August 1942.

For Viktor Frankl's reference to the inner self, see *Man's Search for Meaning*, p. 49.

The *Dandenong Journal*'s report regarding Scott Heywood was published on 15 July 1942.

The *Weekly Times*' report regarding Scott Heywood was published on 29 July 1942.

For Viktor Frankl's message to Tilly Frankl, see *Recollections*, p. 90.

John Garran's references to the guards were drawn from his diary entries for 17 and 28 June 1942.

Keith Murdoch's account of the fall of Singapore was published in *The Herald* (Melbourne), 15 August 1942.

10. Unforgiving

Scott Heywood's letters were dated 19 August 1942; 24 October 1942; 18 October 1942; 26 September 1942; 18 October 1942; 26 August 1942; 20 September 1942; 29 July 1942; 18 December 1941; 26 September 1942; 23 August 1942; 26 September 1942; 23 September 1942; 23 August 1942; 13 September 1942; 13 September 1942; 26 August 1942; 7 November 1942; 23 August 1942; 13 September 1942; 2 September 1942; 6 September 1942; and 13 September 1942.

For additional details of the hellship voyage, see the 2/4th Machine Gun Battalion history website *Remembering the Fallen*, 2nd4thmgb.com.au.

On the Tavoy Eight, see Padre Bashford's statement, National Archives of Australia MP742/1, 336/1/2018. See also Brigadier Arthur Varley's diary entry for 6 June 1942, Australian War Memorial, 3DRL/2691.

The Rohan Rivett quote was sourced from his book *Behind Bamboo*, Angus & Robertson Ltd, Sydney, 1946, p. 214.

11. A Safe Space

Scott Heywood's letters were dated 17 September 1942;
2 September 1942; 24 October 1942; 23 August 1942;
30 August 1942; 23 September 1942; 21 July 1942;
6 September 1942; 7 October 1942; 23 September 1942;
23 September 1942; 2 October 1942; 8 October 1942;
8 October 1942; 23 September 1942; and 9 October 1942.

Captain Charles Cousens was interrogated and brought home to Sydney under arrest after the Japanese surrender. Because no Commonwealth legislation covered treasonable acts committed abroad, he was charged in New South Wales under an obscure English statute; the case was never properly resolved. For more information, see Ivan Chapman, 'Cousens, Charles Hughes (1903–1964)', *Australian Dictionary of Biography*, vol. 13, MUP, 1993.

12. Inner Life

For quotes from Viktor Frankl, see *Man's Search for Meaning*, pp. 50, 52, 59.

Scott Heywood's letters were dated 14 January 1943; 24 October 1942; 23 September 1942; and 30 April 1943.

For Dr Rowley Richards on the beauty of Burma, see *A Doctor's War*, p. 236.

Brigadier Varley's Tavoy Club story was sourced from his diary, 26 May 1943, p. 149.

John Garran's diary entry on his books was dated 12 October 1942.

On the importance of reading for POWs, see Brian MacArthur, *Surviving the Sword*, Abacus, 2005, pp. 187–91.

Dr Rowley Richards' words on books were sourced from an interview he did with Peter Rubenstein.

For Viktor Frankl's account of writing, see *Recollections*, p.98.

13. Doctors' Orders

Scott Heywood's letters were dated 27 October 1942; 24 October
    1942; 27 October 1942; 28–29 October 1942; 15 November
    1942; 13 September 1942; 1 November 1942; 11 &
    13 November 1942; 10 November 1942; 19 November
    1942; 10 December 1942; 18 December 1942; 20 January
    1943; 19 April 1943; 9 November 1942; 15 November 1942;
    22 November 1942; and 17 November 1942.

For the Nagatomo quote, see Gavan Daws, *Prisoners of the
    Japanese,* Robson Books, 1995, p. 185.

Information regarding pay was sourced from Wigmore, *The
    Japanese Thrust,* p. 543.

Details of the rules were sourced from the National Archives of
    Australia: AWM119,122.

Brigadier Varley's account of the Green incident was sourced
    from his diary entries for 5, 7, 11 & 12 October 1942; and
    2 November 1942.

For information regarding the camp sanitary conditions, see the
    2/4th Machine Gun Battalion history website *Remembering
    the Fallen,* 2nd4thmgb.com.au.

Dr Rowley Richards' comments were sourced from Rowley
    Richards & Marcia McEwan, *The Survival Factor,* Kangaroo
    Press, Kenthurst, 1989, p. 99.

14. The Last of Human Freedoms

Scott Heywood's letters were dated 4 December 1942; 5 December
    1942; 17 September 1942; 11 December 1942; 17 December
    1942; 4 December 1942; 10 December 1942; 5 January 1943;
    12 December 1942; and 22 November 1942.

For Brigadier Varley's account of his interaction with Nagatomo,
    see his diary entry for 7 December 1942; for his account of

Whitfield's execution, see his diary entry for 13 December
1942.

For Padre Bashford's account of the execution, see NAA: MP742/1,
336/1/2018.

For John Garran's bridge comments, see his diary entry for
30 November 1942.

The Viktor Frankl quote was sourced from his book, *Man's Search
for Meaning*, p. 75.

15. Eyes Right

Scott Heywood's letters were dated 16 June 1943; 26 November
1942; 3 December 1942; 26 November 1942; 17 December
1942; 19 December 1942; 16 January 1943; 7 December
1942; 12 March 1943; 18 December 1942; 24 March 1943;
4 October 1942; 24 December 1942; 22 December 1942;
24 December 1942; 21 December 1942; 28 December 1942;
and 25 December 1942.

The statement by the Minister for the Army, Frank Forde, was
reported in *The Herald* (Melbourne), 3 December 1942.

Vera White's letter was dated 17 December 1942; it is now held by
Doug Heywood.

16. The Ring

Scott Heywood's letters were dated 25 December 1942;
29 December 1942; 28 December 1942; 27 December
1942; 29 December 1942; 1 January 1943; 20 February
1943; 21 December 1942; 9 January 1943; 3 January 1943;
17 January 1943; 18 December 1942; 16 January 1943;
16 January 1943; and 26 January 1943.

John Garran described Christmas Day 1942 in a diary entry. For his
thoughts on the concert, see his entry for 31 December 1942.

For Varley's account of New Year's Day with the Japanese officers, see his diary entry for 1 January 1943.

For Viktor Frankl's comments about Tilly Frankl, see *Man's Search for Meaning*, p. 48.

17. Hope

Scott Heywood's letters were dated 30 January 1943; 13 January 1943; 21 December 1942; 5 February 1943; 16 April 1943; 16 April 1943; 31 January 1943; 9 January 1943; 23 January 1943; 29 December 1942; 23 February 1943; 7 December 1942; 29 December 1942; 23 January 1943; and 28 January 1943.

Doris Parry's letter was dated 26 January 1943; it is now held by Doug Heywood.

For Viktor Frankl's comments about Tilly Frankl, see *Man's Search for Meaning*, p. 50; on the importance of a sense of purpose, see p. 82.

The Rowley Richards quote was sourced from his book *A Doctor's War*, HarperCollins, Sydney, 2008, p. 84.

18. What Will Be Will Be

Scott Heywood's letters were dated 18 December 1942; 12 February 1943; 17 February 1943; 21 February 1943; 26 February 1943; 3 March 1943; 26 May 1943; 13 March 1943; 17 March; and 15 April 1943.

For an account of Dickinson, Mull and Bell, see the *Bendigo Advertiser*, 24 April 2011.

For details of the escape, see Brigadier Varley's diary entry for 25 February 1943.

For Bell's execution, see Roy Whitecross, *Slaves of the Son of Heaven*, Australian Large Print, Melbourne, 1988, p. 81; see also Brigadier Varley's diary entry for 16 March 1943. For Padre Bashford's account, see NAA: MP742/1, 336/1/2018.

19. The Tree

Scott Heywood's letters were dated 8 March 1943; 8 March 1943; 9 March 1943; 31 March 1943; 15 March 1943; 10 April 1943; 28 August 1943; 22 August 1943; 10 March 1943; 1 April 1943; 9 April 1943; 10 April 1943; 14 June 1943; 2 April 1943; 15 July 1943; 21 December 1942; 1 April 1943; and 28 March 1943.

For Viktor Frankl's comments about humour, see *Man's Search for Meaning*, p. 54.

20. Dying Is Part of Your Job

Scott Heywood's letters were dated: 10 March 1943; 19 & 21 March 1943; 18 March 1943; 24 March 1943; 2 April 1943; 22 March 1943; 9 April 1943; 4 April 1943; 9 April 1943; 29 April 1943; 15 April 1943; 18 April 1943; 21 April 1943; 25 April 1943; 8 May 1943; 27 March 1943; 8 May 1943; 13 May 1943; 20 March 1943; 1 May 1943; and 8 May 1943.

On the work party, see John Garran's diary entry for 10 April 1943; on the issue of competence, see 10 April 1943.

Wal Williams' comments were made in a personal interview, September 2020.

For Brigadier Varley's account of the warning re the sick, see his diary entry for 14 April 1943; on maintaining calm, see 14 May 1943.

On the failure to meet promises, see statement by Lieutenant Colonel Tom Hamilton, NAA: SP459/1, 573/1/434.

On the prophecy by the Minister for the Army, Frank Forde, see the *West Australian*, 30 March 1943.

For Colonel Ramsay's approach to the guards, see A.W. Hence papers, letter, 25 April 1943: AWM PR82/053.

21. Tall Tales

Scott Heywood's letters were dated 11 June 1943; 7 September 1943; 26 September 1942; 4 May 1943; 8 June 1943; 2 June 1943; 22 June 1943; and 6 March 1943.

For Viktor Frankl on rumours about the end of the war, see *Man's Search for Meaning*, p. 45.

For John Garran on sentimental tosh, see his diary entry of 9 December 1942; his account of the concert is dated 29–30 April 1943.

For an account of the film, see statement by Lieutenant Colonel Tom Hamilton, NAA: SP459/1,573/1/434.

For examples of preposterous Japanese military success stories, see *The Herald* (Melbourne), 17 November 1944.

For the humorous bombing story, see Brigadier Varley's diary entry for 25 May 1943.

22. Fighting Despondency

Scott Heywood's letters were dated 13 May 1943; 17 May 1943; 12 & 15 June 1943; 13 June 1943; 14 June 1943; 12 & 22 June 1943; 9 August 1943; 29 June 1943; 15 April 1943; 16 August 1943; 21 October 1943; 16 September 1943; 12 June 1943; 8 June 1943; 8 August 1943; 27 May 1943; 24 May 1943; 10 June 1943; 11 June 1943; 4 July 1943; 25 July 1943; 10 December 1942; 27 June 1943; and 25 July 1943.

On Dr Bertie Coates, see Albert Coates & Newman Rosenthal, *The Albert Coates Story*, Hyland House, Melbourne, 1977, p. 112.

Wal Williams' memories of Bertie Coates were offered in a
personal interview, September 2020.

23. The Gang

Scott Heywood's letters were dated 28 September 1943; 8 October
1943; 26 September 1942; 2 September 1943; 1 August 1943;
8 October 1943; 22 May 1943; 26 August 1942; 22 July
1942; 7 October 1942; 2 March 1943; 22 November 1942;
30 March 1943; 1 July 1943; 21 July 1943; 3 November 1943;
14 November 1943; 19 November 1943; 10 November 1943;
and 18 September 1943.

For Viktor Frankl's account of feeling the presence of Tilly Frankl,
see *Man's Search for Meaning*, p. 52; regarding lice etc., see
p. 57.

For Frank McGovern's memories, see 'Frank McGovern',
Australians at War Film Archive, No. 19, UNSW, 8 May
2003, http://australiansatwarfilmarchive.unsw.edu.au/
archive/19-frank-mcgovern.

Wal Williams' recollection was provided in a personal interview in
September 2020.

The Harold Ramsey quote was sourced from: www.sbs.com.au/
news/former-pows-share-their-memories

The Rowley Richards quote was sourced from Sandy Macleod,
'Psychiatry on the Burma–Thai Railway (1942–1943):
Dr Rowley Richards and Colleagues', *Australasian Psychiatry*,
1 December 2010.

24. White Japs

Scott Heywood's letters were dated 19 August 1942; 26 August
1942; 5 December 1942; 26 August 1942; 14 March 1943;
12 February 1944; 4 October 1942; 9 February 1940;

27 October 1941; 24 July 1942; 15 October 1942; 7 October
1942; 9 November 1942; 28 November 1942; 30 May
1943; 31 December 1942; 9 November 1942; 20 November
1942; 23 April 1943; 12 January 1943; 12 December 1942;
4 September 1942; 13 September 1942; 15 December 1942;
3 December 1942; 27 June 1943; 3 October 1943; 16 October
1943; and 19 July 1943.

On relations between soldiers, see M.J. Pyne, *Relationships
between Officers and Other Ranks in the Australian Army in
the Second World War*, thesis, University of Western Sydney,
2016, especially pp. 160–246.

For Dr Rowley Richards' views on officers, see Rosalind Hearder,
*Keep the Men Alive: Australian POW Doctors in Japanese
Captivity*, Allen & Unwin, Sydney, 2009, p. 133.

For Viktor Frankl's comments on torture, see *Man's Search for
Meaning*, p. 60; on guards, see pp. 93, 94.

25. No Cause to Celebrate

Scott Heywood's letters were dated 16 October 1943; 19 October
1943; 25 September 1943; 19 October 1943; 20 November
1943; 29 November 1943; and 7 November 1943.

Vera Deakin White's letter to Marge Heywood was dated
10 September 1943; it is now held by Doug Heywood.

The War Records Office's letter to Marge Heywood was dated
4 November 1943; it is now held by Doug Heywood.

For his comments on the white crosses, see Brigadier Varley's diary
entry for 24 May 1943.

26. A Promised Land

Scott Heywood's letters were dated 1 November 1943; 3 November
1943; 14 November 1943; 11 November 1943; 29 November

1943; 22 December 1943; 27 & 28 December 1943; 28 &
31 December 1943; 9 January 1944; 13 February 1944;
1 March 1944; 9 January 1944; 21 October 1943; and
14 February 1944.

On food supplies, see Brigadier Varley's diary entries for 7, 15 &
20 December 1943.

27. Three Good Years Lost

Scott Heywood's letters were dated 13 February 1944; 2 May
1943; 27 August 1943; 12 February 1944; 18 January
1943; 2 September 1943; 12 March 1943; 3 March 1944;
15 February 1944; 19 February 1944; 24 February 1944;
15 February 1944; 12 February 1944; 21 February 1944;
22 February 1944; 24 February 1944; 23 February 1944;
22 February 1944; 3 March 1944; 24 February 1944; 4 March
1944; 3 January 1944; 5 March 1944; and 4 February 1944.

On racial attitudes, see Peter Rees, *Bearing Witness*, Allen &
Unwin, Sydney, 2015, p. 476. See also John W. Dower, *War
Without Mercy: Race and Power in the Pacific War*, Seventh
Edition, Pantheon Books, New York, 1993, pp. 9, 259–60.

On the bashing, see Brigadier Varley's diary entry for 1 May 1943.

For Viktor Frankl's thoughts on SS guards, see *Man's Search for
Meaning*, p. 36.

28. The Pact

Scott Heywood's letter was dated 6 July 1944.

For Wal Williams' recollections, see *Pittwater Online News*,
23–29 April 2017.

For Frank McGovern's comments about the journey to Tha
Markam, and then to Saigon, see 'Frank McGovern',
Australians at War Film Archive.

Keith Burrill's comments were made in an undated letter held by Doug Heywood.

29. Cooee

For Wal Williams' recollections, see *Pittwater Online News*, 23–29 April 2017.

For details of embarkation and the voyage, see Leslie G. Hall, *Blue Haze*, Kangaroo Press, 1996, pp. 208, 294, 295, 297.

For John Flynn's comments, see AWM PR88/110.

For details of the voyage, see Darryl Kelly, *Just Soldiers: Stories about Ordinary Australians Doing Extraordinary Things in Time of War*, Anzac Day Commemoration Committee, 2004.

For Harold Ramsey's story, see Dan McDonnell, *The Sun*, 10 September 1994.

Keith Burrill's comments were made in an undated letter now held by Doug Heywood.

For Frank McGovern's comments, see AWM SO4089, and 'Frank McGovern', Australians at War Film Archive.

For Kitch Loughnan, see Hugh Clarke & Colin Burgess, *Barbed Wire and Bamboo*, Allen & Unwin, Sydney, 1992, p. 143.

30. Slow Boat to China

For Wal Williams' recollections, see *Pittwater Online News*, 23–29 April 2017.

For Kitch Loughnan, see Clarke & Burgess, *Barbed Wire and Bamboo*, p. 143.

For a description of the castaways' experience, see Cameron Forbes, *Hellfire: The Story of Australia, Japan and the Prisoners of War*, Pan Macmillan, Sydney, 2005.

For details of the rescue, see Kelly, *Just Soldiers*.

For Dr Rowley Richards' comments, see *A Doctor's War*, p. 239.

For details of the rescue, see Hall, *Blue Haze*, p. 303.

The Japan POW Group provided details of the numbers who were rescued in personal correspondence, 2020.

Commander Summers' comments were published in *World War II Today*, October 1985.

31. Wretches

For Dr Rowley Richards' comments, see *A Doctor's War*, pp. 247–48.

Keith Burrill's comments were made in an undated letter now held by Doug Heywood.

For Frank McGovern's comments, see 'Frank McGovern', Australians at War Film Archive.

32. A Welcome Diversion

Keith Burrill's comments were made in an undated letter now held by Doug Heywood.

For information on the survivors of the *Rakuyo Maru*, see NAA: B3856, 144/1/128.

On the Australian government's approach to releasing information on the *Rakuyo Maru* survivors, see Michael Sturma, 'Australian POWs and the Sinking of the *Rakuyo Maru*: The Politics of Repatriation', *Australian Journal of Political History*, 20 September 2016.

Details of Harold Ramsey's move to Niigata were sourced from a speech he gave at the friendship meeting in Tokyo on 8 March 2011, courtesy of the Japan POW Group.

33. Rollercoaster

Warrant Officer John Flynn's letter was dated 19 January 1945; it is now held by Doug Heywood.

The *Daily Telegraph* report was published on 25 January 1945.

The Japan POW Group provided details of the issues around the camp situation in personal correspondence.

Keith Burrill's comments were made in an undated letter now held by Doug Heywood.

For Harold Ramsey's recollections, see *Clayton RSL Club Weekly News*, 19 June 1991; Dan McDonnell, *The Sun*, 10 September 1994.

34. Black Friday

The Japan POW Group provided details of a GHQ/SCAP report on the raid on 13 July 1945.

For Harold Ramsey's comments, see *Clayton RSL Club Weekly News*, 19 June 1991.

Frank McGovern's recollections were drawn from a personal interview, September 2020, as well as from 'Frank McGovern', Australians at War Film Archive.

The Argus published a story on the damage to the Yokohama–Kawasaki industrial area on 27 September 1945.

Frank Forde's comments were published in *The Argus*, 15 September 1945.

35. The Shoebox

The account of the return of the POWs was published in *The Argus* on 20 September 1945.

The *Stawell Times*' obituary for Scott Heywood was published on 18 September 1945.

Fred Heywood's obituary was published in the *Stawell News and Pleasant Creek Chronicle* on 21 November 1945.

Vic Duncan's letter was dated 26 September 1945; it is now held by Doug Heywood.

Dave Quick's letter was dated 14 January 1946; it is now held by
Doug Heywood.

Major Jack Parry's letter was dated 25 March 1946; it is now held
by Doug Heywood.

Murray Cheyne's letter was dated 11 February 1946; it is now held
by Doug Heywood.

Wal Williams' recollections were offered in a personal interview,
September 2020.

The Directorate of War Graves Services' letter was dated 4 January
1946; it is now held by Doug Heywood.

36. The Camphor Chest

Scott Heywood's letters were dated 30 July 1941 and 8 June 1943.

For Viktor Frankl's comments, see *Man's Search for Meaning*,
p. 65.

Regarding the trinket, see Frankl, *Recollections*, pp. 90–91.

Regarding Frankl's suffering, see his letter to Wilhelm and Stepha
Börner in Viktor E. Frankl, *Man's Search for Meaning, with
selected letters, speeches, and essays*, 2013.

Doug Heywood's thoughts on his father were offered in a personal
note.

A copy of *Guests of the Uncivilised* has been lodged with the
Australian War Memorial.

For discussion on the importance of music, see Guido Fackler,
'Music in Concentration Camps, 1933–1945', *Music &
Politics*, vol. 1, issue 1, Winter 2007.

See Joy Damousi, 'Living with the Aftermath: Trauma, Nostalgia
and Grief in Post-War Australia', *Journal of Interdisciplinary
History*, vol. 34, No. 4, 2004, pp. 672–74.

Margery Heywood's Department of Veterans' Affairs medical
notes were released to Doug Heywood.

Bibliography

Books

T.W. Britt, B.A. Adler & C.A. Castro (eds), *Military Life: The Psychology of Serving in Peace and Combat*, Praeger Security International, Westport, 2005.

Mavis Thorp Clark, *No Mean Destiny: The Story of the War Widows' Guild of Australia 1945–85*, Hyland House, South Yarra, 1986.

H. Clarke & C. Burgess, *Barbed Wire and Bamboo*, Allen & Unwin, Sydney, 1992.

Albert Coates & Newman Rosenthal, *The Albert Coates Story*, Hyland House, Melbourne, 1977.

Gavan Daws, *Prisoners of the Japanese: POWs of World War II in the Pacific*, Robson Books, 1995.

John W. Dower, *War Without Mercy: Race and Power in the Pacific War*, Seventh Edition, Pantheon Books, New York, 1993.

Colin E. Finkemeyer, *It Happened to Us: The Unique Experiences of 20 Members of the 4th Anti-Tank Regiment*, Melbourne, 1994, https://s3-ap-southeast-2.amazonaws.com/awm-media/collection/MSS2350/document/6187721.PDF.

Peter Firkins, *The Australians in Nine Wars: Waikato to Long Tan*, McGraw-Hill, New York, 1971.

G.W. Fletcher, *Diary of Gunner G.W. Fletcher, NX 29466, 2/15th Field Artillery AIF, World War II, Malaya, 1941–1942*, privately held by the Fletcher family.

Cameron Forbes, *Hellfire: The Story of Australia, Japan and the Prisoners of War*, Pan Macmillan, Sydney, 2005.

Viktor E. Frankl, *Man's Search for Meaning*, Washington Square Press, New York, 1984.

Viktor E. Frankl, *Recollections: An Autobiography*, Basic Books, New York, 2000.

Viktor E. Frankl, *Man's Search for Meaning*, Rider, 2008.

Viktor E. Frankl (translated by Helen Pisano), *Man's Search for Meaning, with selected letters, speeches, and essays*, Beacon Press, 2014.

John Garran, personal diary, privately held by his family.

Leslie G. Hall, *The Blue Haze: POWs on the Burma Railway*, Kangaroo Press, Kenthurst, 1996.

Rosalind Hearder, *Keep the Men Alive: Australian POW Doctors in Japanese Captivity*, Allen & Unwin, Sydney, 2009.

Doug Heywood, *Guests of the Uncivilised: The Letters and Diary of William Scott Heywood, W.O. 1, Australian Imperial Force (1911–1945) POW Thai–Burma Railway and Japan*, privately published for the Heywood family.

Linda Goetz Holmes, *4000 Bowls of Rice: A Prisoner of War Comes Home*, Allen & Unwin, Sydney, 1993.

Darryl Kelly, *Just Soldiers: Stories about Ordinary Australians Doing Extraordinary Things in Time of War*, Anzac Day Commemoration Committee, Aspley, 2004.

Brian MacArthur, *Surviving the Sword*, Abacus, 2005.

Peter Rees, *Bearing Witness*, Allen & Unwin, Sydney, 2015.

Rowley Richards, *A Doctor's War*, HarperCollins, Sydney, 2008.

Rowley Richards & Marcia McEwan, *The Survival Factor*, Kangaroo Press, Kenthurst, 1989.

Rohan Rivett, *Behind Bamboo*, Angus & Robertson Ltd, Sydney, 1946.

Brigadier Arthur Varley, *Diary of Brigadier A.L. Varley, M.C., 12 May 1942 – 26 March 1944*, AWM 3DRL/2691.

Roy Whitecross, *Slaves of the Son of Heaven*, Australian Large Print, Melbourne, 1988.

Lionel Wigmore, *The Japanese Thrust*, Griffin Press, Adelaide, 1957.

Articles

Ivan Chapman, 'Cousens, Charles Hughes (1903–1964)', *Australian Dictionary of Biography*, vol. 13, MUP, 1993.

Joy Damousi, 'Living with the Aftermath: Trauma, Nostalgia, and Grief in Post-war Australia', *Journal of Interdisciplinary History*, vol. 34, No. 4, 2004.

Guido Fackler, 'Music in Concentration Camps, 1933–1945', *Music & Politics*, vol. 1, issue 1, Winter 2007.

D. LaBier, 'A Sense of Awe and Life Purpose Increases Your Mental Health', *Psychology Today*, 15 September 2015.

G. McKenzie-Smith, 'The Army's Grocers and Truckies: Understanding the Australian Army Service Corps in WWII', *Sabretache*, vol. 56, March 2015.

H. Parker, 'The Real Life Benefits of Reading Fiction', *Psychology Today*, 7 June 2018.

Michael Sturma, 'Australian POWs and the Sinking of the *Rakuyo Maru*: The Politics of Repatriation', *Australian Journal of Politics and History*, vol. 62, No. 3, 2016.

World War II Today, 'USS *Sealion* Sinks *Rakuyo Maru* – and 1300 POWs', *World War II Today*, https://ww2today.com/12-

september-1944-uss-sealion-sinks-rakuyo-maru-and-1300-pows (original in *Polaris*, October 1985).

PhD theses

K.L Meale, *Leadership of Australian POWs in the Second World War*, University of Wollongong, 2015.

Michael John Pyne, *Relationships between Officers and Other Ranks in the Australian Army in the Second World War*, University of Western Sydney, January 2016.

Newspapers

The Age, 15 February 1941.

The Argus, 17 December 1941, 15 September 1945, 27 September 1945.

Bendigo Advertiser, 24 April 2011.

Clayton RSL Club Weekly News, 19 June 1991.

Daily Telegraph, 25 January 1945.

Dandenong Journal, 15 July 1942.

The Guardian, 7 May 2014.

The Herald (Melbourne), 16 August 1941, 27 December 1941, 15 August 1942.

Horsham Times, 17 August 1934, 30 June 1936, 7 July 1936.

Pittwater Online News, 23–29 April 2017.

Singapore Times, 16 January 1942.

The Sun, (Melbourne), 10 September 1994.

Stawell News and Pleasant Creek Chronicle, 21 November 1945.

Stawell Times, 18 September 1945.

Sydney Morning Herald, 16 September 1939.

Townsville Bulletin, 27 April 2015.

Weekly Times, 29 July 1942.

Official records

Padre Frederick Bashford: NAA: MP742/1, 336/1/2018.

John Flynn: AWM PR88/110.

Lieutenant Colonel Tom Hamilton: NAA: SP459/1, 573/1/434.

A.W. Hence: letter, 25 April 1943: AWM PR82/053.

Memorandum: Report 554, General Headquarters, Supreme Commander for the Allied Powers, Legal Section, Investigation Division. Report of Investigation of Tokyo POW Camp 11D and 14B. 18 June 1946.

National Archives of Australia, Survivors ex Rakuyo Maru; see: MP729/8; MP1049/5; B3856.

Interviews

Roy Cornford, 'A True Story: Surviving the Sinking of the Rakuyo Maru', DVA Anzac Portal, https://anzacportal.dva.gov.au/resources/roy-cornford-sinking-rakuyo-maru-part-1.

Robin Lindley, 'Witness to an Extreme Century: An Interview with Lifton, Robert Jay', *History News Network*, http://hnn.us/article/141140.

Frank McGovern, personal interviews, 2020; also 'Frank McGovern', Australians at War Film Archive, No. 19, UNSW, 8 May 2003, http://australiansatwarfilmarchive.unsw.edu.au/archive/19-frank-mcgovern.

Dr Rowley Richards, interview with Peter Rubinstein, 8 September 2000.

Walter Williams, personal interviews, 2020–21.

Acknowledgements

This book owes so much to the work of Doug Heywood in painstakingly transcribing the letters of his father, Scott Heywood. It was a true labour of love. We all enjoyed the spirited discussions that ensued, albeit over video link, as the book was researched and written. Thanks to Doug's wife, Alex, for her input into the project.

Doug's son, Thomas Heywood, deserves special recognition for providing valuable family history, which helped to give Scott's life added context.

We're indebted to our good friend Peter Rubenstein for bringing us together with Doug, and also for allowing us to draw on his interview with Dr Rowley Richards.

The Stawell Historical Society, and the Ansett Museum at Stawell, were very helpful in filling in some gaps, as were the staff at the Australian War Memorial's Research Centre, who made a special effort to provide access to the war diary of Scott Heywood's unit.

Jill Wilmott of the War Widows Guild in Melbourne helped with post-war research regarding the experience of war widows, while Robert Winther, at the Austin Hospital, helped with the process of securing Marge Heywood's medical records.

It was a pleasure to have the opportunity to talk to two veterans who survived the Burma Railway, Frank McGovern and Wal Williams, who knew first-hand just what Scott Heywood had experienced. And thanks also to Mike Charteris for drawing our attention to Frank's story.

Thanks go to Robert Garran, for sharing the diary of his father, John Garran, who knew Scott on the railway. And also to Mike Fletcher, for allowing us to draw on the diary of his father, George Fletcher. We'd further like to acknowledge the 2/4th Machine Gun Battalion Association, whose website provided useful background to the Burma Railway.

Taeko Sasamoto of the Japan POW Group, provided detailed information about Scott Heywood's time as a POW in Japan.

We'd like to give a big thanks to Kristen Alexander, and also to Andrew Warland, who provided valuable feedback with corrections and suggestions which considerably improved the overall narrative. Finally we'd like to thank our editor, Scott Forbes, and our publisher, Catherine Milne, for her faith in the story and her enthusiasm in publishing this book.

Index

Note: SH = Scott Heywood.
Page numbers in *italics* refer to photographs.

The Age 18, 23, 63, 300
Amiel, Henri-Frédéric 122
amputations 206–7
Anderson, Charles 61, 159, 195, 206, 245
Anderson, Claude 'Pills' 137–8, 244
Anzac spirit 82
The Argus 45, 278, 280, 295, 299–300
Armistice Day (1943) 235
atomic bombs 294
Attwell, Sam 170
Aungganaung prison camp 202, 237–9, 241–4
Auschwitz-Birkenau concentration camp 2, 90–1, 95, 98, 100, 123
Australian Army Service Corps 21, 40, 64, 66, 89, 102, 166, 283
Australian Imperial Force *see* Second Australian Imperial Force
Australian Infantry Corps 12
Australian militia 9
Australian Prisoners of War Relatives' Association 53, 296
Australian Women's Weekly 33
Australian Wounded and Missing Inquiry Bureau 150

Ban Pong 86, 133
Barb, USS 271
Bashford, Fred 110–11, 178–9
Bathurst Military Camp 25
Bean, Charles 241
Bell, Alex 173–4, 176–9
Bennett, Gordon 29, 45, 47–8, 58, 66, 79, 219–20

Bergen-Belsen concentration camp 309
Black Force 184
Boer War 8
Bonegilla camp 22–3
books 125–7
Briggs, Jack 207
Britain 36, 39–40, 78
British Army, 12th Brigade 71
British Commonwealth Mausoleum, Yokohama 304
Brown, Wally 73
Burma 85, 109, 125
Burma Railway
  0 Kilo mark (Thanbyuzayat) 131
  14 Kilo mark (Thetkaw) 131
  26 Kilo mark 184
  55 Kilo mark 206, 216
  68 Kilo mark 194
  71 Kilo mark 194
  75 Kilo mark (Meilo) 180, 188, 193–4, 202–3, 222
  105 Kilo mark (Aungganaung) 200, 202, 231, 309
  108 Kilo mark 226
  133 Kilo mark 231
  construction of 188, 194, 212, 230–1
  deaths during construction 1, 231
  preparations for 100
  rebuilding of sections 234–5
  route of *130*
  strategic reason for 86
  see also Aungganaung prison camp; Meilo prison camp; Tavoy prison camp; Thetkaw prison camp
Burrill, Keith 187–8, 250, 252–3, 261, 267, 273–5, 289, 294
Byng, Len 62

348

Cameron, Ian 223
Campbell, Alan *38*, 115, *116*, 172,
   215
Campbell, Max 262
Celebes Maru (ship) 87–8
Changi Gaol 76–7, 82–3
Chapman, Bruce 207
Cheyne, Murray 112, 247, 303–4
Chief Little Wolf 22
Churchill, Winston 39, 43, 45, 47, 63
Coates, Albert 88, 206–7, 219–20,
   244
conformism 241–2
Coral Sea, Battle of the 86
Cousens, Charles 119–20
Curly (cook) 136, 161, 163, 170,
   172, 215–16
Curtin, John 51

Daily Telegraph 284
Damousi, Joy 314
Dandenong 11, 15, 17, 25–6, 246
Dandenong Journal 18, 97, 286
Daylesford 8, 17
Deakin, Alfred 150
Dickinson, Jimmy 76
Dickinson, Keith 173–4, 176–9
disease
   in Auschwitz 98
   in Burma 98
   in camp 11D 275
   in Changi prison 83
   Japanese attitude to sickness 189,
      191
   in Meilo prison camp 184–5, 191,
      195, 205, 213
   in Tavoy prison camp 106, 112
   in Thetkaw prison camp 136–7, 172
   in Victoria Point prison camp 100
Donaldson, Alan 112
Dumbrell, Ken 30
Duncan, Vic *259*, 261, 263, 269,
   301–2

Edwards, 'Wimpy' 112, 216
Empire Air Training Scheme 21
Europe, war declared in 16

Fletcher, Evelyn 79–80
Fletcher, George 28–9, 32, 35, 39,
   45, *57–9*, 64, 69–74, 79–80
Flynn, Jack *258*, 260
Flynn, John 283–4
Foley, F.A. 300
Forde, Frank 149, 192, 227, 280, 297
Frankl, Tilly 10–11, 81, 89–90,
   97–8, 307, 309
Frankl, Viktor
   allocated a number in camp 129
   on choosing one's attitude to events
      148
   courts and marries Tilly 10–11
   delouses before bed 213
   describes beatings by SS guards
      245
   discovers his wife has died 309
   feels his wife's presence 212
   finds solace in nature 169
   food in Auschwitz 100
   on good and evil 225
   humour as a survival tool 183
   inner life during captivity 124
   liberated from camp 307
   sent to Auschwitz 2, 89–91, 95
   transcendental experiences 162–3
   witnesses rigours of captivity 122
   worries about wife's pregnancy 81
   writes in captivity 127–8
   yearns for wife 123

Gabbett, Matt 126–7
Gallipoli 8, 150
Garran, 'Long John' 89, 98, 125,
   153, 160, 188, 198
Gemas, Battle of 58
Geneva Convention 86–7, 223, 229
George VI, King 304, 313
German army 12
Germany 36, 40, 290
Gibson, Merv 73
Goulden, Bob 92–4, 99, 103
Greater Asia 200
Greece 21
Green, Charles 87, 92–3, 135, 139,
   146, 191, 221, 223, 242

Green Force 87, 184
Grouper, USS 119
Growler, USS 260–1
Guam 43
Guests of the Uncivilised (Heywood) 151, 313
Guests of the Unspeakable (White) 151

Hague Convention 86, 135, 144, 223
Hamilton 5, 277, 310
Hamilton, Tom 198–9, 204
Harris, George 139
Hawkins, Jack 9–10, 22
Hawkins, Russ 144
Heathwood, Jack 246
Henry (Japanese guard) 98–9, 101, 225
The Herald 101–2, 149, 228
Heywood family 7–8
Heywood, Fred 8, 300–1
Heywood, Ian Douglas (Doug) 23, 24, 62, 306, 310, 312, 313–14, 317
Heywood, Jack 8
Heywood, John 20, 310
Heywood, Margaret 300
Heywood, Margery (née Hawkins)
    death 317
    doubts SH's commitment 15
    farewells SH 26
    in fox fur 49, 51
    gives birth to Doug 22–3
    gives birth to John 20
    joins public service 15
    keeps camphor box of keepsakes 317, 318
    life after SH's death 309–10, 314–17, 318
    marries SH 7, 17–18
    moves back to Stawell 83
    moves to Dandenong 11, 246
    moves to Melbourne 310
    moves to Mildura 150, 166, 227
    notified of SH's death 4, 298–300
    notified of SH's internment in Japan 285–6
    notified of SH's missing status 95, 97
    notified of SH's possible death 279–80
    notified of SH's POW status 4–5, 227–8
    portraits of 14, 49, 96, 167, 308, 311
    reads about defence of Singapore 101–2
    reads of soldiers' return 3
    reads of torpedoed Japanese ship 278
    receives cache of SH's letters 306
    receives letter from SH 227
    receives news of SH from rescued POW 283–4
    receives printed card from SH 229–30
    sends SH a signet ring 48
    as a singer 310, 311, 316–17
    struck by motorbike 10
    unable to attend SH's farewell march 23
    writes for information about SH 83–4, 150, 277–8, 302
Heywood, Scott
    affinity for writing 127
    allocated a number in camp 129
    allowed to write to wife for first time 158–9
    appointed acting camp sergeant-major 237
    appointed company sergeant 66–7
    appointed regimental sergeant major 94
    appointed warrant officer 15
    assures Margery Hawkins of commitment 15–16
    attends debutantes' ball 11
    in Aungganaung prison camp 202, 240–9
    becomes a father 20
    becomes a POW 75
    buries Dave Levick 76–7
    buys earrings for wife 249

in camp 11D (Yokohama) 274–5, 289

in camp 14B (Kawasaki) 289–90, 292–4

celebrates Melbourne Cup 234

in Changi Gaol 82–3

criticises British leadership 62

criticises officers 219–24

criticises politicians 78

discipline in writing 164

experiences first attack 51–2

faith in keepsakes 108

in farewell march in Melbourne 23

farewells wife 26

feels shame at surrender 133

finds solace in nature 123–4, 161–3, 168–9, 186, 211

gives letters to Baldy McFadyen 251–2

grave in Yokohama 305

gripped by malaise 113–15

grows up in Stawell 8–9

has appendix removed 289

has ashes interred in mausoleum 304

hides paper from guards 1

on humanity of guards 225–6

inner life during captivity 122–4

joins militia 9

joins Permanent Forces 11

killed in bombing raid 293–4

loses wedding ring 164

in Malacca 31–3, 34, 37–8, 40, 46, 51–2, 60

marches to Changi Gaol 77

marries Margery Hawkins 7, 17–18

on mateship 215, 217

in Meilo prison camp 180–6, 189–90, 192–4, 207–8, 211–13

mourns dead comrades 237

moves to Bathurst Military Camp 25

ordered to evacuate to Singapore 63–5

portraits of 13, 24, 27, 34, 37–8, 46, 116, 358

as a prolific letter-writer 1–2, 31

reads in Tavoy prison camp 126–7

reassures wife of his safety 52–3

receives letter from friend Lofty 209–10

receives letter from mother 246

receives letters from wife 115, 247

records details of execution 111

reflects on the future 117–18, 170–1, 210

reflects on war 142–3, 177, 204, 207–8

reminisces about Lofty 106, 108

reported as missing 97

rescued by Japanese corvette 269–70

in Saigon 252–4

sails for Burma 87–8

sails for Japan 256–60

sails from Hainan to Japan 272–3

sails to Tavoy 104–5

selected as a kumicho 138–9, 222

sends wife some curls 25

sent to work in Yokohama 274–5

sews letters into pack 249

signs house rules under duress 136

in Singapore 28–30, 254–5

sings in choirs 36, 156, 158

small arms training 16–17, 27

suffers from dysentry 83

suffers from malaria 184, 216, 235–6

suffers from nightmares 242–3

in Tavoy prison camp 105–6, 109, 111, 113

in Tha Markham prison camp 250–2

in Thetkaw prison camp 131–3, 136–40, 144–8, 152–65, 168–72, 174–7

thrown from horse 20

torpedoed and shipwrecked en route to Japan 260–9

trains with Australian Infantry Corps 12

transcendental experiences 123–4, 161–3

transfers to AASC 21
tributes to after death 300–4
in Victoria Point prison camp 89,
   92–5, 98–103
volunteers for overseas service 21
witnesses execution of POW 92, 94
worries about losing letters 175–6,
   185
writes to wife on Christmas Eve
   46, 47–8, 50
hierarchy of needs 171
Higuchi, Doctor Tomizo 191–2, 198,
   204
Hirado (ship) 260
Hiroshima 294
Holocaust 81
Hong Kong 43
Horsham Times 10, 21–2
Hunter, Bill 32, 73, 79

Imperial Japanese Army
   25th Army 47, 57
   Air Service bombs SH's camp
      51–2, 54–5
   ambushed by AIF 2/30th Battalion
      58
   attitude towards POWs 99, 241
   brutality of 109, 113, 134, 143–4,
      146, 152–3, 159, 173–4, 237–8,
      241–2, 244
   conquers Southeast Asia 85
   executes wounded Australians
      prisoner 61–2
   humanity of guards 225–6
   invades Burma 85, 109
   invades Malaya 41, 43, 45, 47,
      51–2, 57
   invades Nanking 11
   invades Singapore 35, 39–40,
      43–5, 47–8, 66–74
   plans Burma Railway 86
   prepares to send POWs to Japan
      251
   propaganda of 198–201, 247–8
   surrenders 3
   takes 130,000 prisoners 75
India 86

Indian Army
   44th Brigade 71
   45th Brigade 59
Ishakawa (Japanese guard) 101, 225
Italy 36
Itsui, Hiroshi 110–11

Japanese Army see Imperial Japanese
   Army
Jews 81
Johnson, Charles 164–5
Johnston, George 295–6
Johor 31, 45, 57
Johor Bahru 63, 65

Kachidoki Maru (ship) 256, 266,
   270, 272
Kanchanaburi 237, 246, 249
Kawasaki camp 2 294
Kawasaki camp 14B 289–90, 292–4
Khonkan 206
Kibitsu Maru (ship) 272–3
Kluang aerodrome 54
Knight, Murray 112, 216–17
Korean guards 134, 146, 224, 241,
   254–5
Kota Bharu 41
Kuala Lumpur 56–7

Levick, John (Dave) 33, 76–7
Lisbon Maru (ship) 119, 121
Longwarry, F.L. 300
Loughnan, Kitch 265, 267

Malacca 31–3, 50, 56, 220
malaria 184
Malaya 32–3, 39–40, 45, 51, 64, 78,
   143, 254
Man's Search for Meaning (Frankl) 2
Martin, 'Curly' 270
Maslow, Abraham 171
mateship 111–12, 213–15
McFadyen, Doug 'Baldy'
   as camp quartermaster 100
   chides SH for working so hard 172
   develops ulcer 137, 207
   finds grub in rice 171

in Malacca *38*
marches to 75 Kilo 186
meets SH at Meilo 181
moved to hospital 216
plans post-war career 170
returns letters to SH's widow 306
sent to work with fever 225
SH gives letters to 251–2
suffers from malaria 184
in Tavoy prison camp 112
McGovern, Frank 213–14, 250, 253,
  259, 262–3, 267–9, 274, 276,
  292–4
Meilo prison camp
  amputations in 206–7
  conditions in 184–5, 187–95,
    202–3
  disease in 184–5, 191, 195, 205,
    213
  guards search camp 212–13
  officers take new boots for
    themselves 222–3
  prisoners celebrate Anzac Day 192
  prisoners chop down tree 182
  rumours in camp 196–7, 209
  sick prisoners forced to work 189,
    191, 195
Melbourne 299–300, 310
Melbourne Cup (1943) 233–4
Mengele, Josef 90–1
Menzies, Robert 16, 68
Mergui 85, 115
Midway, Battle of 86
Mildura 150–1, 227
Mills, Keith 290, 293
Moji 273
Montevideo Maru (ship) 121
Mooney, Jim 195
Moulmein 85, 131, 227, 229
Muar River 59, 108
Mull, Alan 173–4, 176–8
Murdoch, Keith 77–8, 101–2
Mussolini, Benito 36
My Brother Jack (Johnston) 295

Nagamoto, Yoshitada 129, 131,
  134–5, 144–6, 231, 242

Nagasaki 294
Nankai (ship) 260
Nanking 11
Nazis 80, 89
New Guinea 141
Niigata 290
No. 593 (ship) 104
North Africa 21

O'Donnell, Ron 159
Osmand, Laurie 112, 184

Pacific War 85–6
Padang 79, 88, 108
Pampanito, USS 260, 266, 270–1
Parry, Doris 166, 168
Parry, Jack 66–7, 166, 224, 255, 303
Pearl Harbor 43
Penang 45, 47
Percival, Arthur 45, 56, 67–8, 73,
  79
Perth, HMAS 213–14, 259
Philippines 43
Phnom Penh 252
'Pig Iron Bob' 68
Plymouth Argylls 143
Port Swettenham 56
The P.O.W. 296
Pozières 70
Pride of Burma (tree) 182
Prince of Wales, HMS 39–40, 44
prisoners of war
  attitude towards Japanese 241
  brutal treatment of 109, 113, 134,
    143–4, 146, 152–3, 159, 173–4,
    237–8, 241–2, 244, 276
  deaths during construction of
    Burma Railway 231
  despondency of 243–4
  essential factors for survival of
    169–70
  execution of 61–2, 92–4, 109–11,
    145–6, 177–9
  fed by Burmese 118
  food for 100, 118, 136, 152, 171,
    185–6, 224, 236, 238
  as forced labour in Japan 275–6

Hague and Geneva Conventions on
86–7, 135, 223, 229
importance of humour 183–4
importance of mateship 111–12,
213–15
included in propaganda films
198–200
inner life of 122–3
Japanese attitude towards 99
killed in US bombing raid 293–5
prison libraries 125–7
return to Burma in 1990s 315
survivors' stories reach Australia
280–1, 296
on torpedoed Japanese ships 119,
121, 260–5
transferred to northern Japan 290
see also Aungganaung prison camp;
disease; Meilo prison camp;
Tavoy prison camp; Thetkaw
prison camp
Puckapunyal 17, 19, 22

Queenfish, USS 271
Quick, Dave 302–3

racism 32–3, 240–1
Rakuyo Maru (ship) 256, 257,
259–61, 265, 272, 278–80, 285,
304
Ramsay, George 184, 195, 231
Ramsey, Harold 214, 264, 286, 290,
292
Rangoon 159
Red Cross 85, 150–1, 228–9, 235,
277, 286, 289
Red Cross Bureau for Wounded and
Missing Prisoners of War 150
Repulse, HMS 40, 44
Richards, Rowley
appreciates beauty of Burma 125
on bad behaviour by officers 224
as a doctor 244
on the essential factors for survival
169–70
gives advice on jumping overboard
263

grateful for militia training 171
on the importance of mateship 214
on the importance of purpose 138
meets Varley's lifeboat convoy 267
on reading in camp 126
separates from Varley's lifeboat
convoy 274
on steamboat to Saigon 252
on the Toyohashi Maru 88
Rivett, Rohan 111
Royal Australian Air Force 30, 41
No. 1 Squadron 41
No. 2 Operational Training Unit
151–2
No. 21 Squadron 41
No. 453 Squadron 43–4
Royal Australian Navy 30
Russia 40

Saigon 252–4
Sasa, Akira 191
Sealion II, USS 260, 271
Second Australian Imperial Force
2/4th Machine Gun Battalion 68,
70, 87, 104
2/6th Field Park Company 28
2/9th Field Ambulance 92, 223
2/10th Australian General Hospital
88
2/10th Field Ambulance 28
2/10th Field Regiment 159, 265
2/12th Field Company 28
2/15th Field Regiment 28, 57,
69–70, 88
2/18th Battalion 70
2/19th Battalion 59, 61, 190
2/20th Battalion 66
2/26th Battalion 28
2/29th Battalion 28, 59, 61, 170
2/30th Battalion 28, 58, 73
4th Anti-Tank Regiment 30, 59,
109
6th Division 21
8th Division 3, 31, 33, 57, 67
8th Division Petrol Company 21,
145
22nd Brigade 68, 71

27th Brigade 25, 28, 68, 71
'A' Force 87, 98, 101, 119
Australian Army Service Corps 21,
    40, 64, 66, 89, 102, 166, 283
  casualties 59, 76, 78, 309
  establishment of 16
  No. 1 Service Corps 66, 71
  No. 2 Service Corps 66, 71
  officer class 218–24
  Special Reserve Battalion 70–1
Second Sino-Japanese War 11
Selarang Barracks 82
Sembawang 43
Seymour 21–2, 220
Shepherd, Frank 73
Shina, Hirayasu 110–11
Singapore 27–30, 35, 39, 66–79,
    101–2, 254–5
Singapore Strategy 39, 47
Singapore Times 58
Slim River, Battle of 58
Small Arms School, Randwick 16
Smith, Harry 110
Solomon Islands 141
Southern Command Training School
    19–20
Stalingrad, Battle of 141
Stawell 7–9, 83, 228, 317
Stawell Times 301
Steele, Ross 73
Strempel, Alf 186
submarines 119, 260–1, 266, 270–1
Summers, Paul 271
The Sun 35, 97, 280

Tanaka, Lieutenant 125
Tanglin Barracks 73, 77, 82, 143
Tatu Maru (ship) 104–5
Tavoy prison camp
  brutality of guards 109, 113
  Coates operates at 207
  conditions in 105–6, 113
  disease in 106, 112
  execution of the Tavoy Eight
    109–11
  importance of mateship 111–12,
    215

library for prisoners 125–7
  officer steals from trust fund 220
  SH sails to 104–5
Tavoy RAF airfield 85
Tengah airfield 68, 70
Tha Markham prison camp 250–2
Thai–Burma Railway see Burma
    Railway
Thailand 86
Thanbyuzayat 131, 133, 198, 235
Theresienstadt Ghetto 89
Thetkaw prison camp
  brutality of guards 134, 144, 146,
    152–3, 159, 173–4
  camp choir 156, 158
  conditions in 133–4, 136–40, 144,
    147–8, 152, 171
  disease in 136–7, 172
  escapes from 173–4, 176–9
  execution of escapees 144–6,
    177–9
  house rules 134–5
  prisoners stage New Year's Eve play
    160–1
  SH arrives at 131–3
  SH tries to get officers to work
    222
  torture of prisoners 144
Three Pagodas Pass 230
Tilley, Don 216
Tokyo 120–1, 228, 288
Toshiba Electric Company 275
Toyohashi Maru (ship) 87–8
tropical ulcers 137, 205–6

United States 40, 51, 86
United States Air Force 276, 288,
    293–4
United States Navy 259–60, 266,
    270–1, 273

Van Boxtel, C.J. 206
Varley, Arthur
  alarmed at prisoners' sickness rate
    191–2
  allocates supplies to most needy
    235

asks about bombing of Australian
cities 201
on Bell's execution 178
as commander of 'A' Force 87
establishes relationship with gaolers
98
invited to watch sumo wrestling
161
on Japanese aims 231
leads convoy of lifeboats 267, 269
negotiates with Japanese officers
221
opposes execution of escapees
144–5
organises library for prisoners 125
protests about brutality of guards
242
protests about food shortages 236
service in the Great War 70
signs house rules under duress
135–6
witnesses execution of prisoners
110–11
wrangles with guards 258–9
The Vatican 228
Victoria Cross 61
Victoria Point prison camp 85, 88–9,
92, 98, 100–1, 103, 215
Victoria Police 9–10
Vienna 10, 81

Wake Island 43
Walker, Jim 31
war crimes 315
Waters, Henry Heath 'Lofty'
at Bathurst Military Camp 25
becomes friends with SH 22
dies of dysentery 300
gets drunk with Jim Walker 31–2
in Padang 108
portrait of 107
SH worries about fate of 62–3, 106
in Singapore 30
survives attack on camp 65
transferred from Padang to Changi
158
writes to SH 209
Weekly Times 97
West, David 170
Western Front (WWI) 150
White Australia Policy 32, 240
White, Thomas 150–1
White, T.W. 'Vera' (née Deakin)
150–1, 228, 286
Whitfield, George 145–6
widows 314
Williams, Wal 190, 206–7, 214, 250,
256, 258, 260, 267, 269–70, 304

Yokohama camp 11D 274–5, 289
Yong Peng 61

To my darling,
with all my love.
Scott
30/10/41

1 in MALAYA.

POST CARD
CARTE POSTALE

K

Warrant Officer 1. W.S. Heywood